TM

References for the Rest of Us!®

BESTSELLING BOOK SERIES

Are you intimidated and confused by computers? Do you find that traditional manuals are overloaded with technical details you'll never use? Do your friends and family always call you to fix simple problems on their PCs? Then the *...For Dummies®* computer book series from IDG Books Worldwide is for you.

...For Dummies books are written for those frustrated computer users who know they aren't really dumb but find that PC hardware, software, and indeed the unique vocabulary of computing make them feel helpless. *...For Dummies* books use a lighthearted approach, a down-to-earth style, and even cartoons and humorous icons to dispel computer novices' fears and build their confidence. Lighthearted but not lightweight, these books are a perfect survival guide for anyone forced to use a computer.

"I like my copy so much I told friends; now they bought copies."

— Irene C., Orwell, Ohio

"Quick, concise, nontechnical, and humorous."

— Jay A., Elburn, Illinois

"Thanks, I needed this book. Now I can sleep at night."

— Robin F., British Columbia, Canada

Already, millions of satisfied readers agree. They have made *...For Dummies* books the #1 introductory level computer book series and have written asking for more. So, if you're looking for the most fun and easy way to learn about computers, look to *...For Dummies* books to give you a helping hand.

IDG BOOKS WORLDWIDE®

1/99

WebTV® For Dummies, 3rd Edition

Cheat Sheet

Important Keys on the Wireless Keyboard

- **Favs.** An abbreviation for Favorites. Use this key to see your list of favorite Web site links.
- **Home.** Press this key at any time to display the WebTV Home screen.
- **Search.** Bring up the search-by-keyword feature and find topics on the Internet.
- **Mail.** Go directly to your e-mail box to read incoming letters or send e-mail.
- **Info.** Need to know the address (called a URL) of the Web page you're currently viewing? Press this key.
- **Go to.** Go directly to any Web page if you know its URL (address). Just press this key and type the URL.
- **Save.** Store a link to the Web page you're viewing in your Favorites collection by using this key.
- **Send.** Want to share a great Web site with a friend? Send a link to any e-mail address with this key.
- **Back.** Use the Back key to display the previous Web page, and keep pressing the key to backstep your way through a Web session.
- **Scroll up and Scroll down.** View long Web pages in segments by scrolling up and down.

Essential Web Sites

www.yahoo.com	Yahoo! — a great Internet directory, with links to all kinds of on-screen services. It's vast and fast.
www.wired.com	A super-cool, ultra-hip, neon-decorated news site for digerati; beginners welcome.
www.eff.org/	Electronic Frontier Foundation — learn about electronic civil liberties and all kinds of online citizenry issues.
cool.infi.net/	Cool Site of the Day — would you visit New York City without seeing the Statue of Liberty? Don't miss this legendary site.
www.thebighub.com	The Big Hub — an astounding search and research tool.
www.realguide.com	A guide to RealAudio events on the Internet. Don't just view the Web; listen to it, too.
www.nytimes.com	*The New York Times* — the grey lady displays new colors on the Web.
www.sportsline.com/	CBS SportsLine — online mecca of sports news, feature articles, and scores.
moneycentral.msn.com/	Microsoft Investor — financial news, stock quotes, and online portfolio management.
www.dummies.com	*For Dummies* Web Site — everything there is to know about the *For Dummies* books plus author chats and e-mail bulletins.
www.bradhill.com	The author of this book — stop in and say hi!

For Dummies®: Bestselling Book Series for Beginners

WebTV® For Dummies, 3rd Edition

Cheat Sheet

Tailor Your Service in Setup

Highlight and select `Setup` on the Home screen to customize the WebTV experience.

- **Text size.** Choose from three sizes of text, depending on your television screen size and the crucial couch-to-TV distance.
- **Music.** Turn the background music on or off, and even select what type of music you like to hear while surfing the Web.
- **Logging on.** Determine how WebTV dials your phone, and even use your own Internet Service Provider to connect with WebTV Network.
- **Options.** Select additional options that appear on the on-screen options panel.
- **E-mail.** Allow WebTV to check your e-mail box for new letters once each day; create a special signature for all your outgoing e-mail; and select the Reply to All feature.
- **The picture.** Adjust the brightness or contrast of your TV picture, or center it on your screen.
- **Add or subtract an account.** Create a new account with its own e-mail address for anyone in your household, or change the properties of an existing account.

Commands for Copying, Cutting, and Pasting Text

- **Cmd+A:** Highlight all the text on a screen.
- **Cmd+Arrow keys:** Highlight portions of screen text.
- **Cmd+C:** Copy highlighted text to memory, leaving it on the screen.
- **Cmd+X:** Cut highlighted text, removing it from the screen.
- **Cmd+V:** Paste cut or copied text to the cursor location.

Chat Commands

- **/msg:** Use this command to "whisper" privately to another chatter.
- **/ignore:** This command, followed by the screen name of another chatter, causes that person's messages to disappear from your screen.
- **/who:** Find out who else is in the chat room with this command, which lists the screen names of participants.
- **/me:** Create an action instead of a line of dialogue. Use this command to indicate smiling, waving, jumping up and down, and so on.

Check Around Town for Local Info

- Get the local weather forecast.
- Browse the Dining Out guide for a restaurant near you.
- Look up sports schedules.
- Let your TV do the browsing — through the Yellow Pages.
- Find a friend from the past in the White Pages.
- Check local movie times and read reviews.

IDG BOOKS WORLDWIDE

Copyright © 2000 IDG Books Worldwide, Inc. All rights reserved.

Cheat Sheet $2.95 value. Item 0742-7.

For more information about IDG Books, call 1-800-762-2974.

The IDG Books Worldwide logo is a registered trademark under exclusive license to IDG Books Worldwide, Inc., from International Data Group, Inc. The ...For Dummies logo is a trademark, and For Dummies is a registered trademark of IDG Books Worldwide, Inc. All other trademarks are the property of their respective owners.

For Dummies®: Bestselling Book Series for Beginners

WebTV®

FOR

DUMMIES®

3RD EDITION

WebTV® FOR DUMMIES®

3RD EDITION

by Brad Hill

IDG Books Worldwide, Inc.
An International Data Group Company

Foster City, CA ◆ Chicago, IL ◆ Indianapolis, IN ◆ New York, NY

WebTV® For Dummies, 3rd Edition

Published by
IDG Books Worldwide, Inc.
An International Data Group Company
919 E. Hillsdale Blvd.
Suite 400
Foster City, CA 94404
www.idgbooks.com (IDG Books Worldwide Web Site)
www.dummies.com (Dummies Press Web Site)

Copyright © 2000 IDG Books Worldwide, Inc. All rights reserved. No part of this book, including interior design, cover design, and icons, may be reproduced or transmitted in any form, by any means (electronic, photocopying, recording, or otherwise) without the prior written permission of the publisher.

Library of Congress Catalog Control Number: 00-102504

ISBN: 0-7645-0742-7

Printed in the United States of America

10 9 8 7 6 5 4 3 2

3O/QX/QY/QQ/IN

Distributed in the United States by IDG Books Worldwide, Inc.

Distributed by CDG Books Canada Inc. for Canada; by Transworld Publishers Limited in the United Kingdom; by IDG Norge Books for Norway; by IDG Sweden Books for Sweden; by IDG Books Australia Publishing Corporation Pty. Ltd. for Australia and New Zealand; by TransQuest Publishers Pte Ltd. for Singapore, Malaysia, Thailand, Indonesia, and Hong Kong; by Gotop Information Inc. for Taiwan; by ICG Muse, Inc. for Japan; by Intersoft for South Africa; by Eyrolles for France; by International Thomson Publishing for Germany, Austria and Switzerland; by Distribuidora Cuspide for Argentina; by LR International for Brazil; by Galileo Libros for Chile; by Ediciones ZETA S.C.R. Ltda. for Peru; by WS Computer Publishing Corporation, Inc., for the Philippines; by Contemporanea de Ediciones for Venezuela; by Express Computer Distributors for the Caribbean and West Indies; by Micronesia Media Distributor, Inc. for Micronesia; by Chips Computadoras S.A. de C.V. for Mexico; by Editorial Norma de Panama S.A. for Panama; by American Bookshops for Finland.

For general information on IDG Books Worldwide's books in the U.S., please call our Consumer Customer Service department at 800-762-2974. For reseller information, including discounts and premium sales, please call our Reseller Customer Service department at 800-434-3422.

For information on where to purchase IDG Books Worldwide's books outside the U.S., please contact our International Sales department at 317-596-5530 or fax 317-572-4002.

For consumer information on foreign language translations, please contact our Customer Service department at 1-800-434-3422, fax 317-572-4002, or e-mail rights@idgbooks.com.

For information on licensing foreign or domestic rights, please phone +1-650-653-7098.

For sales inquiries and special prices for bulk quantities, please contact our Order Services department at 800-434-3422 or write to the address above.

For information on using IDG Books Worldwide's books in the classroom or for ordering examination copies, please contact our Educational Sales department at 800-434-2086 or fax 317-572-4005.

For press review copies, author interviews, or other publicity information, please contact our Public Relations department at 650-653-7000 or fax 650-653-7500.

For authorization to photocopy items for corporate, personal, or educational use, please contact Copyright Clearance Center, 222 Rosewood Drive, Danvers, MA 01923, or fax 978-750-4470.

LIMIT OF LIABILITY/DISCLAIMER OF WARRANTY: THE PUBLISHER AND AUTHOR HAVE USED THEIR BEST EFFORTS IN PREPARING THIS BOOK. THE PUBLISHER AND AUTHOR MAKE NO REPRESENTATIONS OR WARRANTIES WITH RESPECT TO THE ACCURACY OR COMPLETENESS OF THE CONTENTS OF THIS BOOK AND SPECIFICALLY DISCLAIM ANY IMPLIED WARRANTIES OF MERCHANTABILITY OR FITNESS FOR A PARTICULAR PURPOSE. THERE ARE NO WARRANTIES WHICH EXTEND BEYOND THE DESCRIPTIONS CONTAINED IN THIS PARAGRAPH. NO WARRANTY MAY BE CREATED OR EXTENDED BY SALES REPRESENTATIVES OR WRITTEN SALES MATERIALS. THE ACCURACY AND COMPLETENESS OF THE INFORMATION PROVIDED HEREIN AND THE OPINIONS STATED HEREIN ARE NOT GUARANTEED OR WARRANTED TO PRODUCE ANY PARTICULAR RESULTS, AND THE ADVICE AND STRATEGIES CONTAINED HEREIN MAY NOT BE SUITABLE FOR EVERY INDIVIDUAL. NEITHER THE PUBLISHER NOR AUTHOR SHALL BE LIABLE FOR ANY LOSS OF PROFIT OR ANY OTHER COMMERCIAL DAMAGES, INCLUDING BUT NOT LIMITED TO SPECIAL, INCIDENTAL, CONSEQUENTIAL, OR OTHER DAMAGES.

Trademarks: WebTV is a registered of WebTV Net, Inc. For Dummies, Dummies Man, A Reference for the Rest of Us!, The Dummies Way, Dummies Daily, and related trade dress are registered trademarks or trademarks of IDG Books Worldwide, Inc. in the United States and other countries, and may not be used without written permission. All other trademarks are the property of their respective owners. IDG Books Worldwide is not associated with any product or vendor mentioned in this book.

is a registered trademark under exclusive license to IDG Books Worldwide, Inc., from International Data Group, Inc.

About the Author

Brad Hill has worked in the online field since 1992, and is a preeminent advocate of the online experience. As a bestselling author of many books and columns, Brad reaches a global audience of consumers who rely on his writings to help determine their Internet service choices. He served as WebTV's national media spokesperson when WebTV was introduced to the public.

Brad's books include a Publishers Weekly bestseller and a Book of the Month catalog selection. Brad's titles in the "...*For Dummies*" series include *Internet Searching For Dummies*, *The Internet Directory For Dummies*, and *Yahoo! For Dummies*. As a columnist, Brad writes about cyber-cultural trends and online destinations. His work appears regularly in *ComputorEdge Magazine, Online Investor Magazine,* Raging Bull, and TipWorld.

Brad is often consulted in the media's coverage of the Internet, and appears often on television, radio, Webcasts, and as quoted in publications such as *Business Week, The New York Times,* and *PC World.*

Brad doesn't get outdoors much. As compensation, he is listed in Who's Who and is a member of The Author's Guild.

ABOUT IDG BOOKS WORLDWIDE

Welcome to the world of IDG Books Worldwide.

IDG Books Worldwide, Inc., is a subsidiary of International Data Group, the world's largest publisher of computer-related information and the leading global provider of information services on information technology. IDG was founded more than 30 years ago by Patrick J. McGovern and now employs more than 9,000 people worldwide. IDG publishes more than 290 computer publications in over 75 countries. More than 90 million people read one or more IDG publications each month.

Launched in 1990, IDG Books Worldwide is today the #1 publisher of best-selling computer books in the United States. We are proud to have received eight awards from the Computer Press Association in recognition of editorial excellence and three from Computer Currents' First Readers' Choice Awards. Our best-selling ...For Dummies® series has more than 50 million copies in print with translations in 31 languages. IDG Books Worldwide, through a joint venture with IDG's Hi-Tech Beijing, became the first U.S. publisher to publish a computer book in the People's Republic of China. In record time, IDG Books Worldwide has become the first choice for millions of readers around the world who want to learn how to better manage their businesses.

Our mission is simple: Every one of our books is designed to bring extra value and skill-building instructions to the reader. Our books are written by experts who understand and care about our readers. The knowledge base of our editorial staff comes from years of experience in publishing, education, and journalism — experience we use to produce books to carry us into the new millennium. In short, we care about books, so we attract the best people. We devote special attention to details such as audience, interior design, use of icons, and illustrations. And because we use an efficient process of authoring, editing, and desktop publishing our books electronically, we can spend more time ensuring superior content and less time on the technicalities of making books.

You can count on our commitment to deliver high-quality books at competitive prices on topics you want to read about. At IDG Books Worldwide, we continue in the IDG tradition of delivering quality for more than 30 years. You'll find no better book on a subject than one from IDG Books Worldwide.

John J. Kilcullen
John Kilcullen
Chairman and CEO
IDG Books Worldwide, Inc.

WINNER
*Eighth Annual
Computer Press
Awards ≥1992*

WINNER
*Ninth Annual
Computer Press
Awards ≥1993*

WINNER

WINNER
*Tenth Annual
Computer Press
Awards ≥1994*

WINNER
*Eleventh Annual
Computer Press
Awards ≥1995*

IDG is the world's leading IT media, research and exposition company. Founded in 1964, IDG had 1997 revenues of $2.05 billion and has more than 9,000 employees worldwide. IDG offers the widest range of media options that reach IT buyers in 75 countries representing 95% of worldwide IT spending. IDG's diverse product and services portfolio spans six key areas including print publishing, online publishing, expositions and conferences, market research, education and training, and global marketing services. More than 90 million people read one or more of IDG's 290 magazines and newspapers, including IDG's leading global brands — Computerworld, PC World, Network World, Macworld and the Channel World family of publications. IDG Books Worldwide is one of the fastest-growing computer book publishers in the world, with more than 700 titles in 36 languages. The "...For Dummies®" series alone has more than 50 million copies in print. IDG offers online users the largest network of technology-specific Web sites around the world through IDG.net (http://www.idg.net), which comprises more than 225 targeted Web sites in 55 countries worldwide. International Data Corporation (IDC) is the world's largest provider of information technology data, analysis and consulting, with research centers in over 41 countries and more than 400 research analysts worldwide. IDG World Expo is a leading producer of more than 168 globally branded conferences and expositions in 35 countries including E3 (Electronic Entertainment Expo), Macworld Expo, ComNet, Windows World Expo, ICE (Internet Commerce Expo), Agenda, DEMO, and Spotlight. IDG's training subsidiary, ExecuTrain, is the world's largest computer training company, with more than 230 locations worldwide and 785 training courses. IDG Marketing Services helps industry-leading IT companies build international brand recognition by developing global integrated marketing programs via IDG's print, online and exposition products worldwide. Further information about the company can be found at www.idg.com. 1/26/00

Dedication

This book is dedicated to Ian Yellin. His encouragement during our ongoing work with the launch of WebTV Networks was inspiring. It's unusual for a business association to develop into a valued friendship, and I'm lucky to have both with Ian.

Author's Acknowledgments

Every book is a partnership between author and editor, and rarely does a collaboration work so well as in this case. Susan Pink is the editor of this book, and I'm lucky to work with her. Besides being an unusually fine editor, Susan has a gift for remaining calm during the most intense deadline crisis. She also laughs at all the right times.

Ed Adams and Steve Hayes at IDG Books Worldwide got this third edition rolling. Thanks to both of them for their efforts.

Clark Scheffy, Jennifer Ehrlich, and Mary Bednarek headed up the IDG team that launched the first edition of this book, and their influence is part of its success. Mary is also responsible for my writing all these bright yellow books in the first place, so please address letters of complaint directly to her.

Mark Pedley at Philips Consumer Electronics went beyond the call of duty to help make this book happen. His initiative and quick responsiveness to my queries are invaluable.

Claire Haggard and Lisa Blair at Waggener Edstrom were unfailingly gracious in the face of my repeated, sometimes urgent requests for information. Their contributions to this book are essential.

Many thanks to Cecile Chronister at WebTV Networks for working beyond office hours (on the weekend, no less) to satisfy our fearsome deadlines. Cecile has probably blocked the experience out of her mind, but I won't forget her crucial assistance.

Publisher's Acknowledgments

We're proud of this book; please register your comments through our IDG Books Worldwide Online Registration Form located at http://my2cents.dummies.com.

Some of the people who helped bring this book to market include the following:

Acquisitions, Editorial, and Media Development

Project Editor: Susan Pink

Acquisitions Editor: Steven H. Hayes

Proof Editors: Teresa Artman, Dwight Ramsey

Technical Editor: Allen Wyatt

Editorial Manager: Constance Carlisle

Editorial Assistant: Candace Nicholson

Production

Project Coordinator: Maridee Ennis

Layout and Graphics: Amy Adrian, Brian Drumm, Jason Guy, Gabriele McCann, Shelley Norris, Tracy K. Oliver, Kristin Pickett, Jill Piscitelli, Jacque Schneider

Proofreaders: Laura Albert, Corey Bowen, Susan Moritz, Marianne Santy, Charles Spencer, York Production Services, Inc.

Indexer: York Production Services, Inc.

General and Administrative

IDG Books Worldwide, Inc.: John Kilcullen, CEO

IDG Books Technology Publishing Group: Richard Swadley, Senior Vice President and Publisher; Walter R. Bruce III, Vice President and Publisher; Joseph Wikert, Vice President and Publisher; Mary Bednarek, Vice President and Director, Product Development; Andy Cummings, Publishing Director, General User Group; Mary C. Corder, Editorial Director; Barry Pruett, Publishing Director

IDG Books Consumer Publishing Group: Roland Elgey, Senior Vice President and Publisher; Kathleen A. Welton, Vice President and Publisher; Kevin Thornton, Acquisitions Manager; Kristin A. Cocks, Editorial Director

IDG Books Internet Publishing Group: Brenda McLaughlin, Senior Vice President and Publisher; Sofia Marchant, Online Marketing Manager

IDG Books Production for Branded Press: Debbie Stailey, Director of Production; Cindy L. Phipps, Manager of Project Coordination, Production Proofreading, and Indexing; Tony Augsburger, Manager of Prepress, Reprints, and Systems; Laura Carpenter, Production Control Manager; Shelley Lea, Supervisor of Graphics and Design; Debbie J. Gates, Production Systems Specialist; Robert Springer, Supervisor of Proofreading; Trudy Coler, Page Layout Manager; Troy Barnes, Page Layout Supervisor, Kathie Schutte, Senior Page Layout Supervisor; Michael Sullivan, Production Supervisor

Packaging and Book Design: Patty Page, Manager, Promotions Marketing

◆

The publisher would like to give special thanks to Patrick J. McGovern, without whom this book would not have been possible.

◆

Contents at a Glance

Cartoons at a Glance

By Rich Tennant

page 101

page D-1

page 185

page 9

page 269

Fax: 978-546-7747
E-mail: richtennant@the5thwave.com
World Wide Web: www.the5thwave.com

Table of Contents

Introduction

Few aspects of the information age have enjoyed as much publicity and furor as the Web, and this excitement is all the more remarkable when you consider that the Web is less than ten years old. The Web, with its easy hyperlinks, is primarily responsible for bringing the Internet to mainstream public awareness. In less than a decade, it has created a new media realm. The Web has profoundly affected the lives of individuals and the stability of the stock market. Throughout all the hype, delirium, and controversy, the challenge for many people has been access.

Technology has a way of doubling back to collect those who didn't catch the first wave. Millions of people have heard about the Internet and the Web and might even be intrigued and eager to see what all the hype is about. But many of these people don't have a computer, much less an online access account, and have no interest in joining the online revolution with those traditional tools. Even as the price of computers spirals down to unprecedented levels, many folks remain steadfastly uninterested in mastering the complexities of computers.

WebTV was created for exactly that type of person, and there are other reasons to love WebTV as well. Anyone interested in a more recreational, less task-oriented approach to the Internet than that afforded by computers appreciates the reality of the Internet in the living room, available for couch-potato surfing.

Furthermore, WebTV is not just an Internet service — it's an *interactive TV service*. Interactive TV is one of those buzz phrases that doesn't mean anything at first. In this case, it means enhancing your TV viewing, planning, and recording (in the case of WebTV Plus, the more advanced version of WebTV) and merging it with the Internet. It adds up to a convergence of the Internet and television — a futuristic concept that is finally attaining reality.

So there are several aspects to WebTV's coolness and many types of people who have adopted it as their information appliance of choice. From basic e-mail to creating Web pages, from online chatting to easily recording TV shows, from searching the Web to clipping pictures from the VCR, WebTV represents the convergence of home, Internet, and television.

About This Book

This book is your companion to the entire WebTV experience. In addition, I realize that many new WebTVers are new to the Internet as well, so I've included lots of site recommendations. Some chapters of this book can be considered a guide to cyberspace as viewed through WebTV.

WebTV Plus is a television-enhancement service that also provides Internet access. This book explains the features that make WebTV Plus unique and instructs new users in setting up their systems.

One more point. This book will always be there. (Unless you accidentally toss it under a steamroller.) Don't feel like you have to remember anything. There are no tests. It's best to use the book as a reference or, as I said before, as a companion.

Conventions Used in This Book

For the sake of clarity, this book uses certain typefaces and other layout properties to indicate particular things that appear on your screen. To make following along with the book while using WebTV easy, I've been consistent with these conventions.

- ✔ URLs (Uniform Resource Locators, the addresses of Web pages) are indicated with this kind of type: www.webpage.com.

- ✔ When I introduce a new term for the first time, I *italicize* it to get your attention and to reassure you that there's no reason you should know what it means.

- ✔ On-screen buttons and other links seen on the WebTV service screens appear like this: On-screen Button.

What You're Not to Read

Hey, this book isn't a novel. It doesn't even have an exciting ending. (No butler, whatsoever.) You shouldn't feel like you must read the whole book straight through. In fact, there's no need to read even a single chapter straight through. For that matter, think twice before reading an entire paragraph. Don't finish this sentence! Okay, I'm getting carried away. My point is that you can find out a lot, and probably have more fun, by choosing what to read from the Table of Contents. This isn't school.

Most of the book is useful to owners of both the basic WebTV and WebTV Plus systems. Exceptions, though, are Chapters 4 and 5, which cover in detail the distinct Home screens found in the two services, and Chapter 11, which covers interactive TV features of WebTV Plus.

Occasionally, I betray my geekish side by talking in technobabble. I sometimes can't resist explaining a particular point in technical terms. Just ignore me — I always return to normal quickly. As a public service, the reader-friendly editors of this book have marked all geekish paragraphs with the Technical Stuff icon. You're at liberty to read those paragraphs or not; nothing in them is necessary to have a good WebTV experience.

Paragraphs marked with a Plus! icon only make sense to Plus subscribers. So if that doesn't apply to you, skip those paragraphs.

Foolish Assumptions

In this section, I ask, "Who are you?" Well, if that isn't a rude question, I don't know what is. To save you the embarrassment of being rude right back at me, I'll answer it for you. You have probably bought a WebTV system, or are considering doing so, or know someone who has. Perhaps you've bought a unit for a family member — many computer users give WebTV to parents or children just for the e-mail features. If the system is yours, you might not own a computer or have any experience using one, and it's possible you've never surfed the Internet.

If you do own a computer and are an experienced Netizen (that's an informal way of referring to someone who hangs out online), WebTV represents an inexpensive way to put a second online machine in your home, perhaps for other members of your family.

You might be an experienced WebTV subscriber looking to develop new skills. If that's the case, the chapters on HTML, using Page Builder, unusual tips, and finding value in the Internet at large might pull you more strongly than others.

Finally, it's possible that you have no interest in the Internet and picked up this book by accident while searching for a cultural history of Siamese cats. I have nothing to say on that subject except that cats in general have no appreciation for ballet. I wish you well on your search.

This book is a detailed owner's manual for both WebTV systems. WebTV isn't hard to use, but figuring out any new gadget involves mysteries and frustrations when any kind of knowledge is assumed, so I don't assume you know anything about WebTV, computers, or the Web. I explain every on-screen item you're likely to see as well as every button on the remote control. All WebTV features are described to the hilt, with many of them illustrated. Gosh, what a terrific book! Perhaps you should buy one for each room of your home.

WebTV For Dummies, 3rd Edition, is more than a technical guide to the WebTV system. Because many WebTV users are newcomers to the Internet, I've taken the opportunity to provide a guided tour to the sights, sounds, and culture of the Web. Furthermore, the cluster of yellow pages later in the book provides a directory to Web sites of particular interest to WebTV users as well as Web sites of general interest.

How to Read This Book

First, how the book should *not* be read. Don't read it under the covers with one of those little reading lights attached to it. Don't read it while driving. Above all, don't read it while operating heavy machinery. Your best bet is to keep the book near your WebTV system so that you can refer to it while you're online. It's not a thriller. Reading it straight through causes drooping eyelids and fits of yawning. Avoid these medical complications by reading the sections you need help with and exploring the recommended Web locations, or sites.

To help you maintain sanity and health, I've divided the book into parts. (I'm hoping to win an award for choosing such an imaginative name.) The following sections tell what's in the parts.

Part I: Starting from Scratch

This part is where you discover the basics of the WebTV system, starting with what in the world it really is and continuing with an overview of its online features. Along the way, you figure out how to set up WebTV with whatever kind of TV system you have; how to log on to the Web for the first time; how to use the remote control and the wireless keyboard; and how to create accounts for each member of your family. In this first part, you find out about all the WebTV screen options and all the features of the Home screen (WebTV Plus has two Home screens) you see when you log on.

Part II: Getting Comfortable

In Part II, I go into more depth about the main features of WebTV. The part's first chapter (Chapter 6) introduces you to e-mail and describes the way e-mail works through WebTV and some of the ways you can use it. Chapter 7 is dedicated to the Favorites section — that's where you store Web sites you want to visit again. The next chapter is about meeting people — WebTV members and others — in the Community portion of the service, through chatting and messaging.

The Search feature is the subject of Chapter 9. Search is where you use keywords to locate specific topics on the Web. In addition to describing the ins and outs of Search, I make a point of introducing you to other keyword-based search services on the Web.

Part III: Cruising with WebTV

Part III describes how multimedia works on the Internet as seen (and heard) through WebTV, including RealAudio and MIDI music. I introduce the Internet community and describe how to find and use message boards and chat rooms. There's also a chapter on creating your own Web site through WebTV, which you might not have thought possible. It is. Chapter 13 explains the new Page Builder service.

Another chapter in Part 3 describes interactive TV programming available through WebTV Plus. You also find out about the WebTV Information Centers — little home bases on different subjects.

In Part III, I recommend some specific Web sites that are particularly attractive or useful, or just plain fun. I can't emphasize enough that even if the book were five times as big (making it very awkward to carry home), it wouldn't be nearly large enough to cover all the Web sites worth visiting. My recommendations barely scratch the surface of what's available and worthwhile, so you should take them as starting points for your own discoveries. Need more suggestions? Get hold of *Internet Directory For Dummies*. (Modesty prevents me from divulging the author.)

Part IV: The Part of Tens

The great *...For Dummies* tradition continues in Part IV, where I offer tips and recommendations for maximizing the WebTV experience. You get all kinds of unusual recommendations and hidden controls that you might never find on your own.

Special Feature

A clump of yellow pages lurks in the middle of the book. They are directory pages and make up a recurring feature in some *...For Dummies* books. In this case, "The WebTV For Dummies Online Directory" furnishes short reviews of Web sites that are explicitly useful to WebTV users. Places where you can build a site through WebTV; digital storehouses of pictures and sounds that you can link to from your site; WebTV help pages; Web sites built by WebTV members — these categories are all included in the directory pages.

Icons Used in This Book

It just wouldn't feel right to create a ...*For Dummies* book without funny little pictures lurking in the margins. They're so much fun that I use them over and over. Furthermore, each icon serves to direct your attention to the purpose of certain paragraphs.

This icon appears whenever I'm drawing a distinction between the way WebTV works and the way a computer performs the same function. For computer users who have acquired WebTV as a second online access method, these comparisons help you get your bearings. For non-computer users, the descriptions in these paragraphs let you know how much easier WebTV is than a computer in many respects.

WebTV is already in its second generation, which is called WebTV Plus. The Plus version of WebTV is a separate product, requiring a set-top box that's different from the original, first-generation set-top box. Whenever I describe a Plus feature that differs from basic WebTV, the paragraph is marked with this icon.

This icon is your signal to put a dollar bill in my tip jar. No, wait — I thought I was in a piano bar. Actually, each tip paragraph gives you a brilliant suggestion that will save you time, ease your learning curve, lower your blood pressure, and double your money. Well, I can't guarantee *all* that.

This icon should be taken seriously because it indicates that I have violated a sacred trust and degenerated into technobabble. My apologies in advance. Sometimes I just can't help myself. Those of you who enjoy technical explanations probably won't be harmed by reading these paragraphs.

Paragraphs highlighted with the Warning icon are your first indication that something is burning on the stove. After you turn off the heat, read the paragraph — it helps you avoid unnecessary difficulties with some aspect of online navigation or WebTV operation.

This icon is very important. It means . . . umm . . . well, I don't recall exactly what it means. It has something to do with keeping an important point in mind. If I remember correctly.

Where to Go from Here

If you feel like reading some more, go to Chapter 1 and find out about the basics of WebTV — what it is and what terms you need to know to make the most of the rest of the book.

If you're more in the mood to get hands-on experience, skip to Chapter 2, which explains how to set up WebTV. Of course, it helps to have a WebTV unit. If you've bought one already, get the box, bring this book over to it, and start your adventure.

If by chance you've already set up your WebTV system, you might not need Chapters 1 or 2 right now. Glance through the Table of Contents to see where you'd like to start. The chapter titles are pretty self-explanatory, except possibly for "Lemming Dreams." Oh, sorry, that's another book.

The convergence of the Internet and TV awaits you!

Part I
Starting from Scratch

The 5th Wave — By Rich Tennant

"Well, there goes the simple charm of sitting around the stove surfing the Web on our laptops."

In this part . . .

The first part of *WebTV For Dummies* is for the WebTV beginner. Chapter 1 describes what WebTV is (and isn't), and it's useful even for someone who hasn't acquired WebTV yet. The first chapter also contains a handy glossary of words worth knowing, especially as you read other portions of the book. The other chapters in this part explain everything you need to know about setting up the WebTV Internet terminal, using the remote control and optional wireless keyboard, familiarizing yourself with the Home screen, and getting acquainted with the TV Home screen in WebTV Plus.

Chapter 1

What WebTV Is and Isn't

In This Chapter

▶ Using WebTV instead of a computer

▶ Discovering how WebTV works

▶ Finding out what's missing from WebTV

▶ Distinguishing between WebTV and computers

▶ Finding out the basics of being a WebTV user

▶ Understanding the Internet and the Web

▶ Comprehending some crucial terms

*B*ecause you're reading these words, you have acquired a WebTV system (congratulations!) or are considering doing so. Either way, you are embarking on a new adventure and are on the frontier of new technologies for connecting people to the digital age. You didn't think it was such a big deal, did you?

The great part is that you don't need to know very much to participate in this exciting development. But it does help to be aware of what you bought and to have answers to a few basic questions. Don't worry, I don't get technical on you — at least not until I get to the part about reverse quantum mechanics.

By the way, in this chapter, I throw in a number of geek-friendly words that you may have heard on the evening news or read in the paper. If you don't know what they mean (or why people are so excited about them), cruise to the section in this chapter titled "Some Words to Know (This Is Not a Test)."

Welcome to a New Era

Long, long ago, in the dark ages of the Internet (that is, before October 1996), the only way to get on the Internet was with a computer. Computers were unusual creatures with strange, troublesome habits. People would buy cute computer puppies, only to watch them grow up into digital monsters, sharp-toothed and incapable of being housebroken. Well, maybe not that bad. But computers are complicated, no doubt about it, and complications tend to multiply over time, leading to frustration and wasted effort. And the expense: Although the price of multimedia computers has dropped, the good ones are still relatively expensive.

WebTV brings a new angle into the picture. With a WebTV Internet terminal or Plus Receiver, complexity and high cost are left in the dust (even though the name *Internet terminal* might sound intimidating). WebTV is a perfect solution for people who don't care to spend irretrievable hours (days? weeks?) wrestling with stubborn software, finicky modems, and rebellious program upgrades.

WebTV has been out for a few years now and has proved its value to hundreds of thousands of subscribers. More than a nifty product, WebTV has had a profound effect on the information age by unlocking the digital doors for nontechnical, practical folks who are interested in the Internet but are understandably unwilling to invest huge amounts of time and money to bring it into their home. Sound like you? Welcome to the new frontier.

An important distinction

WebTV was introduced in the fall of 1996. A little over a year later, a second-generation product hit the shelves. The new version of WebTV was (and still is) called WebTV Plus, and the original version came to be known as Classic.

As I continue to rave about WebTV's capability to deliver the Internet to folks without computers, I must make an important distinction between the purposes of the two versions of WebTV:

✔ WebTV Classic is essentially an Internet device that operates on the TV screen.

✔ WebTV Plus is essentially a television device that delivers the Internet as added value.

The Internet service for Classic and Plus is identical.

As you can find out in later chapters, WebTV Plus adds TV management features that make it easy to schedule your viewing and record programs. Internet viewing is secondary to TV viewing in the Plus universe. For Classic users, the Internet is the main attraction.

Do I really hate computers?

No, I certainly don't. Although I'm not saying nice things about them in this chapter, I'm irrevocably fascinated by computers, and most of my friends think I spend too much time with them. I own several computers and usually have at least one connected to the Internet at all times. Being on such close terms with computers has given me a heightened appreciation for both the wonder and frustration they inspire.

The point is, WebTV isn't trying to replace computers. It is, however, an alternative to the computer as an Internet vehicle. (And WebTV Plus goes way beyond computers in its capability to enhance the TV experience.) As such, WebTV solves the problem of computer intimidation because it's so easy to set up and use. At the same time, WebTV (especially WebTV Plus) brings its users to the forefront of *convergence technology* by merging the television with the Internet.

If you're already a computer user (like me), you still have several good reasons why you may have acquired WebTV (again, like *moi*). WebTV isn't just for beginners. Here are a few reasons for computer-literate, technical folks to go for a WebTV system:

- WebTV is a way to add a second Internet terminal to the house, without investing in a second computer.
- WebTV brings the Internet into the living room, where groups of people can enjoy it more easily than they could with a computer.
- Surfing the Web through a TV is fun, perhaps especially for people accustomed to squinting at a computer monitor. With WebTV, you can slouch and lounge on your couch instead of hunching over a computer keyboard. Using WebTV seems more recreational than using a computer — and I enjoy it immensely for that reason alone.
- WebTV Plus is more than an Internet device — it expands television viewing and planning dramatically. It's a great component to add to your TV system, even if you're not sure whether you want the Internet features.

It's a Bird. It's a Plane. No It's. . . .

WebTV provides the Internet everybody's talking about, only on your television — without a personal computer. The WebTV system includes a set-top box that sits on top of your television (or somewhere near the TV), a remote control, and an optional wireless keyboard for typing e-mail. (*E-mail* is electronic mail, as you can see in the "Some Words to Know . . ." section near the end of this chapter.) The handheld remote control is all you need to surf the Web — that is, the World Wide Web — the most dazzling portion of the Internet.

WebTV through EchoStar

Most WebTV Classic and Plus subscribers use dedicated set-top boxes that connect to the TV as described in this book and deliver service from WebTV Networks. Another on-ramp to the service is provided by a satelite TV system called EchoStar, using a set-top box called the DISHPlayer 500. Just as with the Classic and Plus set-top boxes, an optional wireless keyboard is available.

EchoStar provides WebTV Plus service (not Classic) for an additional monthly fee to EchoStar subscribers. At the time of this writing, the monthly WebTV Plus subscription charge was the same as for regular Plus subscribers. The Plus service is identical in every respect to the features and screens described in this book.

WebTV provides an additional, optional service to EchoStar/Plus subscribers, one that is not (at this writing) available to non-satellite Plus users. Called WebTV Personal TV, it looks similar to the TV Planner features of WebTV Plus described in this book, but with the added capability to record TV programs to a hard drive built into the DISHPlayer 500 box.

Technology that records programs to internal hard drives is called Digital Video Recording (DVR) and lets you perform cool tricks such as stopping a show during a broadcast to see a replay and recording a week's worth of favorite shows for later viewing. The hard drives have much more room than a video tape, but it's not removable, so you can't build a permanent library of shows.

The set-top box of the first version of WebTV is called the WebTV Internet terminal. The Plus box (the second version of WebTV) is called the WebTV Plus Receiver. (But everyone calls the two services Classic and Plus. That's how I refer to them in this book, too.) WebTV Plus has the same functionality as the original WebTV, plus some new features inside the set-top box and in the WebTV Plus Network service. For the most part, the instructions and tips that I give you apply to both the Classic and Plus service. When differences exist, I highlight them with icons like the one next to this paragraph. (Cute, isn't it?) WebTV Plus subscribers get an extra Home screen and some extra features that link the Internet seamlessly to television programming — plus a faster modem. The two services — WebTV Classic and WebTV Plus — are dependent on the set-top box, which means that the only way to get WebTV Plus is to have a WebTV Plus Receiver. You cannot switch from Classic service to Plus service without buying a WebTV Plus Receiver.

For Internet newcomers, WebTV is like a beginner ski slope: gentle and safe. For the experienced *Netizen* (that is, a fine, upstanding member of the Internet community), WebTV offers a recreational alternative to the glaring, in-your-face computer screen. For the TV aficionado, WebTV Plus furnishes a great interface between your television, your cable service (if you have cable), the Internet, and your eyeballs.

Both WebTV Classic and Plus provide everything you need (except for a phone line and a TV set, which you must provide) right from the beginning. The system takes care of all logon details (connecting to the Internet is called *logging on*) — notoriously one of the hardest parts of the Internet for computer users. WebTV also makes the inherently chaotic and disorganized Web coherent by providing menus, directories, topical selections of great Web sites, and a way to search for what you want.

Although WebTV presents an organized version of the Web, you don't have to stick to WebTV's plan, which is good news for Internet veterans who already know which sites interest them. Most of the Web is available through WebTV just as it is with a computer. The system even evolves automatically as the Web changes — and the Web is changing at a maddening pace. Technologies and features are invented and incorporated continuously, but you don't have to go to a store to buy new software as a WebTV subscriber: The WebTV Network periodically updates your terminal, enabling it to display the most recent enhancements to the Web.

WebTV updates itself periodically by sending software upgrades through the phone lines and into your set-top box. These upgrades are accomplished at the beginning of a WebTV session — and only when you initiate a log on. Such software updates can take 15 or 20 minutes, which is inconvenient if you are planning a quick session to get your e-mail, for example. Not to worry — WebTV always asks before beginning the upgrade, and you may always decline it. If you do pass on the upgrade, WebTV continues asking you every time you log on, until you finally accept the download. If you persistently decline, WebTV eventually pushes the upgrade into your system at the beginning of a session, without asking. (This is a good time to clean out the refrigerator.)

WebTV Plus offers a unique type of update — a content update, not a software update. You can set the system to retrieve updated TV listings for your broadcast area (or cable company) every night, automatically. You may also forego the automatic updates and retrieve new listings manually whenever you please. I've put the complete instructions for updating TV listings both automatically and manually in Chapter 5.

What's Missing?

Although WebTV evolves with the Internet by providing automatic updates to the set-top box, it's too much to say that it keeps up with the pace in every respect. The Internet as experienced through WebTV is not identical to the computer experience. You can certainly enter any Web address and order WebTV to take you there. But certain types of Internet content can't be played or displayed through WebTV. You might be frustrated occasionally by WebTV's shortcomings. Don't blame yourself when the system doesn't seem to be working — the shortcomings are in the system, not you.

This section describes Internet technologies (types of content) that, as of this writing, don't work through WebTV.

Java

Java is a programming language. What does that mean to you and other WebTV users? Little programs (called *applets*) written in the Java language are popular among Internet programmers and are found in some popular Web sites. Game and chat sites, in particular, use Java applets, though plenty of locations for interactive game playing and chatting don't use Java. Other types of Internet destinations, especially investment research sites, also use Java quite a bit.

The lack of Java compatibility has been a bone of contention in the WebTV community since the beginning. As Java has become more prevalent on the Net, WebTVers have become more grumpy about not being able to see and use applets. The problem is that Java — contrary to popular conception — requires a program download, not just a browser enhancement. The Classic and newer Plus set-top boxes lack a hard drive to receive such downloads. Even if they could receive a downloaded applet, Java requires software resources that would stretch the capacity of these basic Internet-surfing devices.

Don't confuse Java with JavaScript, which is a lightweight programming code that produces little animations and certain interactive functions. Most types of JavaScript work fine through WebTV.

If you (perhaps inadvertently) attempt to start a Java program by selecting a link, WebTV tells you that you've accessed a type of content WebTV can't process. If a Web site contains Java programming crucial to its display, you might not be able to enter the site at all.

In survey after survey, and throughout the WebTV message boards, subscribers point to the Java-less Web experience as their biggest complaint. Whether WebTV ever produces a new kind of set-top box with enough storage and other resources to handle Java is an open question. But current Classic users and most Plus subscribers shouldn't harbor any hope of seeing Java through their present boxes.

New versions of RealAudio

RealAudio is a format for music and other audio programming over the Internet. This format was created several years ago by a multimedia company called Real Networks. RealAudio is not the only type of audio heard on the Web, but it was one of the first such formats and retains a prominent position — particularly in Internet broadcasts. Many radio stations that offer Internet simulcasts of their programming use RealAudio to deliver the audio stream.

WebTV has worked with Real Networks to include RealAudio in the WebTV experience, right from the beginning in 1996. But Real Networks creates new and improved versions of RealAudio periodically — rather frequently, in fact — and WebTV has always been sluggish in keeping up to date. Each new version of RealAudio must be implemented in one of the automatic, periodic WebTV upgrades, but that doesn't always happen. There are both technical and political difficulties, but the upshot is that WebTV sometimes lags behind RealAudio — sometimes by a little, sometimes by a lot.

You might think this wouldn't be a problem. What's the worst that can happen — the sound of a radio station isn't as good as it could be? Actually, the problem is worse than that. Audio programming created with a new version of RealAudio is not always compatible with older versions of the built-in RealAudio player. So, when radio stations and other programmers update their RealAudio setup, that station or programming stream can no longer be played by WebTV. Hence the frustrating WebTV message, "The item chosen contains a kind of information that WebTV can't use." When you see that message, remember that you didn't do anything wrong!

Over the years, problems between WebTV and Real Networks have been more political than technical. WebTV subscribers have demonstrated the patience of Job in waiting out the situation. That patience was rewarded in the May, 2000 upgrade, which brought WebTV's RealAudio up to the version called G2, just one version behind the version most recently available to computer users. This upgrade improved the previous situation enormously, but you can't rely on RealAudio links *always* working. And if RealAudio continues to evolve, WebTV might lag further behind again.

Downloads

Download is a computer-speak word that means to acquire something (a program, a picture, a song, a story) from an online source. The downloaded item comes through the modem and is stored on the computer's hard drive. From then on, the user can access the stored item at any time, without downloading it again.

WebTV Classic set-top boxes do not contain hard drives, so downloading is clearly impossible. The first Plus boxes did contain hard drives (recent ones are manufactured without them) but nevertheless could not store downloads. The hard drives were used to store special content delivered by WebTV Networks and could not be accessed by users in the same way that computer hard drives are accessed.

The upshot is that downloading is out of the question for all WebTV Classic and Plus users. WebTV is a Web-surfing device and not a collection device. It views, but it doesn't store. Some Internet hobbies — such as trying shareware or collecting MP3 music — can be pursued only on a computer.

The lack of local storage (an accessible hard drive) means that WebTV is not task-oriented the way a computer is. It was never designed to be so — WebTV is decidedly recreational. But wait (you may ask), doesn't e-mail use local storage? Actually, no. Your e-mail is stored on WebTV's central computers, not in your set-top box. (See Chapter 6 to find out about WebTV e-mail.)

Multimedia

The Web is an increasingly multimedia domain, which means that it's getting easier to watch videos, hear music, and see animations. Two factors contribute to this trend. First, Internet programmers are getting better at developing multimedia conten t. Second, home Internet systems are getting better at playing multimedia.

WebTV has evolved substantially in the multimedia arena since it was introduced, and periodic major upgrades to everyone's set-top boxes continue that evolution. Still, some types of online multimedia content make WebTV choke:

- ✔ **Video.** WebTV understands two online video formats: MPEG-1 and VideoFlash. The first format represents a small but significant percentage of Internet video programming. The second is hardly ever used. Two important formats — Quicktime and AVI — can't be played through WebTV. Compounding the problem is the fact that video doesn't work well through a telephone modem even on a computer that can understand the format. The upshot? Don't plan on watching a lot of online films as a WebTV subscriber.

- ✔ **Adobe Acrobat.** Barely qualifying as multimedia, Acrobat is nonetheless an important file format that delivers formatted documents. Acrobat is often used to display spreadsheets and other material that combines text and illustrations. On a properly equipped computer, Acrobat opens up right inside the Web *browser* (the program used to surf the Web). WebTV doesn't have Acrobat built in. For most users, the lack of Acrobat is a minor problem; many people never miss it.

- ✔ **Word viewer.** WebTV's e-mail system can handle many types of *attachments* — that is, files that are appended to e-mail and must be selected separately from the e-mail to be viewed. Many types of text, sounds, and pictures can be displayed in this fashion, enabling WebTV subscribers to share multimedia with the Internet universe through e-mail. But some file formats can't be read in WebTV as attachments, most notably documents created in Microsoft Word, the most popular word-processing program. Ironic, isn't it, because Microsoft owns WebTV? WebTVers are not amused.

- ✔ **Shockwave.** A company called Macromedia invented a slick programming standard called Shockwave for delivering moving images and sound over the Internet. Only a small percentage of sites use Shockwave, but they are among the most dazzling sites around. WebTV can't display Shockwave content. The unfortunate aspect of this incapacity is that most sites that use Shockwave do so at the very front of the site — the animation is the first thing you see before getting to the main site. As a result, WebTV is often prevented from even entering sites that use Shockwave. (WebTV does handle a slimmer Macromedia programming type called Flash.)

✔ **Zip files.** *Zip* is a compression standard in which big files are made smaller so that people can download them quicker. It is, far and away, the most important and often-used file-shrinking method. Because WebTV doesn't allow downloads, you'd think that Zip compatibility would be a non-issue. That would be true if Zipped files weren't sent by e-mail, but they are. Someone might send you several family photos, for example, all Zipped together into a bundle. WebTV can't handle Zip compression in e-mail — although it can unzip music files that if finds on the Web. Tell your friends not to use Zip when sending you things.

WebTV and Computers

So if WebTV isn't a computer, how does it work? Isn't the Internet a computer network? (Yes.) How does WebTV connect to the Internet if it's not a computer?

Good questions, if I do say so myself. The WebTV set-top box is a computing device of sorts but not a personal computer by any stretch. It has circuits inside, just like a computer. But cars have computer circuits in them, and they aren't computers — neither are microwave ovens.

WebTV is a specialty device for getting you on the Internet through your TV and for organizing your TV viewing. (It can't drive you to the store or cook your dinner, though.) WebTV is neither better nor worse than a computer; it's easier in some ways and lacking in others. Table 1-1 outlines several significant differences between WebTV and *personal computers* (otherwise known as *PCs*).

Table 1-1	How WebTV Is Not Like a Computer	
Fact about WebTV	*Advantages*	*Disadvantages*
All the software you can ever use comes packaged right in the WebTV set-top box and is automatically updated periodically by the WebTV Network service. There is no such thing as purchasing new software from a store and then adding it to your WebTV system.	The system is hassle-free. You never have to worry about purchasing software upgrades, doing manual installations, or learning new programs.	You can't install your own software purchases or upgrade the system in personal ways.

(continued)

Table 1-1 *(continued)*

Fact about WebTV	Advantages	Disadvantages
WebTV is devoted to going online and viewing the Internet. The Plus version of WebTV also provides TV listings and adds picture-in-picture capability to any TV.	WebTV is a dedicated, simple, inexpensive, one-stop answer to those who want to get on the Net or manage their TV programming.	You can't do word processing, make a spreadsheet, or perform other tasks that are available on a computer.
WebTV has a built-in modem (the part that you plug your phone line into and that connects to the WebTV Network).	You never have to bother with choosing, installing, configuring, and troubleshooting a new modem (a curse to computer users everywhere).	With WebTV Classic, you can't take advantage of connection enhancements, such as DSL, for greater Internet speed. However, just installing DSL for a computer can cost more than a WebTV system.
WebTV upgrades are accomplished automatically, without your having to do anything, know anything, or (perish the thought) open the box.	You don't have to become a computer technician, which might be the last thing on earth you want to be.	You can't make the system faster or better than it is. Fortunately, the system is already very good at what it does.
WebTV doesn't have a lot of extra component features that add expense and difficulty to your experience. Although you can store letters and pictures in your e-mail box, no hard drive storage exists for collecting software programs. (You can add a printer to any WebTV system.)	The lack of extraneous features keeps WebTV inexpensive and easy to use.	Without a hard drive (the component on computers that stores things), you can't maintain a warehouse of games and other programs on the WebTV Classic system. Some WebTV Plus Receivers have a built-in hard drive, but it holds only material sent automatically by the WebTV Network, not personal files.
WebTV is much less expensive than a powerful multimedia computer.	You don't have to dip into your child's college fund.	Can you think of one?

DSL stands for Integrated Digital Subscriber Line, in case you were wondering — something you really don't need to worry about.

How WebTV Works

So. You have this new device in your home, and you may not have a clue about what you're getting into. Hey, it's not a problem! Most people have a million questions about the Internet and how to get on it, and they don't even know how to begin asking. So in this section I do the asking for you — and the answering, too. (I promise to keep it under a million questions, though.)

Is WebTV the same as cable TV?

WebTV has nothing to do with cable, even though the set-top box looks somewhat like a cable channel box. WebTV Classic doesn't receive cable or TV stations, and the WebTV Classic Internet terminal isn't involved with TV reception. (It doesn't interfere with reception, either.) WebTV works with whatever cable TV system you might have installed, without getting in the way of the cables. You can also have WebTV and a cable system plugged into your TV at the same time. Chapter 2 tells you how to set up WebTV in all types of configurations.

The WebTV Plus Receiver has, as the name implies, a built-in television receiver. Having a built-in TV tuner means that you can use the WebTV Plus Receiver to tune in your favorite stations, with the added benefit of limited picture-in-picture capability. *Picture-in-picture* is a feature that displays a second program in a small portion of the TV screen. (The Web goes in the big picture, and the television program goes in the little picture.) The picture-in-picture feature built into WebTV Plus enhances what I describe in the next paragraph.

Do I have to choose between TV and the Web?

No, you don't have to choose between TV and the Web. One of the big selling points of WebTV has always been that you can use it while watching TV. You don't have to shut the set off or even change channels to log on to WebTV. For example, you can log on in the background, so to speak, while you're watching a show and wait to use the Web during commercials. You can then switch back and forth between the TV and WebTV, as if the Web were another

TV channel. If you have a set with the picture-in-picture feature, you can see both at once, with the Web in either the large or the small screen. (WebTV Plus Receivers make any television capable of limited picture-in-picture, in which the Web must be the big picture.)

Are there different brands of WebTV?

Yes, you can buy different brands of WebTV. WebTV Classic has two brands: Sony and Philips-Magnavox. Things get even more varied with WebTV Plus. Sony and Philips-Magnavox both make Plus set-top boxes, as do Mitsubishi and RCA.

If you've already bought your WebTV system and are suddenly feeling like you might be missing out on a better brand, relax! Each service (WebTV Classic and WebTV Plus) provided by WebTV Networks is identical regardless of the system brand you choose (or already chose). You see the same things on the screen whether you're using WebTV Classic from Sony or Philips-Magnavox. Same deal with WebTV Plus service from any of the four manufacturers.

Certain distinguishing features exist in the hardware (the remote controls, the set-top boxes, and the peripheral devices attached to the boxes). For the sake of simplicity, I've written this book from the perspectives of a Plus subscriber using the Philips-Magnavox system and a Classic subscriber using both the Sony and Philips systems.

The DISHPlayer 500 system described in a previous sidebar in this chapter is manufactured by just one company, EchoStar. You must subscribe to EchoStar satellite TV to receive Plus service and WebTV Personal TV.

Do I have to get a special phone line?

Absolutely not. WebTV works with regular phone lines. You don't have to dedicate a line to WebTV, and it even works with the call-waiting feature available from most local phone companies, allowing you to take phone calls when they come in — even during a WebTV session. If you end up using WebTV quite a bit, you might want to get another phone line just for the Web, as many computer users do, but a separate line is not required.

Does the Internet cost money?

You pay a monthly fee for using WebTV to access the Internet, although the Internet itself doesn't charge a fee. It's kind of like taking a cab to get to a museum on the other side of town: The museum might be free, but you still have to fork over the cab fare to get to it. WebTV is your cab to the Internet, just as computer users pay America Online, Earthlink, or some other *Internet service provider (ISP)*. You pay for this cab every month. The monthly subscription fee gives you unlimited access — the museum never closes.

If you live outside the range of a local WebTV access telephone number, you must either pay a long-distance telephone charge to connect through the WebTV phone access system or pay a monthly rate to a local Internet service provider for your WebTV connection. If you log on to the WebTV Network through a local Internet service provider, bypassing the WebTV telephone network, you get a discounted monthly rate for the WebTV Network. (See Chapter 2 for an unforgettable description of how to use your own Internet service provider.)

Some Web locations do charge money for viewing. They are like the planetarium that charges for its shows in our metaphorical museum. Such sites feature special content that is (according to the site administrator and perhaps some customers) worth paying for. An example is *The Wall Street Journal Interactive Edition* — an online version of the newspaper. However, Web sites that charge a subscription fee for information or services are few and far between. Signing up for such services is entirely at your discretion, and it's virtually impossible to be inadvertently roped into spending money.

Does WebTV run up the phone bill?

In most cases, your home phone account doesn't even know that anything new is going on. WebTV provides local telephone access to the Internet, and you don't even have to find the number yourself. The system determines your local access number the first time you connect. In some infrequent cases, when subscribers live in remote areas, a local access number might be unavailable. In those cases, WebTV finds the closest number and informs the subscriber that the connection is not a local call.

Finding out what your access number is before setting up your account is a good idea. To do so, simply call the WebTV customer service number at 1-800-GO WEBTV (1-800-469-3288).

In many cases, WebTV assigns two access phone numbers to your account — a main number and a backup. The system automatically uses the second number when the first is busy. That backup number might be a toll call, even if the first number is a free call. Plus users can keep an eye on the screen during the logon process to see what number is being dialed. If the first number bombs out, the second number is displayed, including an area code if the number is outside the local calling area. (If you want to prevent WebTV from dialing that second number, select the on-screen Stop button.)

You may use dialing codes when logging on through WebTV. Chapter 4 describes how to customize your account to do so. Dialing codes can lower your phone bill if WebTV doesn't provide a local dial-in number.

Is getting connected difficult?

Getting connected could hardly be easier. If you've ever connected to an online service or the Internet — for example, on a friend's computer or at work — you know that it can be troublesome. I'm not exaggerating when I say that WebTV makes the process completely pain-free. The system is designed for people who don't know anything about computers or Internet service providers — and don't *want* to know anything about them. At the same time, easy connection appeals to anyone, even an online veteran who has wrestled with the aggravating hassles of getting a computer and a modem set up to behave correctly. To this day, I sometimes have trouble logging on with one of my computers, and I have just about every utility, software package, and hardware gizmo a person can spend money on. WebTV has been an absolute breeze from day one.

Because you don't have to acquire or configure any software and because the system automatically finds your local access phone number for you, all that's left is to push a button on the remote — connecting is that easy. This book goes to great lengths to describe the various on-screen WebTV features and explain how the Internet can fit into your life, but very little explanation is required to get you logging on (that is, connecting to the Internet) successfully. Any instruction you might need to log on is in Chapter 2.

Can I see TV programs on the Web?

For the most part, no. The Internet is an information and entertainment medium (sometimes called infotainment — really, I'm not making that up) that relies mostly on pages of text, pictures, sound, and animation. A few TV stations do feed their broadcasts into the Web or provide video clips of shows. WebTV is not currently equipped to view most of that TV programming on the Web.

You can, however, hear broadcasts of certain radio stations on the Web. I cover some Web features related to *Netcasting* in Chapter 12.

WebTV Plus integrates television and the Internet to a greater degree than WebTV Classic, thanks to some special features. The WebTV Plus Receiver can link you directly to Web pages related to the program you're watching. The integration of TV and the Internet might make it seem as if you're watching TV *through* the Web, but in fact you're simply watching TV in the normal fashion *while* surfing the Web. At present, very little special Internet content is embedded in this fashion.

WebTV isn't supposed to replace TV viewing — it's meant to enhance it. In Chapter 11, I describe many ways to make the best use of the Internet as a television "channel" that augments regular TV shows.

The big question: Should I buy Classic or Plus?

The most common question among people shopping for WebTV is whether to go for a basic unit (sometimes called WebTV Classic) or spend the extra money for a Plus system. Many WebTV Classic users also wonder whether to upgrade to Plus. The answer in both cases depends on how much you would value the features bundled into WebTV Plus, most of which are television features as opposed to Internet features. Here's the rundown:

✔ WebTV Plus provides a second Home screen that is all about your television reception and TV programming. (Chapter 5 describes this distinct Home screen.)

✔ WebTV Plus displays TV listings for your area or cable programming from your cable company, complete with brief show descriptions. So you can see, for example, who's on *The Late Show with David Letterman* or which *Seinfeld* rerun is on later.

✔ WebTV Plus integrates television programming with related Web sites, eliminating the need for a lot of Web searching when it comes to TV topics. This integration, however, is still somewhat undeveloped, with little crossover content. This feature should get better — more mature — over time.

✔ WebTV Plus lets you keep a small television window in the corner of your screen while surfing the Web, even if your TV doesn't have the picture-in-picture feature.

✔ WebTV Plus has a faster modem, which provides quicker displays of Web sites.

The upshot is that WebTV Classic is an Internet device that uses your TV, and WebTV Plus is a television device that accesses the Internet. The seamless integration of the TV and the Web that you get with Plus is very cool (you may control the whole shebang from a single handheld remote) but not important if you just want an inexpensive way to get e-mail. Likewise, if you're a pure Web surfer who likes to keep TV and Internet activities separate, go for the Classic system.

The World's Briefest Internet Primer

If you've spent some time on the Internet, you don't need to read this section. But if WebTV is your first brush with the online world and you're about to wade into the Internet for the first time, you might wonder just what you are joining. Very few things in this world are both as well publicized and as undefined as the Internet, and even after seeing hundreds of references to it in the news and in magazines, it's easy to wonder, "Just what exactly is this Internet thing?" It's one of the best questions you can ask as you venture into WebTV, and you've come to the right place to get the answer.

The foundation

The Internet consists of millions of computers connected to each other over telephone lines. It's enormous and growing constantly as new Internet computers (called *servers*) are added to the global network. You may be accustomed to thinking of a network as having a centralized hub maintained by whatever organization runs the network. The Internet doesn't work quite as you'd expect, though, because no one owns it or is charged with the responsibility for maintaining it. It is too vast and dispersed to be centralized, and tiny portions of it are owned by whoever installs a server and links it to the Net.

The Internet wasn't built recently, even though it might seem new with its newfound mass popularity. The Internet computer network was started decades ago by the United States Department of Defense. The Net has also long been used by academia to exchange research and information. Because the Internet rides on the shoulders of global telephone cables, it quickly became an international, nonpolitical network.

In the mid-1990s, the existence of the Internet suddenly caught the imagination of the wider population, which had already become enamored with online computing through services such as America Online, CompuServe, and Prodigy. The Internet is much more enormous than an online service and much more disorganized. (Remember, no company owns it, so no one whips it into shape.) The Internet is to an online service what the Wild West was to a frontier town.

The Web phenomenon

The Web is largely responsible for the sudden surge in Internet popularity. The Web is a software invention that makes the Internet easy to navigate. It is based on something called a *hyperlink,* or just *link* for short. Hyperlinks are things that appear on your screen that, when you select them, make something happen. Usually what happens is that your screen displays a new Web location. Because links are so easy and fun to use, browsing the Web from one link to the next has become a cultural pastime of the digital age.

Web locations are called *sites* and consist of pages with words, pictures, animation, sounds, music, and movies, although not all these things appear on each Web site and no Web site is as fluid or slick as a TV program. Web sites are big on information; they also contain some entertainment value. I describe some fun, informative, and service-oriented sites through much of this book. (Check Chapter 12 for multimedia sites and Chapter 14 for financial sites and for places to shop on the Web.)

Web sites are created by large corporations, small companies, and individuals. Anyone can add a Web site to the Internet. As you become familiar with the Web through your own explorations, you might encounter the whole range of quality and usefulness, from totally trivial sites, such as the *Star Trek* sing-along, to beautiful and evocative ones, such as those provided by the Internal Revenue Service. (Gulp.)

What to do on the Net

The Internet can be the biggest time bandit that the world has ever seen but also one of the most useful, timesaving inventions that you ever bring into your home. Most people strike a balance somewhere between the two extremes, investing some time exploring the Net's vast expanse to find what has value for them.

You can *surf* (that's Internet parlance for poke around) the Internet to get current news, order chocolates, hear a new album, chat with strangers, check your stocks, shop, take classes, write and send letters, read the newspaper, preview a new movie, get sports scores, shop some more, listen to the radio, join a fan club, do homework, learn about health, find old friends, participate in celebrity interviews (insert deep breath here . . . now proceed), check neighborhood movie times, shop a bit more, get your local weather, browse classified ads, visit a virtual museum, find a lawyer, research almost any topic that you can imagine, get soap opera updates, play on-screen games, and — in case I forgot to mention it — shop. And no matter how long I make this paragraph, I can show only the tip of the iceberg. The Internet is, for all practical purposes, endless.

Some Words to Know (This Is Not a Test)

New hobbies and certainly new technologies require new vocabularies. Don't worry, I don't require that you rant in technobabble at parties. You can pick up new words as needed right from the source — the Internet — while you explore it. But in this book, I use certain terms specific to WebTV, its features, and its controls, so it would be good for you to know what I'm talking about. Some of these words are generic to the online experience, and some are specific to WebTV. The following terms are all useful, delightfully funny, and profoundly enlightening — well, useful, anyway:

- **Connection.** I use the word *connection* to refer to your hookup to the Internet through WebTV. When you press the Web button on the remote, your set-top box dials your phone and connects you to the WebTV service, just like the phone company connects you to a friend when you make a phone call. In this case, the connection is between your set-top WebTV box and a computer at your local WebTV service. When you press the Web button again or use the Hang up option on the screen, you disconnect from WebTV.

- **Cyberspace.** A once-futuristic but now-commonplace term, *cyberspace* has its origins in science fiction. In the real world, cyberspace has come to mean any electronic realm that presents an alternative to the physical world. The Internet is a large part of cyberspace, as most people perceive it (as are virtual reality systems of the near future). Even playing an online video game represents a foray into cyberspace. In this book, I use *cyberspace* to denote the online world in general, including the Internet, the Web, and the entire on-screen WebTV experience. The metaphor of a physical space is probably the easiest way to imagine moving around the Web.

- **E-mail.** *E-mail* is the same as electronic mail. Chapter 6 describes e-mail to such an extent that you'll be dreaming about it. Electronic mail is a way of writing letters to anyone else who has an online account, either through WebTV or a computer. The mail is transferred right through the phone lines, bypassing the post office. E-mail is paperless and almost instantaneous. Because it's so fast, you can have e-mail conversations that go back and forth from here to, say, Japan several times during a day.

- **Highlight box.** A *highlight box* appears on your screen at all times when you are connected to WebTV. Use the Arrow buttons on the remote to move the highlight box around the screen. The box moves from link to link on the screen you're currently viewing. (See the definition for *link* in this section if you're confused.) When you select a particular link using the Select button in the middle of the Arrow buttons on the remote, the highlighted item on the screen makes something happen — in most cases, it displays a new screen. The highlight box takes the mystery out of determining what is a link and what isn't because it highlights only links.

I often use the phrase *highlight and select* in the instruction lists. This means you should move the highlight box to the specified link and press the Select button on the remote. The highlight box is present if a link exists somewhere on the screen.

✔ **Home page.** On the Web, *home pages* are the main, first, or front screens of multipage Web sites. People started referring to home pages when the Web was used mostly by individuals, especially college students, to share personal information online. Visiting early home pages was like entering a person's virtual home. Now that Web sites contain several, hundreds, and even thousands of individual pages (screens), the term has lost its original quaintness. I use *home page* when referring to a site's main page, the screen you first see when linking to that site.

✔ **Image map.** An *image map* is an on-screen picture that is also a collection of links. Highlighting and selecting different places within the image map takes you to different pages. Viewed through WebTV, image maps appear as big links, with the highlight box surrounding the whole picture. Selecting the image map turns the highlight box into an arrow that you move around the image map with the Arrow buttons on the remote. Select any portion of the image map by pointing the arrow at it and pressing the Go button of the remote. Although I call image maps *pictures,* they are not necessarily picturesque pictures — far from it in some cases! Image maps can be lists of text links, as in a table of contents, or a collection of icons that indicate where you go if you select the icon.

✔ **Link.** *Links,* also called *hyperlinks,* make the Web so easy and so much fun to browse. Links are the invisible cables that string the Web together — in fact, they make it a self-connected web. The main purpose of links is to connect one Web page to another, letting you travel among them without bothering with individual page addresses. Just select a link, and off you go. Most Web pages contain several links that lead to other pages both within the Web site you're exploring and outside it to other Web sites. On WebTV, links are identified by the highlight box that moves from one link to another on a page as you press the Arrow buttons on the remote.

✔ **Logging on.** Connecting to WebTV (or any online network, for that matter) is accomplished with a process called *logging on.* The WebTV logon procedure is initiated with the Web button on the remote, which connects the set-top box to the WebTV network through your phone line.

✔ **Network.** In this book, *network* does not refer to a group of television stations. In the fun and frenzied world of computers, a *network* is a bunch of computers, or computer services, that are connected. Online networks, such as WebTV, enable members to join and access the connected services. In this context, WebTV is itself a computer network (connecting many members) that, in turn, is part of a much larger network — the Internet.

✔ **Online.** The Internet, online services, and the Web are all part of the online world. *Online* refers to being connected through a personal device to a large network shared by many people. Connecting in this fashion has come to be known as *going online.* I refer to the entire WebTV connection experience as *being online,* whether you are exploring the Web or just checking your e-mail.

✔ **Online service.** Any network that provides network access to customers is called an *online service.* Famous online services include America Online, CompuServe, and the Microsoft Network, each of which provides members with online access, software, content (sites) to explore, and Internet access. The WebTV Network is an online service that provides access to the Internet without the need for a computer, uses the television to display Internet screens, and organizes Internet content in a useful way.

✔ **Search engine.** Services on the Web that help you find specific topics by entering keywords are called *search engines.* WebTV has a built-in search engine called, appropriately enough, Search. In Chapter 9, I describe how to use Search and point you toward other search engines on the Web, just for variety. You work each search engine in much the same way, but they perform their searches differently, yielding different results.

✔ **Surfing.** Browsing from link to link on the Web evokes images of riding the digital wave, and the word *surfing* has come to mean browsing the millions of interconnected Web pages. Surfing, cruising, and browsing all mean the same thing: exploring the Web.

✔ **Terminal.** A *terminal* is any device used to connect an individual to a network. Computers that access the Internet are called computer terminals. WebTV is not a computer, but the set-top box is a terminal, and in this book I sometimes refer to it that way.

✔ **URL.** This is an acronym for Uniform Resource Locator. *URLs* are the computer addresses of the Web. Every Web page has a distinct URL. URLs are long, cryptic strings of letters, numbers, and punctuation marks that threaten to choke you if you ever try to read one out loud. Fortunately, WebTV hides URLs from you for the most part, except when you want to see one. If you ever need to know the URL of the page you're viewing, press the Options button on the remote and select Info to see a display of the URL. You might be sorry that you asked for it. Most of the time, you don't need to tangle with URLs.

✔ **Virtual.** Anything that is nonphysical but still real (or seems real) can be called *virtual.* An online friendship, for example, in which two people have never met face-to-face but still talk regularly through e-mail or in chat rooms is called a virtual friendship. A *chat room* is a virtual room, because people can gather in it even though it doesn't have walls or physical features. Taken to the max, virtual reality is any technology-induced perception that mimics physical reality without any physical attributes. Because the entire online experience is essentially virtual, I occasionally use the term in this book.

✔ **Web directory.** Any organizational list of Web sites is a *Web directory.* The WebTV directory is bundled into the Search feature (see Chapter 9). The Search directory consists of selected Web sites divided into subject categories; this directory is especially helpful for Internet beginners. Other directories on the Web are larger, containing millions of links to Web sites accumulated by automated software that scours the Web for new additions. Whether big or small, most Web directories operate similarly, by dividing links into topics and letting you move from broad categories to narrower ones until you find the exact topic you're looking for.

✔ **Web page.** Every location on the Web consists of at least one page and usually many more. A *Web page* displays text, pictures, and sometimes other elements, such as sound or animation. A single page may be larger than your TV screen, extending far below it. (Use the Scroll buttons on the remote to see the whole page, as I explain in Chapter 3.) The page never extends off the side, however. All pages of a single Web site are connected with on-screen links.

✔ **Web site.** *Web sites,* like individual buildings in a city, are the essential structures of the Web. You can visit any site on the Web by linking to it or by directly entering its URL in the Go To screen. Most Web sites consist of many individual Web pages linked together. Web sites are sometimes purely informational and sometimes service-oriented. In the overwhelming majority of cases, they are free for anyone to access, although a few charge for a subscription.

✔ **WebTV Classic.** This is the first version of WebTV, as opposed to WebTV Plus (defined at the end of this list). WebTV Classic provides Internet access and the capability to switch between the Internet and television programming. WebTV Classic is made by Sony and Philips-Magnavox, both of which connect to the same service.

✔ **WebTV Network.** The online service you connect to through your WebTV set-top box is called WebTV Network. Subscribers to the Plus service connect to WebTV Plus Network. The company that provides both these services as well as your telephone access to the Internet is called WebTV Networks. It is also the company to which you pay your monthly subscription fee.

✔ **WebTV Plus.** The second generation of WebTV, featuring greater integration of Internet and television programming, as well as a faster modem.

Chapter 2

Everything You Need

- -

In This Chapter

▶ Unpacking your new WebTV components

▶ Connecting the WebTV set-top box to different TV systems

▶ Making your first call

- -

*T*his chapter tells you all you need to know about setting up WebTV and integrating it into your present television-cable-VCR system. Just look for the section in this chapter that applies to you (you don't *need* to have cable or a VCR) and follow the instructions.

Fortunately, WebTV comes with everything you need to get started. The only thing that's not necessarily included is the optional wireless keyboard. You do need to make a few cable connections before logging on to the Web, but connecting everything is only about as hard as setting up a new VCR. Keep reading to discover the purpose of everything that comes in the WebTV package and then continue to the next sections to hook it all up.

Opening the Box

When you open the box, you find the following items:

✔ **The set-top box.** You wouldn't get too far without the set-top box. The front has a SmartCard slot and the lights, which of course are not lit. (If they are, it's because you have an electrifying personality.)

The back has several jacks where you insert the cables. Look at the back and notice where everything will get plugged in.

The audio and video jacks are color-coded to match the cables. (Red and white are for audio; yellow is for video.) There's an S-video jack, which I talk about a little later in this chapter. You can see a standard telephone jack back there and, on the extreme right as you're looking at the back, the power jack.

The WebTV Plus Receiver has some extra plugs in the back and side of the box. A WebTV port adds future expansion capabilities. An extra set of video and audio plugs — again, gearing up for the future — enables hookup with a video camera, a VCR, or another audio or video device. Furthermore, a microphone input is not for karaoke, but for interaction with specialized Web sites that take audio input. Most important of all, the Cable In and Out jacks allow hookup directly to your cable system, as I describe later in this chapter.

✔ **The remote control.** You can put the remote aside until later when you read Chapter 3, where I describe it in exquisite detail.

✔ **Audio cable.** This is the black cord with red and white tips and two plugs on each end. The plugs match up with the audio inputs on the back of the set-top box.

✔ **Video cable.** This is the black cable with the yellow ends. It matches up with the single yellow jack on the back of the set-top box.

✔ **S-video cable.** This cable is black, with a multipin end. It is used with televisions that feature an S-video outlet in the back. The S-video connection to WebTV provides a slightly better picture than the yellow video cable. You should use only one or the other. If your TV has S-video, you can use either S-video or the regular yellow video cord, but the S-video input typically gives you the best picture. If you don't have an S-video television, you must use the yellow video cable.

✔ **Telephone cord.** The included phone cord looks like any other phone cord running from a wall outlet to a telephone.

✔ **Phone cord splitter.** The splitter is a phone wall outlet adapter that enables you to plug two devices into one phone wall outlet.

✔ **Power cord.** The power cord for WebTV is not permanently wired into the set-top box — it's detachable. One end goes in the wall electrical outlet, extension outlet, or power strip like any other plug, and the other end matches up with the power jack in the back of the set-top box.

The WebTV Plus Receiver comes bundled with some extra stuff that helps you make the more complicated hookups described later in this chapter. Following are the extras you get with Plus:

✔ **Coaxial cable.** Coaxial cables are the cords that connect cable TV to in-home devices such as VCRs and televisions. The plugs have one thin metal prong sticking out from the center. WebTV Plus includes a coaxial cable for hooking cable TV directly to the Plus Receiver.

✔ **IR Blaster.** Is this a cool name or what? The IR (InfraRed) Blaster is a device that relays remote control signals from the Plus Receiver to your cable box and VCR, enabling you to control the entire WebTV-VCR-television setup with a single control or the keyboard. The IR Blaster is a single plug on one end and two plastic sensors, about 2 inches long, on the other end. As I describe later in the chapter, you attach the plug to the back of the Plus Receiver and then position the plastic doodads underneath the Receiver and your VCR, if you have either or both of those components.

The IR Blaster that comes packaged with the Sony WebTV Plus Receiver has only one of the plastic gadgets at the end. This means you can use the IR Blaster to control either your cable box or your VCR, but not both. The Philips-Magnavox Plus Receivers, with the dual-action IR Blaster, provide a more complete integration of a cable-VCR setup.

✔ **Webeye (Philips-Magnavox WebTV Plus only).** The Webeye is a distinguishing feature of the Philips-Magnavox brand of WebTV Plus, and a terrific little feature it is. The Webeye is a remote-control sensing device that allows you to move the set-top box out of sight. With the small Webeye attached to the set-top box, you can point the remote to the Webeye while the larger Plus Receiver remains hidden.

Hooking Up WebTV Classic

Here's what you do with all that stuff that comes in the WebTV Classic box. You can connect the set-top box either directly to a television or to a VCR that's connected to your television. The order in which you make the connections — whether you plug in the audio cables or the video cable first — doesn't matter, but it's always safest to plug power cords in last.

Read on to find out how to connect WebTV Classic directly to a television. Skip to the next section to find out how to connect a WebTV Classic set-top box to a VCR.

Connecting to a TV directly (no VCR)

The following process is for people who are connecting WebTV directly to a television. (Skip to the next set of steps if you already have a VCR connected to your television.)

1. **Plug in the audio cables.**

   Pick up the cord with the red and white plugs at the end. The two ends of the cable are identical, so you can insert either end in the TV and the WebTV set-top box. Just make sure that you match each red plug with a red jack on the TV and the WebTV set-top box and match each white plug with the white jack on each unit. (It's not the end of the world if you don't match them correctly, but you get better sound if you do.)

2. **Plug in the video cable.**

   If you have a TV with an S-video connection, use the S-video cable and run it from the S-video connector on the television to the similar jack on WebTV. If you don't have an S-video TV, use the yellow-tipped video cable. Connect it from the television's video jack to the yellow jack of the set-top box.

   If at first you can't find the necessary connections, look for them on both the front and back of your television. Some TV sets hide the RCA jacks under a hinged panel.

3. **Plug in the phone line.**

   If you, like most people, don't want to completely disconnect your phone to use WebTV, you can use a simple adapter that turns a phone wall outlet into two outlets. The adapter is included in both the Sony and Philips-Magnavox versions of WebTV. It doesn't give you two phone lines, mind you, but it does allow you to share one phone line between two devices. (You can use only one at a time; either you're connected to WebTV or you're talking on the phone — never both at once on a single phone line.)

   Plug the adapter into the phone wall jack. Then plug your telephone line into one of the adapter's openings and plug WebTV's included phone line into the other opening. Finally, connect the other end of WebTV's included phone line into the telephone jack on the back of the set-top box.

   Telephone extension cords are also available so you can avoid the unsightly display of a phone line straggling across the room — that is, if you have a long enough extension cord. Given a long enough cord, you can run it along the baseboard and still reach the wall outlet.

4. **Plug in the power cord.**

   Plug the smaller end of the thick power cord into the WebTV set-top box. The cord fits only one way, and it's not reversible. Look closely at the plug, and you can see that one side is flat — match that side with the flat side of the jack and plug it in. Then plug the other end into a wall outlet, an extension cord, or a power strip. (Power strips with built-in circuit breakers protect all kinds of electronic equipment from power surges and are generally safer than standard extension cords.)

WebTV and Windows 98

Some people have the impression that there is an integration of WebTV and Windows 98: That is, if you have a computer running the Microsoft Windows 98 operating system, you can connect to the WebTV Network without a set-top box. Although it's true that WebTV has a limited presence in Windows 98, the notion of total integration is not true at this point. Here's the scoop.

The Windows 98 computer operating system does have a feature called *WebTV for Windows 98*. Understandably, this has caused some confusion. The truth is, *WebTV for Windows 98* is an entirely separate (and very limited) product, not connected to the WebTV Network enjoyed by WebTV Classic and Plus subscribers. This book is about the WebTV experience of connecting to the WebTV Network and accomplishing the unique interaction between the Internet and TV that the WebTV set-top box provides.

If you have access to a computer running Windows 98, however, you might want to explore the *WebTV for Windows 98* feature. You must have two things:

- A TV card installed in the computer. Such a card enables the computer to receive television broadcasts (and even cable reception) and display it on the computer monitor. Some new Windows 98 computers have TV cards built in; other computers must have them installed.

- *WebTV for Windows 98* installed as part of the operating system.

Windows 98 is a large, multifaceted operating system, and users have some choice about which portions get installed. To install *WebTV for Windows 98*, follow these steps:

1. **Click the Start button.**

2. **Point the screen cursor at Settings and then click Control Panel.**

3. **Double-click Add/Remove Programs.**

4. **On the Windows Setup tab, click the WebTV For Windows check box to select it and then click OK.**

5. **If you are prompted, insert your Windows 98 CD-ROM.**

6. **When prompted, restart Windows 98.**

WebTV for Windows 98 furnishes interactive television listings and some other special features. You don't even need an Internet connection to see some of *WebTV for Windows 98*. In fact, even the TV card isn't necessary to see the TV listings — you just can't use them on your computer without the card.

At this point, the complete WebTV experience is available only through a Classic or Plus set-top box, as described in this book. *WebTV for Windows 98* is an operating system add-on that gives computer users a small taste of a few WebTV features, without access to the WebTV Network online service.

Connecting to a TV through a VCR

Connecting the WebTV set-top box to a VCR is similar to connecting a set-top box to a television, as I describe in the preceding section. Follow these steps:

1. **Plug one end of the audio cables into the audio jacks of WebTV; connect the other end to the Audio In jacks on your VCR.**

2. **Plug one end of the yellow video cable into the yellow WebTV video jacks; plug the other end into the VCR Video In jack.**

3. **Plug a phone line into the WebTV set-top box.**

4. **Plug the power cord into WebTV and then into a wall outlet, an extension cord, or a power strip.**

5. **Make sure that the VCR is connected to the TV with a standard coaxial cable, or use an S-video cable if your VCR and TV have S-video connections.**

Connecting to a TV with cable (no VCR)

Adding WebTV to a cable-enhanced TV system gets a bit high-tech, but the rewards (great cable reception, a hundred or so channels, and millions of Web pages) are worth it. There are two basic cable setups: with a VCR and without a VCR.

Here's how to hook up WebTV to a basic, non-VCR home cable system:

1. **Leave the cable conversion box connected to the TV exactly as it is.**

   The cable that connects a conversion box to a television is called *coaxial,* or *coax* for short. It is the cable entering the home from outside and leading to the conversion box somewhere near the TV. The cable is plugged into the conversion box, and then another coax cable leads from a different jack on the conversion box and is plugged into the television.

2. **Plug in the yellow video cable from the video jack of the TV to the yellow video jack of WebTV.**

   Use the S-video cable if your TV is an S-video model.

3. **Connect the red and white audio cables from the WebTV audio jacks to the television audio jacks.**

   Be sure to keep the color-coding correct, matching the ends of the cables with the colors of the jacks.

4. **Plug a phone line into the WebTV set-top box.**

   Make sure that the other end is plugged into a telephone wall jack.

5. **Plug the power cord into WebTV and then into a wall outlet, an extension cord, or a power strip.**

Connecting to a TV with cable and a VCR

The most complex setup is a cable and VCR setup, but it's still not too difficult. If you have a cable TV conversion box and a VCR, adding WebTV gives you a darn dynamic home entertainment system with a ton of options. With a cable/VCR setup, it's best to treat the VCR as the nerve center of the system. You plug both the cable conversion box and the WebTV cords into the VCR, and then use a coaxial cable to connect the VCR with the television (which is how you normally hook a VCR to a TV).

Just follow these steps and you're ready to go:

1. **Connect the coaxial cable from the cable conversion box to the coaxial input of the VCR.**

   Most likely, this connection has already been made because most cable/VCR systems are set up in this fashion.

   If you're searching for the coaxial input of the VCR, be aware that it's sometimes labeled simply "IN," as if words were dollars and the manufacturer didn't want to spend too many of them. It's sometimes also labeled "Antenna," for systems that receive non-cable television broadcasts through the VCR. Whatever the darn thing is called, make sure you have a coaxial cable leading from the cable conversion box to that jack.

2. **Connect the yellow video cable from the WebTV video jack to the VCR's video jack.**

   If the VCR has a choice of Video In and Video Out (or similarly named) jacks, plug the yellow video cable into the Video In jack.

3. **Connect the red and white audio jacks from the WebTV audio jacks to the television audio jacks.**

   Be sure to keep the color-coding correct, matching the ends of the cables with the colors of the jacks. If you have a choice between Audio In and Audio Out jacks on the VCR, choose In for both the red and white cables.

4. **Plug a phone line into the WebTV set-top box.**

   Make sure the other end is plugged into a telephone wall jack.

5. **Plug the power cord into WebTV and then into a wall outlet, an extension cord, or a power strip.**

Using WebTV Classic with a VCR

Why would anyone connect the WebTV Classic set-top box to the VCR instead of to the television? With some older televisions, you don't have a choice. If you have a TV without audio or video inputs in the back, you need some way of getting the WebTV signal to the television. The VCR can fill that role, but it makes operating WebTV slightly more complicated.

When using WebTV Classic through your VCR, all functions operate identically to hooking it up directly to the television — except for switching back and forth between TV and WebTV. When WebTV is hooked up directly to the TV, switching is a simple matter of pressing the TV button on the remote. When WebTV is hooked up through the VCR, you must juggle three remotes to get from TV to WebTV, as follows:

1. **With your TV remote, change the channel to the one you normally use to watch a movie with your VCR (usually channel 3 or 4).**

2. **With your VCR remote, press the TV/VCR button.**

   The button might not be called exactly that, but it's the one you use to switch between a tape and the TV.

3. **With the WebTV remote, navigate the Web or log on.**

   Logging on for the first time is covered later in this chapter. Chapters 3 and 4 give you lots of basic information about using the remote and venturing into WebTV's basic features.

To get from WebTV to TV, just reverse the first two steps:

1. **With the VCR remote, press the TV/VCR button (or whatever it's called) to return to the television broadcast.**

2. **With the TV remote, change the channel to whatever you're watching.**

The main disadvantage of connecting WebTV Classic through the VCR is that you must change TV channels every time you switch to WebTV — unless, by chance, you're watching a show on the channel assigned to your VCR, usually channel 3 or 4. But with a little practice, you can juggle those remotes like a circus artist. Besides, juggling the remote is a lot easier than washing the dishes.

Hooking Up WebTV Plus

Setting up a WebTV Plus system is more complicated than setting up WebTV Classic, but the extra complications are worth it. In some cases (depending on your exact cable-television-VCR setup at home), the result is a beautifully integrated home-viewing and Internet-access experience, all controlled with a single remote.

To make the setup process clear, I've divided it into two stages. First, you must connect the TV signal (not the TV itself) to the WebTV Plus Receiver (the set-top box). A television antenna or a cable TV wire can carry the TV signal. (WebTV Plus works fine whether or not you subscribe to cable TV.) Second, you must connect the WebTV Plus Receiver to your television set. Through this two-stage procedure, you bring the TV signal from outside your house into the WebTV Plus Receiver and from there to your television set. If you have a VCR, it can get into the act, too. Read on to proceed with your setup.

Connecting WebTV Plus to the TV signal

Your first step is to get your TV signal, whether it's from a television antenna, cable TV, or a satellite, flowing into the WebTV Plus Receiver. This section looks complicated at first glance, but that's just because I'm covering all the options for every type of TV setup. Only one applies to you. Look over the headings to the following sections, find the one that describes your home TV setup, and follow those instructions. After you get to the part that applies to you, the setup isn't so difficult.

If you have a standard TV antenna (no cable or satellite TV)

If you're not a cable TV subscriber, you probably have some kind of signal-grabbing device attached to your TV. Antennae come in several shapes and sizes — some attach directly to the TV set, and others proudly survey the neighborhood from your building's roof. Whichever is the case, the antenna must connect to the back of your TV set. Your job is to remove the antenna wire from the TV and attach it to the back of the WebTV Plus Receiver.

The antenna wire has one of two types of plugs at its end, as you discover when you detach it from the television. Here's what to do with each type:

- ✔ **Coaxial plug.** If your antenna wire terminates in a coaxial plug, identical to the type of wire used by cable TV setups, your job is easy. (The coaxial plug is circular, with a single, straight, thin piece of metal sticking out from the center.) Pull the plug out from the television and plug it into the Cable In jack of the WebTV Plus Receiver. Never mind that you don't have cable TV — that's still the correct jack.

- ✔ **Twin antenna leads.** Some antennae wires terminate in a pair of U-shaped clips that get screwed into place on the TV. If that's the type of antenna you have, you need to purchase an adapter that converts those twin leads into a coaxial plug. (You can buy such adapters at most electronics stores, such as Radio Shack.) Screw the twin leads into the adapter just as they were screwed onto the TV and then plug the adapter into the Cable In jack of the WebTV Plus Receiver.

Hooking up a satellite system

If you use a satellite system for your TV reception, follow the instructions for connecting WebTV to a cable system. Simply exchange your satellite box for the cable box, and adjust the cables in the same way.

If you have cable TV with a cable box (no VCR)

Cable TV systems come in two flavors: with a set-top box and without one. (You don't have a choice of which kind you have; it depends on how your cable company prefers to deliver the signal.) The cable set-top box controls channel selection and receives input from the cable remote control. It also receives the cable signal from outside the house, and relays it through a coaxial cable to your television. Your job now is to change the signal's path — you want it relayed to the WebTV Plus Receiver instead. It's easy:

1. **Follow the coaxial cable from the Out jack of your cable TV set-top box, and unplug the other end.**

   The other end is probably plugged into your television set. Don't unplug anything from the cable box itself.

2. **Plug the removed coaxial cable into the Cable In jack of the WebTV Plus Receiver.**

If you have cable TV without a cable box (no VCR)

If your cable system doesn't include a cable set-top box and if you also don't have a VCR, the coaxial cable bringing the cable signal into the house is plugged directly into your cable-ready television set. Your job is to divert the cable signal by putting it into the WebTV Plus Receiver before allowing it into your TV set. Here's how:

1. **Unplug the coaxial cable from the back of your TV set.**

2. **Plug the cable into the Cable In jack of the WebTV Plus Receiver.**

If you have cable TV without a cable box, plus a VCR

If your cable TV subscription comes without a set-top box and if you have a VCR, your coaxial cable is plugged into the VCR first; then the cable signal is routed through another coaxial cable to your television set. You need to arrange the signal's path so that the WebTV Plus Receiver gets the signal before the television set. Just follow these steps:

1. **Unplug the coaxial cable from the In jack of your television set.**

   Leave all the other connections intact. The coaxial cable in your hand is connected to the Out jack of your VCR, and you are about to plug the free end into the WebTV Plus Receiver.

2. **Plug the free coaxial cable into the Cable In jack of the WebTV Plus Receiver.**

   Now your cable TV signal comes from outside your house into the In jack of your VCR; then another coaxial cable takes the signal from the Out jack of the VCR to the Cable In jack of the WebTV Plus Receiver.

If you have cable TV with a cable box, plus a VCR

This setup has everything. You are a cable TV subscriber; the cable company has provided a set-top box; you have a VCR connected to the system; and now you're adding the WebTV Plus Receiver.

Currently, your TV signal proceeds from outside the house to your cable set-top box; from the cable set-top box to the VCR; and from the VCR to the television set. Your job is to insert the WebTV Plus Receiver between the VCR and the television set. It's not hard:

1. **Unplug the coaxial cable from the In jack of your TV set.**

2. **Take the coaxial cable you just unplugged, and plug it into the Cable In jack of the WebTV Plus Receiver.**

This is the most complicated of all possible setups, so it's worth reviewing all the connections. You should now have three coaxial cables in the following arrangement:

- ✔ The first coaxial cable runs from outside the house to the In jack of the cable TV set-top box.

- ✔ The second coaxial cable runs from the Out jack of the cable TV set-top box to the In jack of the VCR.

- ✔ The third coaxial cable runs from the Out jack of the VCR to the Cable In jack of the WebTV Plus Receiver.

Connecting WebTV Plus to the TV

One of the previous sections applies to your home TV setup; by now, you should have your TV signal (broadcast or cable) connected to the WebTV Plus Receiver. The final step is to bring the television set itself into the picture (so to speak). You do this by connecting the WebTV Plus Receiver to the TV set, so that the TV set is the final component to receive the TV signal.

Tying things together with the IR Blaster

The IR Blaster, a remote signal-sensing device, is included in the WebTV Plus package. But you don't have to use it. It adds convenience to the WebTV setup and activates some of the coolest television features of the Plus sytem, but it's not a requirement. The IR Blaster has nothing to do with the Internet portion of WebTV viewing. The Blaster's function is to let you control your entire system (television, cable or satellite channels, and VCR controls) with a single remote or the keyboard.

The IR Blaster is a long Y-shaped wire with a small plug on one end and two plastic devices on the other end. The plastic devices are on separate wires, so they can be separated by a few feet. The purpose of these little plastic devices is to relay infrared signals from the Plus Receiver to your cable box, your VCR, or both. Here's how to set up IR Blaster:

1. **Insert the Blaster plug into the IR Blaster jack on the back of the Plus Receiver.**

2. **Slip one of the plastic devices underneath your cable or satellite box.**

   Disregard this step if you don't have a cable or satellite box. If you do, position the Blaster near the infrared sensor of the box. (Shine a flashlight at the front of the box if you have trouble discerning where the sensor is.) The raised portion of the plastic device remains in front of the cable box.

3. **Slip the other plastic device underneath your VCR.**

   Disregard this step if you don't use a VCR. Again, position the Blaster near the VCR infrared sensor.

You're now ready to use the IR Blaster. Don't do anything with it just yet. You need to make your first logon call and establish an account first, as I describe in this chapter. Then check out Chapter 5, where I explain the features activated by the Blaster.

You have three options for connecting WebTV Plus to the TV set. Which one you use depends on what kind of television set you have — specifically, what plugs are on its back panel. Following are the three options:

- ✔ **Using the S-video cable.** If your TV set is equipped with an S-video jack, this option provides the clearest picture. Take the S-video cable included in the WebTV Plus package, and connect one end to the S-video jack on the WebTV Plus Receiver and connect the other end to the S-video jack on your TV set.

- ✔ **Using the audio and video cables.** If your TV set has audio and video jacks (two Audio Ins and one Video In), you may use the color-coded audio and video cables. This option might provide the second-best picture quality. (I can't see much difference between this option and the following one — and the following option is simpler.) Plug the audio and video cables into the Audio and Video Out jacks of the WebTV Plus Receiver, and then plug the other ends into the Audio and Video In jacks of the TV set.

✔ **Using a coaxial cable.** If your TV set lacks audio and video jacks, or even if it has them, you may use this simple option. (An advantage to this option is that it leaves the audio and video jacks free for auxiliary input, such as from a camcorder.) Plug a coaxial cable into the Cable Out jack of the WebTV Plus Receiver, and then plug the other end into the coaxial In jack of the TV set.

After you have completed one of the preceding options, you're finished! With the essentials, anyway. (See the sidebar "Tying things together with the IR Blaster" for instructions on using the IR Blaster.) Congratulations! At this point you may proceed to making your first logon call to WebTV Network and establishing a WebTV account.

Your First Call

Having made all the wire connections, the fun can really begin. You are ready to make the first logon call, sign up for the WebTV service (Classic or Plus, depending on which hardware you bought), and begin exploring the Internet. Kind of makes you shiver with anticipation, doesn't it? If not, take a moment to drop an ice cube down your shirt.

Making that first call is easier than operating a telephone. You do it with exactly one step:

> **Pick up the remote control, point it toward the set-top box, and press the Web (Classic) or Power (Plus) button.**

You probably don't need any help because the system walks you through the first call and the subsequent sign-up process. There is a slight wait the first time you dial in — here's what's going on:

1. **Waiting for an answer.**

   WebTV has dialed your phone and is waiting implacably for an answer. Don't worry; it isn't calling someone in Prague. It's dialing a toll-free number belonging to WebTV Networks.

2. **Starting communication.**

   A friendly computer answers on the other end, and the two systems are chatting happily.

3. **Connecting to WebTV.**

   You're almost there, right?

4. **Starting to dial.**

Wrong. Now it's starting over. What gives? In the first call, WebTV determined your location and found a local number for your set-top box to use from now on. Now it's dialing that local number.

5. **Waiting to connect.**

Whistling or tapping your fingers greatly enhances the performance of your system at this point.

6. **WebTV answering.**

Yeah, yeah — you've seen it all before.

7. **Connecting.**

Aha! Now you're getting somewhere. All the previous scintillating repartee is about to pay off.

8. **Connected to WebTV.**

Wake up — you're connected!

You're almost on the Web, but first, you have some signing up to do. The following process establishes your main household account. It unfolds as a succession of screens, some containing information and others asking for it. If you bought the optional wireless keyboard, you have reason to celebrate when you fill out the Sign-up screens. If you didn't, the opening screens don't require all that much typing, and you can use the on-screen keyboard with no problem.

The opening screens are all self-explanatory. But I would like to emphasize these points:

✔ **If you don't have the wireless keyboard, you can use the on-screen keyboard.** Simply press the Select button on the remote (sometimes called the Go button), which is located in the middle of the four Arrow buttons, whenever an information form is highlighted on the screen. An information form is any empty field that looks like it wants you to type into it.

✔ **You can pay the monthly charge for the WebTV Network with a credit card or by check.** Just remember that if you pay by check you must always buy six months of service in advance. If you choose to pay by check, WebTV Networks will bill you through *snail mail*. (Get used to that term — it's what Internet users call the U.S. Postal Service in comparison to the almost instant response of e-mail.)

The service agreement

Right after you enter your billing or payment information, WebTV offers you an opportunity to read the service agreement. It's a standard agreement like the ones you find in all online services. It is also 50 screens long! You're responsible for knowing the contents of the service agreement if you ever have a legal discussion with WebTV Networks. I completely understand if you don't want to dive into it now, when you're on the verge of attaining full Webness. You don't have to read the service agreement at this stage, and you can always refer to it later.

Finishing up

The final screen in the sign-up process is a review screen showing you all the information you've entered about yourself. To change anything, use the Back button on the remote or the keyboard to return to a screen you want to change. Then, after making your changes, select the Continue button on the screen to move up through the pages.

When you get to the You've Finished Signing Up screen, highlight and select the Continue button. In a few seconds, one of the Home screens is displayed, which I elucidate in Chapters 4 and 5 with the kind of transcendental clarity normally associated with religious revelations.

Disconnecting

You can disconnect from WebTV — basically, hang up the phone — in three ways:

- ✔ **Do nothing.** If you keep doing nothing for a while, WebTV disconnects *you!* The process is called *timing out,* and it takes effect when WebTV hasn't received any commands from the remote control or the keyboard for ten minutes.

- ✔ **Press the Web or Power button.** Doing so turns off the power to the set-top box. An effective, if abrupt, way of disconnecting.

- ✔ **Press the Options button of the remote and then select the Hang up option.** The features of the Options button are described in Chapter 3. But you can try it now to disconnect. The advantage to disconnecting this way is that the set-top box continues to be powered on, making your next logon procedure faster.

Chapter 3

Using the Remote and the Keyboard

. . . .

In This Chapter

▶ Using the Web button to log on

▶ Getting a grip on the remote control

▶ Understanding the remote's buttons

▶ Using the wireless keyboard as a remote control

. . . .

The WebTV remote control is the heart of the system. Without it, the set-top box is useless. The remote (or the optional keyboard, which contains most of the functions of the remote) is your interface to the Internet through WebTV. With nothing but the remote in your hand, you can surf the Web and even do some limited typing with the help of an on-screen keyboard. This chapter explains the functions of the WebTV remote control, the keyboard, and how to highlight and select on-screen items.

Firing It Up

Connecting with WebTV is ridiculously easy. Well, it might not seem ridiculous if you haven't wrestled with computers very much. To anyone who has spent a delightful summer evening struggling to install software, train a modem, or establish contact with an unwilling online network, the WebTV system is a solution from paradise.

The key to the city, so to speak, is right on your remote control in the form of the Web (or Power) button. (Different manufacturers make WebTV equipment, so sometimes the same buttons are labeled with different names.) The Web/Power button is all you need to connect to the Internet. Pressing it initiates the following sequence of events:

1. The set-top box's power is turned on (if it was off).

2. The box dials your local access number and connects with the WebTV Network.

3. After you're connected, the system takes you to a Home screen, the starting point of each session.

If the power is turned off when you press the Web (or Power) button, WebTV might display a screen asking whether you've moved. It's not asking whether you've changed position on the couch. The system wants to know whether your box is still at the same address, and if it should dial the same phone number to log on. If you're in your home, just press the Select button on the remote (sometimes called the Go button) to continue the logon process.

Plus users have the pleasure of viewing an advertisement while logging on. You know the era of interactive TV has arrived when commercials play while you're connecting to the Web. Welcome to the twenty-first century.

Three easy steps! On a computer, connection can require several clicks, menu pulls, program boots, and if it's the first time you connect, considerable time configuring all your software. Reducing connection to a single button-push is something anyone can live with.

One-Thumb Browsing

I didn't invent the expression *one-thumb browsing*. WebTV promotions featured the idea of one-thumb browsing when the device was first introduced, and I liked the ring of it. It has the ring of truth. You can now surf the Web — and in high style, in my opinion — with your thumb hovering over the remote as you languish in living-room luxury. No other digits are required or even encouraged. (Unless you decide to use the wireless keyboard, which is described later in this chapter.)

This section describes how the remote works and what all the many implementations of thumbage do. I've written this book from the viewpoint of someone using the Sony or Philips-Magnavox WebTV Classic remote and the Philips-Magnavox WebTV Plus remote. (See Figure 3-1 for a picture of the remote that comes with the Sony WebTV Classic.)

Figure 3-1:
The remote control for the Sony WebTV Classic Internet terminal.

Taking remote aim

The natural impulse when holding a remote control is to aim it at the TV. Remember that the WebTV remote is sending its invisible signals to the set-top box, not the television. This is not a problem if the box is placed directly above or below the TV set. If you're clicking the buttons to no avail and the terminal box is placed at a slight distance from you (such as on the bottom shelf of a television stand), remember: Aim for the box, not the tube!

The only exception is if you have the Philips-Magnavox WebTV Plus Receiver, which comes with the Webeye that I describe in Chapter 2. In that case, aim for the Webeye, and feel free to hide the set-top box out of sight.

Making things happen: The Arrow and Select buttons

If, six months from now, your remote control has a thumb trail worn in it, the trail probably leads to the Arrow buttons because they are by far the most-used selectors. The remote has four Arrow buttons representing the four sacred directions of pagan ritual ceremonies. The truth is, they point only up, down, left, or right, which is vaguely traditional. In this case, the Arrow buttons make the highlight box move around the screen.

The Arrow buttons and highlight box fulfill the function of the mouse and cursor on a computer, but they operate differently. In both cases, the goal is to select something on the screen. A computer achieves this goal by providing a smooth moving on-screen cursor that responds to movements of the mouse as you slide it around the desk. Using the mouse, you can position the cursor at any point of the screen, even if selecting that point does nothing. By contrast, on WebTV, you can position the highlight box only on a Web link. (If you are viewing a screen that has no links — which is very unusual — there is no highlight box.) When you use the Arrow buttons on the remote, the highlight box jumps from its current link to the one above (if you use the Up-arrow button), below (if you use the Down-arrow button), and so forth. Because the highlight box is always positioned on a link, something always happens when you use the Select button.

The Select (or Go) button lies in the middle of the Arrow buttons, like an egg in a nest. Use it to activate any link currently in the highlight box. Selecting a link with the Select button is how you move from one Web location to another. With a little practice, you should be able to perform most Web journeys with the merest movements of your thumb among the five buttons — shifting the highlight box with the peripheral Arrow buttons and going places with the central Select button.

Most of the time, your thumb should nestle in the cradle formed by the four Arrow buttons. (On some remotes, the Select button is recessed cozily within the four Arrow buttons; on other remotes, it's raised.) In that position, it's easy to lean your thumb against an Arrow button suggestively enough to make the highlight box jump to its next position (especially with the Sony remote). You need to develop the right feel for the subtle highlight maneuver so that you don't press too heavily against the center Select button and accidentally activate a link. Of course, the other reason to practice with the Arrow buttons is to develop utter coolness and suave surfing habits — you want to convey an appearance of effortless screen navigation to impress your friends.

Sometimes, you reach screens with a link that's already highlighted as a default selection. On a style survey page, for example, you might be asked a question such as, "Do you wear socks most days of the week?" Because the creator of the Web site assumes that, indeed, most people do wear socks on most days of the week, the Yes link is highlighted as a default response. In such situations, you can simply press the Select button and your link is made. If no default-highlighted selection exists for a certain link, simply follow the instructions in the previous paragraphs. Then put on some socks.

Back to the future

Wandering the Web is best accomplished by simply following links; you can experience a certain delight in going deeper into the dense online jungle, getting more lost with every blithe, information-soaked minute. Many times during such roamings, moving forward from link to link isn't desirable. Specialized buttons on the remote help you retrace your steps and even give you a fresh start instantly.

The most important of the dedicated buttons for retracing your steps is the Back button. Pressing the Back button takes you one step backward in your convoluted trail through the Web. It works on the breadcrumb theory. (How many breadcrumbs does it take to change a light bulb? That's not the theory, but if you know the answer, e-mail me.) WebTV keeps track of your movements and lets you recapture them with the Back button. Press this button whenever you want to redisplay the preceding screen, and keep pressing it to continue stepping backward.

The Back button is notably useful when exploring the multiple pages of a single Web site — a common situation. Suppose you arrive at a shopping site's home page and select a link that displays a menu of gift categories within which you can do some online shopping. You choose one and follow that link to a small catalog of food-related gifts. After browsing for a while (and buying some imported chocolate to send me in appreciation for writing this book), you want to return to the menu of gift categories. Simply press the Back button — and step backward to the preceding menu. You may continue this way indefinitely, ordering gifts for everyone you know, until your credit card begs for mercy.

Computer users are accustomed to Back buttons as they're represented in Web *browsers* — a type of software program for accessing the Internet. These users are also familiar with Forward buttons that send them, well, forward — after first using the Back button. In other words, a computer browser's Forward button steps you forward through sites you've just backstepped through. The two browser commands (Back and Forward) are useful together, letting the browser shuffle back and forth between Web pages. WebTV has no Forward button, but having backtracked, it's easy enough to find and select the link that originally took you forward by simply using the Recent button, which I describe next.

Messages from an untalkative system

WebTV doesn't usually pester you with a lot of system feedback in the form of on-screen messages. It just lets you go about your Internet business. But no feedback at all can be disconcerting at times, leaving you wondering whether anything is happening. This is especially true on the Internet, where slight delays between pages are inevitable.

When you select a link, a small box appears in the upper-left corner of the screen indicating that WebTV is accessing the page represented by that link. (See the figure.) Words such as Contacting publisher or Connecting reassuringly appear in the box. If a delay lasts too long, WebTV stops trying, under the assumption that you don't want to spend the entire evening staring at nothing happening. After about a minute of unsuccessfully trying to access a page, the system displays a message,

such as That Web page kept you waiting and waiting and allows you to try another link. (Long delays and unsuccessful page accesses are caused by Internet traffic jams, not by some problem with the WebTV system.)

The surfing experience is also accompanied by soft, inconspicuous system sounds that cue you in to what is happening on the screen. Most of these sounds are audio responses to buttons you press on the remote. When you select a link, a slight chirping sound lets you know that WebTV received the request. A pillow-soft sound reminiscent of a machine politely saying "no" emanates when you try to scroll past the bottom of a page. These audio hints are welcome to most people, but if they get on your nerves, you can mute the television or turn down the volume.

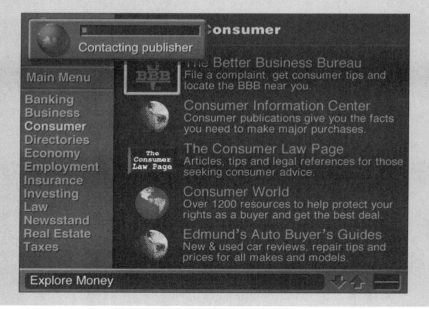

When you select a link to access a new page, WebTV begins displaying the page quickly, even before it has received the whole thing, and you can begin reading and scrolling while pictures are still appearing along its length. A small indicator at the lower-right corner of the screen lets you know whether the page is complete. When the green line is jagged and moving, parts of the page are still loading. When it's horizontal and motionless, you have the whole thing.

You don't have to wait for the page-loading indicator to go flat before selecting a new link and moving past that page. If you see a link you want to follow and the page-loading indicator on the bottom-right of the screen is still jagged and moving, simply highlight and select the link as if the page were completely loaded. You can't do any harm or confuse the system in any way.

The recent past

The Back button is great for moving one step at a time, but what if you want to jump back two, three, or more steps? Picture yourself in that shopping site again. (What do you mean you never left?) You're at the gift category menu. You go to the food catalog, but you can't decide what kind of chocolate to send me. You follow a link that describes a particular gift package more completely, including showing you a picture. It looks like the perfect author gift. (My birthday is in March.) Deciding to order, you select the Order button, which takes you to another page. The ordering process actually takes two pages, plus a confirmation page that displays when you're finished. Whew!

Now you are several pages removed (forward) from the gift category menu, and you want to return to it so you can start the whole grueling process anew. This is where the Recent button comes in handy. It's more than just handy — it's essential. Press it, and a panel pops up showing you the last 12 screens in your travels. WebTV, ever so helpfully, shows you a small picture of each of the 12 recent pages to remind you visually of where you've been. You can highlight and select any one of the images to return to the page instantly, leapfrogging over the intermediate stops.

The Recent button works similarly to the History or Go lists in computer-based Web browsers. WebTV's version is better in one way and lacking in another. First, the bad news: Using the WebTV Recent button, you can look back in time only 12 steps. On a computer, the length of the History list is variable, depending on how you set up the browser. The good news is those little pictures of your recent Web visits. The pictures let you see the screen you're looking for and get back to it much more easily than staring at a bunch of cryptic page titles or URLs in a Web browser. Also, WebTV is designed to be easy at every stage, and it's probably just as well that there's no way to fiddle with the settings.

Oh, Auntie Em, it's good to be home!

Like the tornado-tumbled Dorothy, whose adventures in Oz might be likened to a romp through the Web, sometimes the best thing is to click your heels three times and get home as quickly as possible. WebTV cuts to the chase when it counts most by providing a dedicated Home button that zips you back to the Web Home screen instantly, from anywhere that you happen to be.

WebTV Plus has two Home screens. (See Chapter 5 for a description of TV Home, the other Home screen in Plus.) Using the Home button takes you to the Web Home screen. You can always get to the TV Home screen by pressing the View button of the remote or the keyboard.

Use the Home button whenever you want to get to one of the basic services — Mail, Explore, or Search — from deep within the Web. The remote has no dedicated buttons for those areas (although the buttons exist on the keyboard), but these services are only one selection away from the Home screen. This means no basic aspect of the service is ever more than two button-pushes away.

Options

The Options button is the multifunction button on the remote. You can press it from anywhere on the Web, and it displays a panel with on-screen buttons that represent several choices. Just highlight and select any of the following options:

- ✔ **Info.** Select `Info` to display the URL (address) of the page you're currently viewing. I can think of few occasions when this is desirable, but if you want to write down the URL for some reason, perhaps to give to a friend, the `Info` option is how to get it. Computer Web programs always display the URL atop the page, and the `Info` feature keeps apace with that tradition. Furthermore, in many cases, the Info panel tells you when the current page was last modified, which can be handy when viewing a news or sports page. But for practical purposes, `Info` is probably the least-used option.

- ✔ **Find.** `Find` enables you to look for a specific item in a Web site. Suppose you're reading a news story on-screen. You know that a public figure you're interested in is mentioned in the story somewhere, and you want to jump right to that section. Highlight and select `Find` on the Options panel. An entry form pops up in which you can type the words(s) you're looking for. After entering the word you're searching for, highlight and select the `Find on Page` button (or simply press the Return key on the keyboard). The Web page scrolls down (if necessary) to the point at which your word is located, and highlights the word in a different color so you can spot it right away.

If the page you're on doesn't contain any instances of the word(s) you're searching for, a message appears saying `Could not find the word on this page`.

✔ **Save.** This incredibly useful feature functions like a treasure chest, saving the page you're on in your collection of Favorites. (See Chapter 4 for a complete description of Favorites.) When you highlight and select `Save`, a window appears, enabling you to select the Favorites folder in which to save the page. Select the folder and then select the `Save Page` button; a small panel appears with a treasure chest on it. The chest opens, glitters, and closes, indicating that the page has been stored under lock and key in your Favorites collection.

✔ **Send.** You can e-mail nifty Web pages to your friends with the `Send` option. Actually, the page itself doesn't get e-mailed anywhere, but its URL does in hyperlink form. The address can simply be highlighted and selected by other WebTV users to visit the page. It's really better than sending the actual page, which would clog up the recipient's mailbox.

After clicking the `Send` option, type the e-mail address of a recipient, and then highlight and select the `Send Page` button (or simply press the Return key on the keyboard).

You can use `Send` to deliver an e-mail page link to any electronic address, even if it's outside WebTV. The result is the same: A selectable URL is placed in the recipient's mailbox with your return address. Most computer folks use e-mail programs that recognize Web links, and they can click these links to visit the page you want to show them. Even if a user's e-mail does not display the URL as a link, he or she can copy the address and visit the Web site you suggest.

✔ **Go to.** If you know the URL of any Web location, you can enter it directly using the `Go to` option. For example, you could determine the URL of a Web page using the `Info` option, copy it down, and enter it in the `Go to` option at some later time. But it would probably be easier to just save the page and link directly to it from Favorites. Some Web sites have easy-to-remember URLs. In fact, many of the big ones do. For example, the URL for Yahoo! is `www.yahoo.com`. Well, that might not seem too easy at first glance, but after you get the hang of using URLs, it is indeed a simple task. In addition, many companies and organizations are now including URLs in television and magazine advertisements — and the `Go to` option is the quickest way to visit those Web sites.

Speaking of learning URLs, WebTV makes it very easy. You really don't have to learn much because the system encourages you to use a kind of shorthand when entering addresses with the `Go to` option. The standard parts of the URL that remain unchanged in most Web addresses are assumed to be part of what you're entering. (That would be the `http://` prefix, the `www` part, and the `com` part, plus the periods that separate the parts.) All that you need to type is the organization name that usually falls between the `www.` and the `.com`. In the case of the Yahoo! example, that's `yahoo`. The rest of the URL is filled in for you.

✔ **Reload.** This choice is available when you select the Advanced options portion of Setup (see Chapter 4 for more information). Reload takes the current Web page and simply loads it into your TV screen again. This is useful when updating sports scores or any other page information that changes frequently or when a page seems to load only halfway.

The Reload option corresponds to the Refresh or Reload button found on Web browsers. Computer users click the Refresh button when they want to see updated content on a page or when a page stalls, partly loaded. (Always a frustrating experience, for computer users and WebTVers alike.) The Reload option on WebTV isn't quite as convenient because it takes at least two clicks of the remote or the keyboard instead of one click on a computer. Nevertheless, it's a handy feature.

✔ **Hang up.** The second Advanced option, Hang up, lets you disconnect from WebTV without turning off your set-top box. Disconnecting this way is best when you've set up Automatic mail checking and you want to have the red light inform you of e-mail that has arrived. (See Chapter 4 for more information about the automatic mail check feature.)

✔ **Print.** Using the Print option creates a paper copy of the screen currently in view — but only, of course, if you have a printer connected to your WebTV set-top box. Chapter 4 describes how to set up your system for using a printer and which printers work with WebTV.

✔ **TV Window.** One option is available only on the WebTV Plus screen — the TV Window option. Selecting TV Window brings a small version of the current TV channel to the screen while you're using the Web. This picture-in-picture (PIP) feature works on all television sets, even those that don't have PIP built in. If you find that the TV Window screen gets in the way (it does obscure a corner of the Web screen you're looking at), just call up the Options panel and select TV Window again to get rid of it. By the way, using this feature automatically mutes the WebTV soundtrack (see Chapter 4), if you have it playing.

When you use the TV Window option in WebTV Plus, a small picture-in-picture version of the current TV channel appears in the lower-right corner of the Web screen (and the small light on the TV Window option button turns green). Sometimes the TV Window screen obscures a portion of the Web page you want to see. One tip is to scroll the Web screen down a bit, revealing what was underneath the TV Window screen. A second tip is to press the Enter button on the remote, which moves the TV Window screen to the bottom-left corner of the Web screen. You can keep pressing Enter to shuttle the TV Window screen back and forth across the screen as needed.

Seeing beyond the edges: The Scroll buttons

Some Web pages are long — quite long. In fact, there's no limit to how long a Web page can be. (I've never heard of one extending forever, but if there is such a thing, some poor soul is probably still trying to find the end of it.) WebTV formats Web pages to ensure that they don't spill out beyond the sides of the television screen. But the pages can't be shortened, so the remote gives you two Scroll buttons for seeing what lies above and below the limits of your TV screen. (On rare occasions, a Web page has too much information, requiring hundreds of scrolls, and WebTV truncates the page.)

When you first arrive at a Web page, you can see whether it extends beyond the screen by noticing whether two arrows (up and down) are in the lower-right portion of the screen. If so, the downward-pointing arrow indicates that more of the page can be seen beneath the screen, and you can scroll down to it using the lower of the two Scroll buttons. When you scroll downward, the upward-pointing arrow also becomes green, indicating that the page is now upward scrollable as well. Whenever you reach the top or bottom of the page, the system lets you know by emitting the pillow-soft "no" noise.

You can also use the Arrow buttons to scroll up and down a long page, but this method takes longer than using the Scroll buttons. Pressing the Down-arrow button repeatedly eventually forces the highlight box below the lower edge of the screen, at which point the next portion of the page will come into view — how many clicks this process takes depends on how many links the highlight must pause at before it reaches the bottom of the screen. The Arrow button method is not as fast as simply pressing the lower Scroll button, but if you hold your thumb on the Down-arrow button, you zip through the links pretty quickly. For that matter, you can apply the same tactic to the Scroll button, and hold it down while the screen zippingly lurches toward the bottom or the top. The Scroll buttons offer the express view of the Web.

When viewing a very long Web page, it's handy to shortcut to the top or bottom of the page, rather than scrolling incrementally up or down. The optional keyboard allows such a shortcut with the use of the Cmd key. (That's short for *Command.*) At the top of any Web page, press the Cmd key and hold it while you press the downward Scroll button on the keyboard. You arrive immediately at the bottom of the page. When at the bottom, you can reverse the process by holding the Cmd key while you press the upward Scroll button of the keyboard.

On computers, scrolling is performed a number of ways, including holding a mouse button and dragging the scroll bar next to the Web page up or down. The page moves smoothly and in much finer increments than on WebTV. The advantage with a computer is being able to set the page in the exact preferred position. The advantage to the WebTV system lies in not having to find the scroll bar and drag it — a simple press of a button accomplishes the job.

From Web to prime time: The TV button

One of the greatest, most groundbreaking features of WebTV is its capability to operate while the television is tuned to regular TV programming. If you're not yet logged on to the Web, you can log on while watching TV simply by using the Web button. Then, using WebTV Classic, you can switch back and forth between a television show and the Internet by pressing the TV button (called the TV/Web button on some models). Use the TV button whenever you want to check out the Web during shows, commercials, station breaks, or boring parts of the news.

 For WebTV Plus subscribers, the View button switches back and forth between the Web and the TV Home screen. (See Chapter 5 for a scintillating description of the TV Home screen and how it interacts with the Web.)

 If you leave WebTV unattended for over ten minutes, it automatically breaks your connection. (Surprise!) It's for your own protection, actually. Your connection closes down so that your phone line doesn't remain tied up indefinitely if you forget to log off. You can keep the connection going indefinitely by selecting a link from time to time. If your connection is automatically broken (called *timing out*), the power remains on for your set-top box and, after another five minutes, a screen saver appears, saving the picture tube of your TV from the stress of displaying an unchanging image for long periods. Currently, the screen saver is a WebTV logo bouncing around the screen, but this might change.

The screen saver doesn't prevent you from watching TV; WebTV Classic users see it only when the television has been displaying the same Web page, without any scrolling, for 15 minutes. WebTV Plus systems also revert to a screen saver when the TV Home screen is displayed, in which case the television program also gets "screen saved," with results that might be described as trance inducing. Whenever you tire of gazing at the screen saver, just click the Select button — the screen saver is deactivated.

The Remote Off the Web

Ease is a high ideal in WebTV land: Maneuvering two remotes would require too much exertion, so the remotes for some models even have controls that determine your television's normal, non-Web operation. The information in this section applies specifically to the Sony WebTV Classic and Philips-Magnavox WebTV Plus remotes. The Sony Plus remote has minor cosmetic and functional differences. The Philips-Magnavox Classic remote doesn't contain television controls.

✔ Notice the bank of numbered buttons on the remote. These buttons can be used to enter numbers into a Web page (for example, when using your credit card to purchase something) or to change TV channels. (On the Sony Classic remote, the function of the Number buttons is determined by a small switch directly above them labeled num/ch. If this switch is set to num, the Number buttons enter numbers in the Web environment. If this switch is set to ch, the Number buttons become channel switchers.)

WebTV Plus remotes do not have the num/ch switch that I describe in the preceding paragraph. Instead, the Philips Plus remote has two buttons: TV Mode and WebTV Mode. Press TV Mode to make the numbered buttons change the channel. The Sony Plus remote has a TV/WebTV switch. Move it to TV, and the numbered buttons change the channel when pushed.

✔ The Volume (Vol) buttons at the lower left control the television loudness.

✔ The Channel (Ch) buttons at the lower right increase or decrease the channel number by one.

To use any of the TV functions available on any of the remotes, you must enter the remote code for your television. Do so by pressing the Code set button on the remote and then entering the code, using the Number buttons on the remote. The remote code for your set is printed in your television owner's manual as well as in any manual that you might have for a universal remote.

Two . . . Two . . . Two Keyboards in One!

It's a typing keyboard . . . and it's a remote control! If I could hold the keyboard to my cheek and smile into the camera, I would. The optional wireless keyboard is one nifty device (to put it in technical terms) — it can do everything the remote does and more. In fact, the Classic and Plus keyboards can replace the remote entirely when it comes to surfing the Web. (The WebTV Classic keyboard is shown in Figure 3-2.) The disadvantage to using the keyboard all the time lies in its size — compact as it is, you can't fit it into one hand and use your thumb for browsing.

Figure 3-2:
The WebTV
Classic
wireless
keyboard.

The Navigation buttons on the keyboard aren't laid out as intuitively as on the remote, but they're all there. When writing e-mail messages and moving among the various screens in the Mail section, it's best to keep the keyboard perched on your lap. I usually have the remote next to me on the couch because the process of highlighting and selecting links doesn't fall under the fingers as readily on the keyboard as on the remote.

A dedicated approach

The keyboard contains all the buttons on the remote, plus several timesaving specialized ones. This section is based on the Philips-Magnavox keyboard; the Sony keyboard has minor cosmetic differences.

- **Favs.** A dedicated Favorites button, this takes you directly to the Favorites collection for your account. (With the remote, you must highlight and select Favorites from the Home screen.)

- **Home.** The Home button takes you directly and conveniently to the Home screen. On the WebTV Plus keyboard, the Home button displays whichever Home screen (Web or TV; see Chapter 5 to clarify the difference) corresponds to the side of WebTV you're using at that moment.

- **Search.** The Search key displays the Search screen, without having to highlight and select Search from the Home screen.

- **Mail.** When you want to type some e-mail or check your mailbox for any messages, the quickest route is to grab the keyboard and press the Mail key, which takes you directly to the Mail List screen. (With the remote, you must highlight and select Mail from the Home screen.)

- **Find.** The Find key lets you search for a word or a phrase on any Web page. (With the remote, you must press the Options button and then select Find.)

- **Info.** Pressing the Info key displays the URL of the Web page you're viewing.

- **Go to.** When you want to go directly to a Web site and you know its URL, press the Go to key and then type the URL. The system assumes the www. prefix and the .com suffix — you need to type only the organization name that goes between them. If you read a URL in a print ad or see one on TV, the Go to key is the easiest way to check out the Web site.

- **Save.** The Save key saves the current Web page to your Favorites collection. (See Chapter 7 for a rundown of the Favorites feature.)

- **Send.** Use the Send key to e-mail the URL of the currently viewed Web page to someone. The recipient of this fabulous gift can be another WebTV subscriber or anyone with a valid e-mail address.

- **Edit.** Ready for an easy button? The Edit button does nothing whatsoever. Zilch. Nada. Why is it there? Only the WebTV gods know for sure. Perhaps a function will be assigned for it soon. In the meantime, don't waste any energy scratching your head over it — it's guaranteed to be useless.

Several keys that I mention in this list are replacements for the on-screen selections you get from pressing the Options button on the remote. They're swell shortcuts for the keyboard surfer. But if you enjoy the sight of the Options panel rising from the bottom of the screen (some people are easily pleased), you can use the Options key on the keyboard instead of the dedicated keys. The Options key is located near the lower-right corner, just to the left of the Left-arrow button. After you have the Options window on the screen, you can highlight and select options with the Arrow keys on the keyboard.

The WebTV Plus keyboard is enhanced by a row of switches above the function buttons. These switches duplicate many of the functions found on the remote, as I describe in the previous section. With these enhancements, Plus users can switch between a Web screen and the TV Home screen (by using the View button), change channels, adjust the volume (assuming you've entered the TV code into the keyboard, as I describe previously for the remote), and turn the Plus Receiver's power on and off.

Highlighting and selecting with the keyboard

You can use the Arrow keys on the keyboard just like the Arrow buttons on the remote to move the highlight box around the screen. The Arrow keys are located in the lower-right corner (the usual place for most keyboards). They're not positioned in the same circular arrangement as on the remote, making them slightly less friendly to the thumb, but a little practice makes them quite usable. (I use the first three fingers of my right hand.)

When a link or an option is highlighted, the Return key (located above the Up-arrow key on the keyboard) functions the same as the Select (or Go) button on the remote. If you're accustomed to typing, especially on a computer, this arrangement makes sense and probably feels comfortable to you. You might want to use the keyboard when surfing, just to navigate the Web. If you're more comfortable with the remote, you're probably going to stick to it unless you really must type something.

Chapter 4

The Web Home Screen

In This Chapter

▶ Finding the Web hub of WebTV

▶ Locating all those settings

▶ Customizing the WebTV experience

▶ Changing your account

▶ Checking out the main WebTV areas

▶ Giving someone else a turn

▶ Seeking help

*E*ach time you log on to WebTV Network, the first thing you see is the Web Home screen. (It's called Home in WebTV Classic and Web Home in Plus. Otherwise, the screens are almost identical. See the next paragraph for details.) You can think of the Web Home screen as the centerpiece — the headquarters — of your Internet experience. You don't need to do anything special to find it. Just log on, and the Home screen finds you. If you want to return to it at any time in your Web session, just press the Home button on the remote or the keyboard.

Subscribers to the WebTV Plus Network see a Web Home screen almost identical to the Home screen of WebTV Classic. WebTV Plus subscribers also have a second Home screen, called TV Home, that appears even when the WebTV Plus Receiver is not online. (Of course, the Plus Receiver must be turned on to see a screen. See Chapter 5 for the lowdown.) The following minor differences distinguish the Web Home screens of Classic and Plus:

    ✔ In WebTV Plus, the Home screen is called Web Home; in Classic, it's called just Home.

    ✔ In Plus, the Web Home screen contains a link to TV Home.

Starting Point and Launching Pad

The Web Home screen, shown in Figure 4-1, has links to the following main areas of WebTV:

- **Mail.** From this area, you can send, receive, and read e-mail. (See the section at the end of this chapter called "What kind of mail?" If that's not enough, Chapter 6 tells you more than you probably want to know about e-mail.)

- **Community.** The Community section leads to online chatting, online message boards, and the WebTV Page Builder. (See Chapter 13 for an exhilarating rundown of Page Builder, a Web-site creation tool.)

- **Favorites.** Favorites is where you store links to Web sites you want to revisit regularly. (See Chapter 7 for a bunch of tips for making the most of Favorites.)

- **Search.** With a little practice, you can find almost anything on the Web with Search. (Chapter 9 shows you how.)

Figure 4-1: The Web Home screen.

Although WebTV has many other features, the sections just listed contain the meat and potatoes of the WebTV Internet experience: Web sites, community interaction, and e-mail. (E-mail is a type of potato.) From the preceding main areas, you can exchange e-mail with anyone on the Internet, chat socially with other Internet users, and get to anywhere on the Web.

Think of Web Home as the hub of an enormous wheel of information and fun. When you explore a giant wheel, you never want to lose your place with respect to the hub, no matter how far away from it you wander. Not to worry. With the Home button, you're never more than a single button-click away from Home. No matter how tangled your path through the Web, you can always start over with a single click.

In addition to sending you to the main sections of WebTV, the Home screen also

✔ Provides an area for setting up the details of your WebTV experience, including screen options that tailor WebTV to your preferences.

✔ Allows you to locate your subscription information and view your billing account.

✔ Has some on-screen instructions in case you (gasp!) accidentally glue together all the pages of this book.

✔ Includes a page for switching from one household account to another.

✔ Shows you a few featured Web links selected by the glassy-eyed selection team at WebTV for your viewing pleasure.

✔ Links you to information areas provided by WebTV (look at the bottom of the Home screen).

Three Important Selections

The Home screen (Web Home for Plus users) features three important links directly underneath the four major icons (Mail, Community, Favorites, Search) atop the page. Each of these three links allows you to adjust certain settings that affect your viewing, your account parameters, your dialing information, and your subscriptions status. It's not easy to remember which settings are located beyond each link. So Table 4-1 is a quick rundown of where things are located. Note that the Use an ISP feature is located under both Settings and Account. The reason? Sheer duplicity.

Table 4-1	Set-Up and Account Features	
Settings	*Account*	*Switch User*
E-mail settings	Address change	Switch to different household account
Password	Payment method	
Text size	Use an ISP	
Surfing music	Billing statements	
Print settings	Terms of service	
On-screen keyboard settings	Privacy policy	
Add household users		
Dialing features		
Use an ISP		

Setting Things Up

WebTV allows you — in fact, encourages you — to tailor your WebTV experience to your taste in a few ways. First, you can use the Settings page to alter the way WebTV looks on your screen, the way it sounds, how it prints, how your e-mail works, and several other significant details. The following steps enable you to use the Setup page:

1. **Click the Home button on your remote.**
2. **From the Home screen, highlight and select** Settings.

The Settings page contains several links to screens of options. Just keep reading to see what you can do.

Setting up MSN Messenger

MSN Messenger is WebTV's one-to-one chatting program. With it, you can talk in real time with other WebTVers and even with computer users running the computer version of MSN Messenger. See Chapter 8 for more discussion about how MSN Messenger works.

The MSN Messenger settings let you turn Messenger on and off, change your availability for chatting, change your chatting name, and see who is blocked from chatting with you. Follow these steps to adjust these settings:

1. **Click the Home button on your remote.**

2. **From the Home screen, highlight and select** Settings.

3. **On the Settings screen, highlight and select** MSN Messenger.

4. **On the MSN Messenger Settings for *YourName* screen, highlight and select the setting you'd like to adjust.**

   MSN Messenger has four settings. Select any of the following and follow the instructions on each settings screen:

   • **Turn MSN Messenger off.** Use this setting to disable MSN Messenger. When turned off, Messenger doesn't notify you when a preselected chatting friend is online and doesn't send chat messages to your screen. In other words, it leaves you alone. If you like receiving invitations to chat, leave Messenger on most of the time. Feel free to switch it on and off as the chatting mood strikes.

   • **Change how available you are.** Use this selection to determine whether any Messenger user or only those on your chatting list can reach you. If you don't like hearing from strangers, select the latter. If you want to meet new people and build a bigger list of chat friends, it's best to allow everyone to contact you, at least for a while.

   • **See people you've blocked.** You may prevent selected individuals from contacting you, even if you have Messenger set to allow chats with everyone. This screen merely shows you who (if anyone) is blocked — it doesn't allow you to put a block in place. See Chapter 8 for more information about how to use MSN Messenger.

   • **Change your name.** Your name, in this setting, is different from your e-mail address. Here, you change the way your identity appears in an e-mail heading, a newsgroup post, or a Messenger chat. One name covers all three functions, but you may change that name whenever you like.

Creating family accounts

One of the great family features of WebTV is the multiple-account feature. Each WebTV terminal can hold six accounts — one main account and five others. This means everyone in the family can have a separate logon account (unless you have a large family).

Household accounts are autonomous. This simply means that each account has its own settings, list of Favorites, and e-mail box and can be assigned its own password. The master account setup (called the *subscriber*) determines the basic features of each of the other accounts (called *additional users*). The subscriber account, which should be the responsibility of a parent if WebTV is for family use, can also bypass all the passwords and change settings for additional users at any time.

To add an account to your WebTV subscription, just follow these steps:

1. **Click the Home button on your remote.**

2. **From the Home screen, highlight and select** Settings.

3. **On the Settings screen, highlight and select the** Extra users **item.**

4. **When the WebTV users screen appears, select the** Add User **button.**

   If you've come to this section to delete a household user (the account, not the actual family member), select the Remove User button instead.

   On the next screen, it's time to do some typing.

5. **On the User's Name screen, fill in the family members' first and last names where indicated.**

   If you have the optional remote keyboard, just use that to enter names and preferences. If not, simply press the Select button on the remote when any typing box is highlighted, and the on-screen keyboard pops up. Use the Arrow buttons and the Select button to operate the on-screen keyboard, as described in Chapter 3.

6. **Press the Down-arrow button to highlight the** Continue **button, and select it.**

7. **On the User's Internet Name screen, type an Internet name.**

   The chosen name can't contain any spaces, but don't worry — it's not a name that will follow you around in cyberspace. It does, however, serve as the name in your e-mail address. For the sake of friends who want to remember your e-mail address, the Internet name should bear some resemblance to your actual name — but any sequence of letters, numbers, hyphens, or underscore characters (_) works fine.

8. **Highlight and select the** Continue **button.**

   At this point, if another WebTV subscriber has already taken the Internet name you chose, you're asked to select another one. Continue this process until you find a free Internet name. You may have to get pretty imaginative.

9. **On the Password screen, choose an optional password for the account and then type it again in the lower box.**

   The letters and numbers of a password do not appear on your screen as you type them. Asterisks appear instead — this is standard practice with Internet services. This way, someone lurking over your shoulder can't see your password.

You don't need to assign a password to any household account. If you create an account without a password, however, the account will be accessible to anyone who turns on your TV and WebTV system. If you create an account for another family member, you're probably best off leaving the password blank — the family member can add his or her own password at any time. Creating a password makes the account more private, of course. If you're concerned about not having access to a child's online activities and e-mail — relax. You can set up the account with disabled e-mail, which I discuss here. In addition, if you have access to the subscriber account, you can override the password of any additional user accounts.

Take a moment to think about how you want to set up personal e-mail for one of your children. (Unless you don't have any children, in which case you should spend very little time thinking about it.) Following are two considerations you may have (and which seem to conflict):

- E-mail is a fun and worthwhile feature at any age, but you want to protect your kids from receiving inappropriate e-mail material.

- Disabling e-mail may seem too restrictive, but setting up the account with a password leaves the child completely unsupervised because the parent can't gain access to the child's e-mail.

A compromise is to leave e-mail enabled but set up the account without a password. This way, you can supervise your child's use of e-mail without depriving him or her of electronic correspondence.

10. **After typing the password twice (or leaving both fields empty), highlight and select the** Continue **button.**

11. **On the User Restrictions screen, select the range of access allowed for the new account.**

   The User restrictions screen is used primarily to protect kids from adult Internet content. The descriptions next to each choice give you a summary of the selections; see the "Making safe accounts for kids" sidebar for the complete lowdown.

12. **After selecting the access restriction (or lack of restriction), highlight and select — you guessed it — the** Continue **button.**

13. **On the Electronic Mail screen, select whether the new account will have e-mail functions.**

   If you check the Block e-mail box, the person controlling the account can't send or receive electronic mail. Like the restrictions on the User Restrictions screen, disabling e-mail contributes to a kid-safe Internet experience, making the account invulnerable to unsolicited (or requested) material currently in circulation on the Internet.

14. **You know what to do — highlight and select the ol'** `Continue` **button.**

    The Adding a User screen displays all your choices for confirmation.

15. **If everything looks correct, highlight and select the** `Done` **button.**

    The WebTV Users screen appears, listing all current household accounts associated with your terminal.

16. **If everything is in order, highlight and select the** `Done` **button.**

Making safe accounts for kids

Ever since the Web became popular, a great deal of apprehension has arisen about the Internet being dangerous for kids. Some of the anxiety is justified, and some is alarmist hype created by people resisting change and new frontiers. (This unsolicited opinion has been brought to you free of charge.) The point is, parents are justified in their concern for their children's well-being and safety in every environment, online and offline. WebTV lets parents control the parameters of a child's Internet experience with the following features:

✔ **Separate accounts.** You can create a new account for your child.

✔ **Account restrictions.** You can use SurfWatch or Kid-friendly restriction plans. Each is effective in its own way. SurfWatch uses a comprehensive keyword system to block any adult Internet site from appearing on the screen. Kid-friendly takes the opposite approach by placing the account within a preset online service that contains only kid-appropriate sites.

SurfWatch lets your child enjoy a wider Internet experience, including inoffensive adult sites that might not be included in Kid-friendly. However, SurfWatch is slightly more risky because a site might slip through the keyword guardians.

✔ **Disabled e-mail.** On the Internet, it's sometimes easy to find someone's e-mail address and send that person an unsolicited letter, picture, or URL (Web site address). Disabling the e-mail capacity of a household account removes that slight risk but denies the child an e-mail experience. And the e-mail experience is one of the best parts of being online. Just think, if you have e-mail at work, it might be nice to get e-mail from your kids at home.

✔ **Restricting chat:** Any account can have its chat features turned off or restricted to public rooms only. Beware of that last feature if you're uncomfortable with your child's exposure to chatting. Public rooms are no more savory, on balance, than private rooms. If you don't want your kids meeting people in the chat environment, turn it off completely in their accounts.

✔ **Restricting Page Builder:** This obscurely protective feature is of dubious value. Preventing your kids from making Web pages deprives them of Internet-age creativity. But if you want their Web experience to be perceptive only, this feature is available.

Customizing your screen

You can change a few of the different characteristics of how WebTV appears on your screen. You can customize the on-screen keyboard, alter the size of text, configure the Options panel, and even change the picture quality of WebTV.

QWERTY — an Australian mammal?

No, QWERTY is an abbreviation for the way a typical typewriter or computer keyboard is laid out. The top row of the keyboard starts with the letter *Q* and continues with *W, E, R, T,* and *Y.* For people who know how to type, the QWERTY layout, with letters scattered in seemingly random order, works just fine. For those who never sat through Miss Orshensky's typing class in junior high, QWERTY is an incomprehensible mess.

The optional remote keyboard is configured in the standard QWERTY layout and can't be changed, but you have a choice with the on-screen keyboard. If QWERTY doesn't fit your hunt-and-peck style, you can follow these steps to change the keyboard to the alphabetical layout, which may make more sense to you:

1. **On the Web Home screen, highlight and select** Settings.
2. **On the Settings screen, highlight and select** Keyboard.
3. **On the Keyboard screen, highlight and select either the** Alphabetical **or** Traditional **(QWERTY) layout.**
4. **Highlight and select the** Done **button.**

Stop squinting

WebTV is very clear and easy to see. But part of its legibility depends on the size of your television and how far away you are from it. If you have a 5-inch screen and prefer sitting 30 feet away — well, good luck. But even larger, closer screens may prove troublesome to read due to your eyesight or a simple preference for larger type.

Some Internet text is unchangeable because it's part of an image. (Such text is hard to read on computers, too.) Text that's separate from the pictures of a Web site, however, can be manipulated separately, and WebTV gives you a choice of text sizes. To change the scale of the text, follow these steps:

1. **On the Web Home screen, highlight and select** Settings.
2. **On the Settings screen, highlight and select** Text size.

3. **On the Text size screen, select** small, medium, **or** large **text.**

   This screen tells you which text size is currently selected.

4. **Highlight and select the** Done **button.**

Whistle while you surf

WebTV comes equipped with a soundtrack that can play continuously while you explore the Internet. The default music setting is Off, so you must activate this feature to hear the music. Follow these steps to play the soundtrack:

1. **On the Web Home screen, highlight and select** Settings.

2. **On the Settings screen, highlight and select** Music.

3. **On the Music screen, highlight and select the** Background music **box.**

4. **If you'd like to select music categories, highlight and select the** Choose Music Styles **button. On the Background music styles page, highlight and select any (or all) music styles.**

   Only the music styles you select are played while you surf. If you don't select any styles, you're liable to hear anything.

5. **Highlight and select the** Done **button.**

6. **Back on the Settings screen, highlight and select the** Done **button.**

The soundtrack consists of several musical excerpts, none longer than a few minutes. They rotate among themselves, seemingly at random, and present a good variety of mood — from a streetwise scrap of funky groove to ethereal New-Age air candy and from an ornate baroque piano composition to what sounds like a French serenade from the turn of the century.

The selections are designed to provide a smooth background to your surfing activities, and for the most part, they succeed. If you stay connected for hours, however, you might become jaded by the soundtrack. And long-time users are no doubt thoroughly sick of the songs, some of which have been part of the mix since 1996. Don't shoot the WebTV box. Either mute your TV or follow the preceding procedure and clear the Background music box.

Don't worry about the soundtrack interfering with other sounds or music you pick up from the Web, such as MIDI music, MP3 streams, or RealAudio presentations you want to enjoy. The music soundtrack automatically shuts off when you begin playing any other Internet programming.

Setting up your mailbox

Your mailbox is ready and waiting for you after your first connection to the WebTV Network. You don't need to prepare it in any way to begin sending and receiving e-mail. You can, however, determine how the mailbox works using a few options, which are conveniently clustered in one place. Follow these steps to get there:

1. **On the Web Home screen, highlight and select** Settings.

2. **On the Settings screen, highlight and select** Mail.

   The Mail Settings screen appears, with a few choices.

You can make eight categories of adjustments to how you write and receive e-mail through WebTV. Following is the rundown. All these screens are available as selections from the Mail Settings page:

✔ **Extras.** The Extra Features screen gives you access to three e-mail options. First, you can create a storage area for letters you've sent or even discarded, plus the ones you want to save. Second, you can set up your e-mail functions to always quote the original message when you're replying to the message. (This is standard practice with Internet e-mail.) Third, you can add a cc: line to your address header at the top of every outgoing e-mail, so you can send copies of any letter to multiple recipients. (A Reply all button is included when the third feature is activated, so you can automatically send a reply to everyone in the cc: list of an e-mail you receive.)

To select any or all of these extra e-mail features, just highlight and select the corresponding check boxes and then select the Done button.

✔ **Listing.** This screen is where you choose the order in which your mail is listed — newest mail first, or the reverse.

✔ **Message Light.** This link takes you to a convenient option called the Automatic Mail Checking screen, which invites you to set a time of day at which your WebTV unit will check for new mail. This auto-retrieval function occurs once every twenty-four hours. I have mine set at 4:00 A.M. The red light on your set-top box illuminates if new mail is found. (The light is on anyway if you leave any message unread in your mailbox.)

The Automatic Mail Checking works for only the account currently logged on to WebTV. If your household has more than one account, the light indicates that mail is waiting in the mailbox of the account currently in use. If no one is currently logged on to WebTV, the light indicates that mail is waiting for the account that last logged on.

The system can tell you whether you have mail waiting, but it doesn't deliver it. Automatic mail checking simply dials into the network, looks in your mailbox (it can keep a secret, don't worry), and illuminates the red light on your WebTV box if something is waiting for you. You must connect to WebTV as usual to read what awaits you.

✔ **Word List.** This screen is where you add words you want recognized by the built-in e-mail spell-checker. Now, don't spend the next few weeks adding every word in your vocabulary. WebTV already knows most of them. Add unusual words that you use frequently, so that the spell-checker doesn't keep tripping over them. Words like *splatsticky* (what happens when you drop a bottle of maple syrup), or *furfly* (a disagreement between a cat and a dog). Click the Add Word button and then type your words on the next screen. Be sure to spell them correctly!

✔ **Signature.** This text is more like a little farewell message: You can include a famous quote, your e-mail address, or maybe your profession. The text is placed at the end of every e-mail message you send. An e-mail signature text is a little different from the signature you put on a check or a pet license.

Personalized signatures saved as files (called *sig files*) are common in Internet e-mail and other types of messaging. They often consist of the author's name and e-mail address, perhaps a quote (either famous or fabricated), or even a little picture made from typed characters. A personalized signature has nothing to do with a handwritten signature that you may put at the end of a business letter. Remember that your *sig* is attached to all your e-mail, so make sure it's universally appropriate to whomever you may address a letter.

Some WebTVers get very fancy indeed, creating extravagant signatures complete with graphics, backgrounds, and fancy typefaces. That kind of signature is on the complicated side, but lots of fun if you're ambitious. Look in Chapter 13 for ideas and instructions.

✔ **Mail Name.** Your WebTV identity consists of two parts: Your e-mail address and the name that follows the address, in parentheses, located in the e-mail header. Most people do not use their real or full name in the e-mail address, either for the sake of anonymity or because the name was already taken. Nothing stops you from putting your real name in parentheses if you choose to. It's the parenthetical name that appears (without the parentheses) in the mail list of WebTV users (and most outside recipients) that get your mail.

✔ **Remote Mail.** Providing an advanced feature, this screen allows you to set up retrieval of e-mail from non-WebTV mailboxes. The other address must use the Post Office Protocol (POP3) standard, which most Internet addresses do. If you use another Internet service provider or online service, chances are you have another e-mail address outside WebTV. You can retrieve that mail through WebTV, either removing it from the out-side server or leaving it there for later retrieval by another means. For people who use multiple addresses, this feature proves very handy. You need all the account information for your outside e-mail address and its server, for which you may need to contact your ISP or online service.

A check box at the bottom of the screen asks whether you'd like to leave the messages on the server of your non-WebTV e-mail account. I always leave that box checked, so I can retrieve my mail all over again on a computer, where I may need to process it. If you don't want to receive your e-mail a second time, make sure the box is unchecked.

When the preceding feature is activated, a Fetch button appears in the sidebar of your Mail page. Highlight and select Fetch to get your remote mail, which is mixed in with your WebTV mail on the Mail List for *YourName* screen.

The Remote Mail feature doesn't apply to Web-based e-mail accounts as found in Yahoo!, Hotmail, Rocketmail, Netcenter, or other popular free mail sites. Those accounts are established on a Web page, and you retrieve your mail from a Web page — not in the WebTV Mail area.

✔ **Junk Mail.** WebTV keeps track of organizations that send unsolicited e-mail advertisements. That's not to say that WebTV knows about *every* organization that sends junk mail. But if you dislike receiving virtual come-ons for cable descramblers, sex sites, and bulk-mail lists, you should select to have junk mail blocked. It's no guarantee that you'll never receive another *spam* (slang for bulk-mail junk in cyberspace), but the option cuts down the load.

The key to your kingdom

Passwords — secret words that give access to an online account — are an option in WebTV. Each household account may have its own password, and using one keeps that account private to those who know the password. If you didn't establish a password when setting up the account you're presently using, you may add one at any time. If the account does have a password, you may change it or eliminate it at any time, as follows:

1. **On the Home screen, select** Settings.

2. **On the Settings screen, select** Password.

3. **On the Password screen, type the same password in each of the two boxes, or leave them both blank to eliminate a password.**

The best connection

Telephones weren't designed to dial into computer networks, go online, or surf the Internet. If they were, Alexander Graham Bell's famous first phone call would have been, "Watson, send me e-mail." There's almost never a problem with WebTV — I have been working with the system since before it was released to the public, and it has been foolproof in all my experience. (Naturally, I'm a good person to test how the system responds to fools.)

The Settings area offers you a few options to customize WebTV to your particular phone system. First, highlight and select Dialing to reach the Dialing Options screen, where you have the following five options at your command:

- ✔ **Basic.** Highlight and select Basic to enter a prefix that must be dialed to access the phone line. For example, when using WebTV in a hotel, you must dial 9 to get a dial tone, so you would type 9 in the Prefix box on the screen. (Use the wireless keyboard, select the box to use the on-screen keyboard, or use the numbers on the Sony terminal remote.) Below the Prefix box is a Pulse dialing box, which must be highlighted and selected if your phone service is pulse rather than tone. After making these selections, highlight and select the Done button and you are dropped back off at the Dialing Options screen.

- ✔ **Call waiting.** Select Call waiting to reach the Call Waiting Options screen, where you select the option that fits your telephone service and preference. If you don't have call waiting, highlight and select the top item, No call waiting on my phone line. If you have call waiting, you may let WebTV interrupt your Internet sessions when a phone call comes in (highlight and select the middle item, Accept calls). The session is temporarily disconnected and then easily reconnected when you've finished talking on the phone. (Just use the Select button on the remote to activate the on-screen Reconnect button waiting on your screen.) Alternately, you may elect to shut off call waiting so that your callers receive a busy signal when you're using WebTV. (Highlight and select the bottom item, Block calls.)

When disabling call waiting for a WebTV session (the Block calls selection), you must type the code that your phone company requires to turn off call waiting. If you're not sure what that code is, don't call WebTV — they don't know either. Check in the front pages of your telephone book or call your local phone company and ask how to temporarily turn off call waiting. (If you call the phone company, make sure that the representative doesn't think you're asking to have the feature permanently removed from your line.)

If you elect to accept calls using the call-waiting feature, and if, over time, you discover that it's not working quite right, you might want to return to the Call Waiting Options screen. Highlight and select the

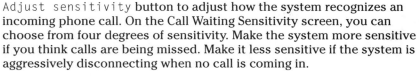

`Adjust sensitivity` button to adjust how the system recognizes an incoming phone call. On the Call Waiting Sensitivity screen, you can choose from four degrees of sensitivity. Make the system more sensitive if you think calls are being missed. Make it less sensitive if the system is aggressively disconnecting when no call is coming in.

Adjusting the call-waiting sensitivity on the Call Waiting Sensitivity screen is tricky. Not that the screen itself is hard to figure out — it's a piece of cake. But the results of your adjustment can be evaluated only over time, as you receive (or don't receive) phone calls during WebTV sessions. There's no instant way to test the settings. My advice is to leave it on the most sensitive setting (the topmost of four on-screen choices), which is the default setting. If, over time, the system isn't responding properly to incoming phone calls (and your friends complain that they can never reach you on the phone even when you have the call-waiting feature set to answer calls), return to this screen and lower the sensitivity by a notch.

✔ **Reset.** Highlight and select `Reset` to display the Reset Dialing Options screen. Select the `Reset` button to return all dialing options to factory settings, negating any changes you may have made.

✔ **Use your ISP.** On the Using Your Own ISP screen, you may dial into WebTV using a preexisting Internet access account (from an Internet service provider — that's what ISP stands for) rather than WebTV's own telephone network. The big advantage is that your WebTV Classic monthly subscription rate goes down when you use your own ISP. Furthermore, your ISP may have more local numbers for you to dial than WebTV does. On the downside, you must pay your ISP *and* WebTV's reduced subscription rate every month.

The first few screens of this feature help you decide whether or not to use an outside ISP. If the answer is yes, keep going until you reach the Use Your Own ISP screen, and fill in the blanks. Then proceed to the next screen with the `Continue` button, and fill in the dial-up phone numbers of your ISP. The `Done` button gets you out of there.

✔ **Advanced.** You'll probably never have to use the advanced dialing options. (I pray on your behalf to the Supreme Being of the Internet that you never have to — not because the screen is difficult, but because it's mainly used to solve a problem.) Highlight and select `Wait for dial tone` if you're having trouble making a connection and you're using a voice mail system that notifies you of waiting messages with a brief broken dial tone. Highlight and select `Audible dialing` if you want to hear the phone dialing and making the WebTV connection. Hearing WebTV use the phone is not very exciting, and it might bother you if you're trying to connect while watching television, but it can help determine why a connection is failing. Highlight and select the `Slow`, `Medium`, or `Fast` item if you think your phone is being dialed too quickly or too slowly.

Don't be alarmed by the Advanced Dialing Options screen. Chances are excellent that you'll never use it. If you do have connection trouble and get surly at the thought of fiddling with a bunch of cold on-screen options, you can always call a warm, live person at 1-800-GO WEBTV (1-800-469-3288) for technical support.

Getting hard copy

When WebTV was first available, you could surf the Web but you couldn't print anything. A mysterious looking interface plug lurked on the right side of early Classic models, but you couldn't do anything with it. The lack of printing was a missing feature that spelled a major difference between an early WebTV Internet terminal and a computer. Now, however, all owners of WebTV terminals (Classic or Plus Receivers) can hook up one of a selected list of printers and get hard copies of any Web screen. Here's what you need:

- ✔ **A printer.** The printer is not included when you buy a set-top box, so you must buy it separately.

- ✔ **A printer cable.** You can't use just any regular printer cable as you'd use with a computer, though. The type of cable you should ask for is known by this catchy name: IEEE-1284. Ask for it wherever you shop for the printer.

- ✔ **An adapter.** The adapter is a special small device that fits into the interface plug of early Classic units, located on the right side of the set-top box. Later Classic boxes and all Plus boxes have a standard printer interface plug (called a parallel port). Sony and Philips-Magnavox each make an adapter for the early Classic units, and they are not interchangeable. You must buy the adapter that matches the set-top box you own. If you buy the wrong adapter, you'll be very disappointed and might start weeping.

The Setup screen has a link for adjusting the system to your printer and printing settings:

1. **On the Setup screen, highlight and select** Printing.

2. **On the Printing options screen, highlight and select the options you want.**

   The Print date and Web info selection refers to the date on which you're printing (naturally) and the URL of the Web site. The Print background images selection tells the printer to include the faint background pictures that lie underneath the text on some Web pages. If you're printing primarily for information, it's best (and much quicker) to leave the Print background images box unchecked.

3. **Highlight and select the** Done **button.**

Which printers work?

This question is a long-standing point of confusion among WebTV owners. Because a printer is not included with the initial WebTV purchase and must be acquired as an add-on component, considerable mystification surrounds the issue of which printers work with which WebTV models.

The first thing to know is that only Canon, Hewlett-Packard, and Epson printers work with WebTV. Begin by narrowing your choices to these three companies and their model lines.

Second, if you have one of the early Classic systems (with the adapter plug on the side) Canon and Epson printers are out of the running. You may use only Hewlett-Packard printers.

All the WebTV models except for the early Classic units can use the same group of printers. If you're unsure of which WebTV model you have, look at the set-top box. Is there an adapter on the side or a printer port on the back? If you have the adapter, you have an early Classic

model. This is the point of distinction when it comes to printers, not whether you use Classic or Plus.

Following is the list of working printer model numbers for both groups of users — early Classic boxes and all other boxes:

- ✔ **Early Classic (with side adapter):** Hewlett-Packard only. Choose from DeskJet models 420C, 610CL, 612C, 400, 400L, 600, 660C, 670C, 670TV, 672C, 680C, 682C, 690C, 692C, 693C, 694C, 695C, 697C.

- ✔ **All others (back-panel printer port):** All of the preceding plus the following. The Hewlett-Packard DeskJet 810C, 812C, 830C, 832C, 840C, 842C, 880C, 882C, 895C. The Canon LR1 PrintStation. The Canon BJC-1000, BJC-1010, BJC-2000, BJC-2010, BJC-6000, BJC-80, BJC-210, BJC-240, BJC-250, BJC-4100, BJC-4200, BJC-4300, BJC-4400, BJC-4550, BJC-610, BJC-620. The Epson 440, 660, and Stylus Photo 750.

Viewing and Changing Your Account

Your account consists of your name, postal address, phone number, the amount you pay for a WebTV subscription, how you pay that subscription, and the method you use to log in. These items define your relationship with WebTV Networks. You can view your account details and, in some cases, change them. Here's how:

1. **On the Web Home screen, select** Account.

2. **On the Your WebTV Account screen, choose one of the selection headings to view aspects of your account.**

Here's what you can do from the Your WebTV Account screen:

- ✔ **Subscriber info.** This page displays the name, postal address, and phone number associated with the account and whether it's protected with a password. Highlight and select any item to change it.

- **How you pay.** You can pay for WebTV access with a credit card or automatic withdrawal from a bank account.

  As of early 2000, WebTV charges a $5.00 fee (per month) for automatic bank withdrawals.

- **Use an ISP.** This feature is exactly as described a bit earlier in this chapter. You may access this feature either here or through the Settings screen.

- **Billing statement.** This is where you view your billing history.

- **Terms of service.** Ah, the infamous Terms of Service (TOS) statement. It's long. It's legal. It's unbelievably tedious. Plow through it if you have reason to think you'll find yourself prosecuted by WebTV for misuses of the service or if you think another member might be violating the TOS.

- **Privacy policy.** Most online services (even Web sites) implement and publicize a privacy policy that determines how the service uses your personal information. Such information includes your name, address, phone number, and any other identifying and locating information you divulge when opening an account.

Peering behind the Home Screen

The Home screen (or Web Home screen for Plus users) is a doorway to information lurking just under the surface, provided by WebTV Networks. This information isn't part of the Web at large, available to anyone — it's just for WebTV users. The Today in WebTV section and the WebTV Centers section give you nicely packaged information to start your online session without forcing you to ferret out Web pages or dive into your Favorites collection. (Of course, you can start your session in Favorites, or Mail, or any way you like.)

Today in WebTV

The center portion of the Web Home screen contains a rotating selection of attractions that change often. In most cases, the sites are WebTV pages — images and information available only to WebTV users. The big space in the middle of the screen links you to what is usually a topical site, related to a news story or an approaching holiday. To its right is an advertisement, which is also a link.

All these links work in regular WebTV style. When you first arrive at the Web Home screen, whether having just logged on or clicked there during a session, the highlight box is on the Mail icon. Use the Arrow buttons on the remote to move the highlight box down to the main site featured in the center of the screen, and select it to visit the site. The same goes for the other featured sites.

WebTV Centers

Along the bottom of the Web Home screen, notice the basic topical headings — Entertainment, News, Sports, Health, Money, and Shopping. Something called WebTV Today and something else called Around Town are listed too.

WebTV Today and Around Town are described with clarity and poise in Chapter 10, startlingly called "Around Town and WebTV Today."

The other WebTV Centers are links to private WebTV content that can't be seen by computer users on the Internet. Basic headlines are the fare, plus links to Web sites (no longer private to WebTV) that you might enjoy.

Figure 4-2:
WebTV Information Centers focus on Health, Money, Sports, and other topics.

It's Someone Else's Turn

Say you've been surfing WebTV for the last hour — two hours, maybe. One of your kids is getting impatient and finally grabs the remote out of your hand. You decide it's time to surrender to the force of impetuous youth. Your youngster is so impatient that you're afraid to even turn off the terminal box to switch accounts for fear of uncontrolled temper. Fortunately, for the peace of your family, you don't have to turn anything off. Just take these steps (as quickly as possible):

1. **On the Web Home screen, highlight and select** `Switch User.`

2. **On the Choose *YourName* screen, highlight and select your eager child's account.**

   WebTV transfers the connection from the master account to the chosen sub-account. Incidentally, you can switch in the preceding fashion between any two accounts, even if neither is the household master account.

You can't get out of the Choose *YourName* screen without choosing an account with which to continue. WebTV assumes you want to change accounts and will not let you use the `Back` button to retrace your steps. If you decide to remain with the present account, simply choose it from the list. WebTV logs you into the service all over again (but without disconnecting the phone and redialing), starting you off on the Home screen.

Along the top of the Home screen are four selections that represent the main content areas supplied by WebTV. Of course, the Internet itself is the biggest content area. The four Home selections are WebTV's valiant efforts to organize the massive content of the Internet, plus e-mail. The following capsule descriptions are provided just to whet your appetite. Part II explains each content area in detail.

What kind of mail?

Electronic mail, computer mail, lightning-quick virtual mail. E-mail has a host of uses, is a great way to stay in touch (frequently and inexpensively) with friends and family, and can be used to get acquainted with new online friends. E-mail knows no geographic boundaries or distance-based pricing. WebTV Mail is included in the monthly subscription cost, regardless of how much you use it (for sending and receiving).

Whose favorites?

Yours. The Favorites section is your own storehouse of great Web sites. It's where you put the places you want to visit regularly or return to at a later date. (See Chapter 7 for information about viewing WebTV's suggested favorites.)

Explore where?

In the Web directory. Explore is WebTV's table of contents for the Web. It's a directory of the best, most interesting, most fun, most educational, slickest, most brilliant Web sites, divided by subject category. Mind you, it's not a total inventory of the Web — such an exhaustive list would number millions of sites — but it's a great start.

Search for what?

Virtually anything. The Search screen lets you type an idea, a subject, a name, a geographical location, a product, or any other topical hint you're interested in. The system searches the Web (not just the Explore directory) for sites related to what you typed. Explore and Search both help you find the good stuff; Explore is for browsing, and Search is for more focused searching. Don't confuse either one with the Find feature, described in Chapter 3. Find locates a word or a group of words on a single Web page.

If You Lose This Book . . .

You must buy two replacement copies as penance. (Just kidding.) In the meantime, you might want to know that WebTV offers on-screen instructions for the various parts of the service. You can get to the on-screen instructions by following these steps:

1. **On the Web Home screen, highlight and select** Help.

2. **On the Help Main Index screen, highlight and select one of the topic headings.**

   Short tutorials follow, walking you through the basics of the WebTV experience.

Chapter 5

The TV Home Screen

*W*ebTV Plus has two Homes. (Sort of like having a house in the country.) In fact, the second Home screen — TV Home — is the main distinguishing feature that sets Plus apart from Classic. The Home screen of WebTV Classic is replicated in WebTV Plus as the Web Home screen (see Chapter 4).

WebTV Plus TV Home is a powerful and attractive integration of the Web and television programming. In Plus, you can flip between the Web and the TV easily, put them both on the same screen, and browse local broadcast and cable listings with program summaries. Furthermore, you can search for TV programming by keyword or category — one of the strongest attractions of the Plus system. In the future, specific TV programs and certain Web sites will be further integrated, making the television a more interactive device.

This chapter leads you through the features of the TV Home screen in WebTV Plus. Classic users, you might want to read up on the features if you're thinking of upgrading or if a friend or family member is considering Plus.

Finding TV Home

You don't need a divining rod to find the TV Home screen because it's the first thing that appears when you turn on WebTV Plus — assuming your TV is turned on. Otherwise, you won't see much of anything.

The key to viewing the TV Home screen at any point in your Web session lies in the View button, located on both the remote and the keyboard. Here's a typical logon scenario for a new user who has set up WebTV Plus and established a WebTV account:

1. **Turn on the TV set.**

   The TV Home screen appears (see Figure 5-1), with a TV program displayed in a reduced middle screen.

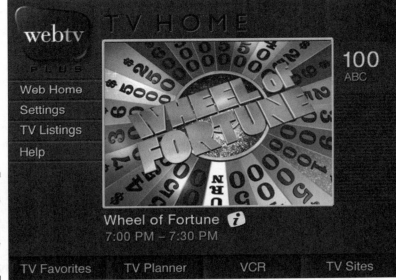

Figure 5-1:
The TV
Home
screen in
WebTV
Plus.

2. **Press the View button to begin a Web session.**

   You may also highlight and select the Web Home link on the TV Home screen. Either way, WebTV Plus now begins its logon procedure to connect to the Web. After you are logged on, WebTV displays the Web Home screen.

3. **Use the View button to alternate between Web Home and TV Home.**

   Alternately, you may highlight and select the Web Home and TV Home links.

   At any point in your Web session, from anywhere on the Web, you may switch to the TV Home screen by pressing the View button.

   When you switch to TV Home, your Web session remains at the page you left, awaiting your return. Even if you log off, the page is displayed when you next log on, assuming you don't turn off the set-top box's power. (Use the Hang up selection on the Options panel.)

Basic Features of TV Home

TV Home is designed to enable you to browse through program listings and view information about shows, without leaving the television screen entirely. To that end, many of the various screens of TV Home present a TV screen of some size. The Search TV screens (covered later in this chapter) do not display a TV screen, although you can still hear the program as you search.

At any time, you may enlarge the TV screen to full size by highlighting and selecting the TV screen window.

The primary TV Home screen, the one you see when you first turn on WebTV, contains the television screen in a central reduced window, with four links beside it:

- ✔ **Web Home.** Select Web Home to switch to the Web Home screen (described in Chapter 4 from the viewpoint of a WebTV Classic user).

- ✔ **Settings.** Select Settings to adjust how your TV listings are presented, which cable company (if any) you use, your telephone dialing settings, which channels you want programming information for, and how the screen appears.

- ✔ **TV Listings.** This link sends you into the Listings area, reducing the TV screen to a small window in the upper-left corner. Here, you may see what's programmed for all your channels, cable and broadcast, for the next 24 hours.

- ✔ **How To.** Select this link for brief tutorials on the TV-integration features of Plus. Subjects include using the remote, controlling the VCR through WebTV, and using the TV Listings area — all of which I cover in this chapter.

Beneath the TV window on the TV Home screen, a snip of information appears about the current show. In most cases, you don't get more than the program title and its duration. In a few cases, particularly with movies, a small *crossover link* icon indicates that a Web page can give you more information. (Look at the *i* icon back in Figure 5-1.) Selecting it automatically switches to the Web and displays that site. WebTV Network promises more crossover links in the future. (See Chapter 11 for more information about Web sites created by WebTV Network that relate to certain shows.)

Getting and Using Listings

The TV listings are one of the best things about WebTV Plus. Before you can enjoy the added dimension they lend to channel surfing, however, you need to tell WebTV what your viewing setup is.

Getting 'em

One of the first things a new WebTV Plus user should do is create a Listings setup. This procedure might seem complex — but only the first time you do it, thank goodness. Follow these steps:

1. **On the TV Home screen, highlight and select** Settings.

2. **On the TV Settings screen, select** Listings setup.

3. **On the Listings Setup screen, select** TV Area.

4. **On the TV Area screen, enter your ZIP code and whether you have cable service, a regular TV antenna, or satellite service.**

5. **Highlight and select the** Retrieve **button.**

   If you selected cable or satellite service, WebTV automatically logs on to retrieve all the possible cable or satellite providers for your TV area. It then displays the list.

6. **From the list of cable or satellite providers, choose the company from which you get your service.**

7. **Highlight and select the** Retrieve **button.**

   WebTV collects your programming listings for the next week. The process can take between two and ten minutes, depending on how many channels you receive. If for some reason you want to stop the retrieval of listings, highlight and select the Stop button. You can get the listings later.

Using 'em

After your listings are retrieved, you probably want to browse through them. Following are a few things to try:

1. **On the TV Home screen, highlight and select** TV Listings.

   If your listings are out-of-date (if you haven't checked them in over a day and don't receive automatic retrievals), WebTV asks whether you want to retrieve fresh listings. Select the Continue button to do so, and follow the instructions in the previous section.

2. **On the TV Listings screen, highlight and select** For today.

   You can also select the second item, By day and time, to choose another day's listings, up to a week in advance. The screen's third option, Search TV Listings, is covered later in this chapter.

If you want to continue watching the current program in a small TV screen window, select the Stay on channel while browsing listings box. If you leave that box unchecked, the channel changes as you browse through the TV listings. After checking the box, move back up to highlight and select the For today link.

3. **Use the Up-arrow and Down-arrow buttons on the remote or keyboard to move the highlight box from one channel to the next.**

4. **Use the Scroll buttons to move through the listings in increments of six channels.**

5. **Use the Right-arrow button to look ahead.**

   You see what's scheduled for up to 24 hours in advance. Use the Left-arrow button to return to the present time.

6. **Select any highlighted channel to switch to that channel.**

   Not only is the channel changed, but also the TV screen window enlarges to full screen. Use the Back button to return to the Listings screen.

7. **From the Listings screen, use the Back button to return to TV Home.**

   On the Listings screen (see Figure 5-2), the channel and program you're currently watching are highlighted.

Figure 5-2: The Listings screen displays the program you're watching.

Setting Up Your Cable Box and VCR

The best way to take complete advantage of the TV Home features is to integrate your cable (or satellite) box and your VCR (if you use one) with WebTV. After you do this, you can control the entire setup with the remote or the optional keyboard. The complexities of this setup are worthwhile for the control and automation you get.

Just take a deep breath and follow along, taking one step at a time. I'll start with the VCR, and then do the cable (or satellite) box:

1. **On the TV Home screen, highlight and select** Settings.

2. **On the TV Settings screen, highlight and select** Hooking up.

3. **On the Hooking Up screen, highlight and select** VCR.

4. **On the VCR connection screen, select whether you have a** Coaxial **or** Audio/Video **hookup.**

   See Chapter 2 for the wiring procedures and a description of coaxial cables.

5. **After making your selection, highlight and select the** Continue **button.**

6. **On the VCR connection screen, select which channel the VCR uses to send out its signal.**

   You might need to look at the back of your VCR to determine the channel setting. In most cases, it's 3 or 4.

7. **When the VCR Signal screen appears, place a recorded tape into your VCR and press the Play button of the VCR.**

   Be sure to use a tape that has something recorded on it but that you don't mind erasing a small portion of! You should see the tape play back in the small TV window. The TV/VCR switch of your VCR must be set to VCR.

8. **After you see the tape playback, highlight and select the** Continue **button.**

9. **On the VCR manufacturer screen, highlight and select your VCR's brand name from the list.**

   If you don't see your VCR on the list, select the More button to see more brands.

10. **On the** *YourBrand* **VCR screen, highlight and select** Continue.

    It's important at this point to do a visual check to make sure the IR Blaster is plugged into the back of the Plus Receiver, with one of its ends positioned in front of the infrared sensor of the VCR. (See Chapter 2.) Note that Sony IR Blasters have only one end, not two. You must choose whether to use it to control your VCR or your cable (or satellite) box.

11. **On the Code Set screen, highlight and select the VCR controls, and observe whether the VCR responds.**

    This screen is used to determine your VCR's remote code so WebTV can learn it. If the controls don't affect your VCR, highlight and select the Next button. Continue this trial process until the on-screen controls affect your VCR. You might need to test a few dozen codes, so be patient. You'll eventually find the correct code. The code must work with *all four* on-screen controls, including Record. That's why it's important to use a tape you don't mind recording over, even if only for a few seconds.

12. **After you find the code, highlight and select the Done button.**

Now it's time to set up your cable (or satellite) box. The procedure is similar, in that WebTV asks for brand information and tests for remote codes. Here's what you do:

1. **On the TV Home screen, highlight and select Settings.**

2. **On the TV Settings screen, highlight and select Hooking up.**

3. **On the Hooking Up screen, highlight and select Cable box if you use cable or highlight and select Satellite box if you have satellite service.**

4. **On the Cable Box Connection screen, highlight and select either Coaxial or Audio/Video, depending on the type of wire your cable box uses.**

   In most cases, the correct answer here is Coaxial. See Chapter 2 for an explanation of different wires used in WebTV's hookup.

5. **Highlight and select the Continue button.**

6. **On the next Cable Box Connection screen, highlight and select the channel used to receive the signal from your cable box.**

   The correct channel probably corresponds to the VCR output channel. If you're in doubt, look at the back of your television set and see which channel is selected.

7. **Select the on-screen Continue button.**

8. **On the Cable Box Signal screen, observe whether you are viewing a program in the small TV window.**

   Make sure that your TV/VCR switch on your VCR is set to TV. If you still don't see a picture, highlight and select the Next button. Repeat this process until a TV picture comes through — it may take several tries! Hang in there.

9. **When you see a picture, celebrate by highlighting and selecting the Continue button.**

10. **On the Cable Box Manufacturer screen, highlight and select the brand of cable box you're using.**

    Look at the cable box to see what brand it is. It's probably shown on the front, but look all over it if you have to. If you can't find a brand name anywhere, call your cable company. If the brand name isn't listed, highlight and select the `More` button.

11. **On the *YourBrand* Cable Box screen, highlight and select the `Continue` button.**

    Make sure that the IR Blaster is set up. It needs to be plugged into the back of the Plus Receiver, and one of the plastic ends should be positioned in front of the infrared receiver of the cable box. (See Chapter 2.) Note that the Sony IR Blaster has only one end. You must choose whether to use it to control your cable (or satellite) box or your VCR.

12. **On the Code Set screen, highlight and select each of the two channels, and observe whether your cable box switches channels to correspond with your selections.**

    This may take several tries to find the correct cable box code. If the channel doesn't change, highlight and select the `Next` button and then try selecting the channels again. Repeat the process until the channel changes with your selections.

13. **Give a shout of jubilation and select the `Done` button.**

You're finished! Now your cable (or satellite) box and your VCR are totally under the control of the WebTV remote and keyboard.

Changing Channels

It's odd to write a tutorial on that most basic of home entertainment skills — changing TV channels — but WebTV gives you a few options, so it's a subject worth reviewing. Following are the basic ways of changing channels when watching TV through WebTV Plus:

✔ **On the Listings screen, use the Up-arrow and Down-arrow buttons on the keyboard or remote to highlight different channels.**

The TV follows your highlights if you use the IR Blaster and if the `Stay on channel while browsing listings` box is *unchecked* on the TV Listings page. (See the "Using 'em" section.) Selecting any channel expands the TV window to full-screen.

✔ **On the Listings screen, use the Up-scroll and Down-scroll buttons on the remote or keyboard to leap among the channels in larger increments.**

Again, the TV follows by changing channels, if you have the IR Blaster hooked up. Select any channel to see it full-screen.

✔ **Use the Channel + and – buttons on the keyboard or the remote control.**

Using these buttons increases and decreases the channel selection by one number at a time.

✔ **If you've entered your television code into the WebTV remote control, use the numbered buttons to change channels.**

You must press the TV Mode button on the remote first. On the keyboard, move the TV/WebTV switch to the TV setting.

✔ **Whether or not you've entered your television code into the WebTV remote, you may use the television's original remote control to change channels, as you did before you had WebTV.**

Notice that changing the channels the old way leaves WebTV behind. Neither the TV Home screen nor the Listings screen can follow channel changes when made with the TV remote, and you won't get any program information. You may resume changing channels with the WebTV remote or keyboard at any time.

Customizing TV Home

The TV Home screen itself (the screen shown in Figure 5-1) always appears the same, and you can't make changes to it. The features of TV Home, however, have a lot of flexibility, and that's what this section is about. You can set up TV Favorites (similar to Favorites on the Web side of WebTV, described in Chapter 7), and set WebTV to remind you of shows at certain times and even record them.

Creating TV Favorites

TV Favorites is designed around the principle that you return to some TV or cable stations again and again. You might not be particularly attached to particular broadcast stations, so if you don't get cable or satellite reception, this feature might be of little interest. But it makes perfect sense for paid-TV subscribers, because so many topical channels carry an explicit type of programming. My Favorites, for example, betray my TV addictions, and include the SciFi Channel, A&E, VH1, the Comedy Channel, and a few others. With a single click of the remote, I can glimpse what's currently playing on each of my TV Favorites, and switch to any of them with another click.

To set up your TV Favorites, follow these steps:

1. **On the TV Home screen, highlight and select** TV Favorites.

2. **On the Favorite Channels screen, select the ungrammatical** Setup Favorites **button.**

3. **Highlight and select all the channels you'd like on your TV Favorites list.**

   Don't worry over your choices too much — you can change your TV Favorites list at any time, as often as you want. Use the `Clear` button at any time to deselect all your choices and start over. Highlight and select any previously selected channel to unselect that one channel.

4. **When you've finished selecting channels, highlight and select the** `Done` **button.**

5. **View your TV Favorites.**

   You may move the highlight box among your selected channels. If you're using cable and have the IR Blaster set up as described in Chapter 2, the channel switches as you highlight one Favorite channel after another. (The channel changes even if the `Stay on channel while browsing listings` box is checked on the TV Listings screen.)

6. **To expand the TV screen window to full size, select any channel.**

Planning couch time

WebTV Plus encourages planned television viewing. Should this be called mindful TV as opposed to mindless TV? Maybe. At the very least, using the Plus TV Planner ensures that you won't miss your favorite shows through carelessness. If you have a VCR connected to your Plus system and are using the IR Blaster, you don't even have to be home when the show airs.

TV Planner has three basic functions:

- ✔ It reminds you of shows you want to watch, with on-screen displays just before the shows begin.
- ✔ It can switch the channel to display the show at its beginning.
- ✔ It records the show on your VCR if you want.

TV Planner can switch the channel and record the show only if you're using the IR Blaster, as I describe in Chapter 2.

In a few other places, I've mentioned the difference between the Philips-Magnavox IR Blaster and the Sony IR Blaster, but this is the spot where the difference becomes really important. The Philips-Magnavox Blaster has two ends, but the Sony Blaster has only one end. The TV Planner feature is one of the coolest and most powerful parts of WebTV Plus, and you need that double-ended IR Blaster to take advantage of it. TV Planner enables you to set WebTV to automatically record a program at its broadcast time, or switch the TV channel to the show when it starts, or both. To accomplish this, the IR Blaster must be positioned in front of both the cable (or satellite) box, and the VCR. The single-ended Sony Blaster can't do this.

You can get started with TV Planner easily. Here's how:

1. **On the TV Home screen, highlight and select the** TV Planner **button at the bottom of the screen.**

   When you first select TV Planner, the TV Planner screen doesn't have any selections listed, naturally. You need to do some serious planning.

2. **On the TV Planner screen, highlight and select the** TV Listings **button.**

   You could have navigated straight to TV Listings from the TV Home screen. Either way, you start your TV planning from the TV Listings screen.

3. **On the TV Listings screen, select** For today **or** By day and time.

   Select the For today link if you'd like to add shows from the current day's schedule to your TV Planning list. Select By day and time to display a calendar one week in advance. Highlight and select a day on the calendar to see that day's listings. Another screen appears, on which you may highlight and select a two-hour period to view for the selected day.

4. **On the Listings screen, highlight and select any show that has not yet begun.**

   If you're viewing listings for a future day, naturally all the shows are in the future. If you're viewing the current day's listings, you must use the Right-arrow button to select a show that hasn't yet started.

5. **On the Program Info screen, highlight and select the** Remind **or** Record **button.**

   This is where you choose between two different TV Planner functions.

   Remind does just that — it reminds you with an on-screen display that your show is about to begin, one minute before the program start time. The reminder stays at the top of your TV screen (it doesn't get in the way too much) until you highlight and select the Continue button, or until the show begins.

   Selecting the Record button sets WebTV to activate your VCR when the program begins and put the show on tape. (You have to provide the tape! You also must make sure that the tape is inserted in the VCR and that the machine is turned off when the program begins.)

   If you select either Remind or Record, another TV Planner screen appears with the date, time, and channel information of the show.

6. **If you selected the** Remind **button:**

   a. **Highlight and select the** Tune to channel when program begins **box to automatically switch to the selected program's channel.**

   b. **Highlight and select the** Remind Regularly **button to lock this program into your regular schedule.**

   c. **You may select daily or weekly reminders.**

7. **If you selected the** Record **button:**

   a. **Highlight and select the** Remind before program begins **box to receive a reminder in addition to automatic recording features.**

   b. **You may also adjust the start and end record times by highlighting and selecting the times under the program name.**

   c. **Use the** Record Regularly **on-screen button to set up a daily or weekly recording schedule. (Then go buy a pile of VCR tapes.)**

8. **After you've finished establishing your TV Planner, highlight and select the** Done **button.**

You may repeat this process as often as you like, building up a formidable TV Planner list. To see your list at any time, highlight and select TV Planner on the TV Home screen. On the TV Planner screen, select any show to adjust its settings or to remove it from your list.

TV Planner works beautifully with the Search TV Listings feature. Don't stop reading now — reading the next section ties it all together.

Searching TV Listings

Conventional television program guides work on a date and time system. You can see everything that's playing at any given time, usually a week in advance. WebTV covers that angle, but offers much more to help you find worthwhile TV shows you might not even know exist.

The Search TV Listings feature is one of the most powerful aspects of WebTV Plus — so much so that it can revolutionize television habits. Used creatively with the IR Blaster and a VCR, this feature can help you provide better TV fare for your kids. In my opinion, the Searching TV Listings portion of TV Home is worth the investment in WebTV Plus by itself — even leaving out the entire Web.

Enough raving. Time to do some searching.

Understanding how the Search TV Listings feature works

Sometimes you want to watch whatever is on at the moment; other times, you want to watch something good regardless of when it's on. The latter preference takes some planning and a bit of searching. WebTV Plus makes both easy.

Searching TV Listings lets you scour the available TV fare for your system (broadcast, cable, or satellite) according to topic, genre, show, character, or several other criteria. The system automatically looks up to a week in advance. After you get the hang of it, and if you're using the IR Blaster with a VCR (see Chapter 2), you may start watching all your favorite shows *on your own schedule*. Even if you're currently recording favorite shows, the addition of powerful search tools can bring great programming into your life.

Searching for TV shows by category

The easiest way to begin searching is by category. Here's how:

1. **On the TV Home screen, highlight and select** TV Listings.

2. **On the TV Listings screen, move the highlight box to the Search TV Listings area, and then highlight and select** By program title or category.

3. **On the next TV Listings screen, highlight and select a category you'd like to search.**

4. **On the next TV Listings screen, highlight and select all the subcategories you'd like to search within your chosen main category.**

   Select the Check All button to select all subcategories or the Clear All button to unselect them all.

5. **After you've made your selections, highlight and select the** Search **button.**

6. **View the results of your search.**

   A listings screen appears with all the hits of your search request for the next week. Scroll among them with the Up- and Down-arrow buttons and Up- and Down-scroll buttons on the remote.

7. **Highlight and select any program to add it to your TV Planner.**

   You may receive an on-screen reminder of the show or automatically record it. See the "Planning Couch Time" section of this chapter to activate those features.

Searching for TV shows by keyword

Searching by keyword lets you type a show title, a character, or descriptive terms such as *horror* or *love*. (This is where you can get creative.) The results are uneven in some cases and dependent on the program and movie descriptions provided by WebTV — because the keywords search the descriptions.

The best way to experience searching by keyword is to play around with it. Here's how to get started:

1. **On the TV Home screen, highlight and select** TV Listings.

2. **On the TV Listings screen, move the highlight box to the Search TV Listings area, and then highlight and select** By program title or category.

3. **On the next TV Listings screen, highlight the** Search **text box, type a keyword, and then select the** Search **button.**

4. **View the results of your search.**

   Just as when you search by category, you can select any program result to add it to your TV Planning list.

As a general rule, searching by category is a good way to find new shows; searching by keyword helps you locate broadcast times for shows you already know about. Searching by category is a feature worth spending some time with. I quickly found a number of musical specials, for example, that I had no idea about. I ran out to buy a box of VCR tapes to capture all the great programming I had been oblivious to. If you use cable or satellite TV, you may well experience the same eye-opening revelation. Just get into those categories and do some experimenting — it's a wide world of TV programming out there, and chances are you'll discover some gems.

Part II
Getting Comfortable

The 5th Wave   By Rich Tennant

"The best thing about WebTV is I'm able to answer 50 percent more 'Jeopardy' questions than before."

In this part . . .

1t's time for a guided tour of the main features in the WebTV Network. Each chapter describes one of the main content areas: E-mail, Favorites, Community, and Search. The chapters in this part give you a good working knowledge of the core WebTV experience and lay the foundation for further adventures with multimedia, interactive TV, and Web page-building. Be sure to check out Chapter 8, which includes a description of MSN Messenger, one of the most significant WebTV upgrades since the last edition of this book.

Chapter 6

Using E-Mail

Despite all the excitement and wonder of the Web, regardless of the revolutionary effect that the Internet is having on our culture, and the many and varied aspects of the cyberspace experience notwithstanding, one simple online feature has been stealing the show right from the beginning: e-mail.

Electronic mail. It sounds cold, like the digitizing of human contact, the roboticizing of human relations. Isn't e-mail just the next evolutionary step in our spiral toward information-age shallowness, instant gratification, and individual isolation? Quite to the contrary! E-mail, in spite of its computer and academic lineage (it was previously used primarily by university faculty members), has evolved into an informal tool for families and friends, inspiring more contact because of its speed, ease of use, and cheap cost.

Cousin Freddy on Your TV

E-mail is not a replacement for all the other ways of connecting with others, including postal mail and the telephone — not to mention face-to-face contact. But e-mail has a few great characteristics:

> ✔ It's fast — really fast. In the online world, postal mail is called *snail mail*. Electronic letters are delivered often within seconds of being sent and almost always within minutes. E-mail sent from one WebTV subscriber to another arrives instantaneously.

- ✔ It's cheap. In fact, e-mail is effectively free, considering that WebTV members have unlimited e-mail use included in the monthly subscription cost.

- ✔ Its speed has created an e-mail culture in which short, informal notes are often exchanged at a rate of several per day. For those unaccustomed to writing letters or who just don't like taking the time to do so, short and frequent e-mailing provides a great alternative. Many people have found themselves to be active e-mailers even if they are notoriously delinquent letter writers.

- ✔ Just about every company and government office in America can be reached by e-mail.

- ✔ Geography is irrelevant — no expensive and nasty-tasting airmail stamps, no length limit for your letters, no waiting until the letter arrives, no waiting until 3 a.m. to call overseas.

E-mail has emerged from being an esoteric tool of academia to a business device to a cardinal social medium of the digital era. Grandparents use it to stay in touch with far-flung family members; parents, with their kids in college; high school students, with each other; and of course, cousin Freddy, with you.

When e-mail goes amiss

Electronic mail is wondrous, but not infallible. Neither is anyone who uses it! From time to time, everyone experiences the mild aggravation of returned mail. Returned mail happens when you send an e-mail and — bam! — it slams back to your own e-mail box, usually within a few seconds of sending it. The returned e-mail appears on your Mail List screen as a letter from Post Office, with a subject that reflects the reason for its undeliverability. For example, if you accidentally type an invalid e-mail address, the subject reads "Returned mail: User unknown."

An unknown user is by far the most common reason for returned e-mails. But something else can happen even if you enter the address perfectly. Some mail servers (the computers that receive your sent letters and deliver them to their recipients) shut down at night, especially servers associated with colleges and universities. (Mail servers at colleges usually have the .edu extension at the end of the e-mail address.) When a delivery is attempted to a closed server, you receive a notice that says, in effect, "The door is locked, but we'll keep knocking." The e-mail system keeps trying to deliver until the letter finally goes through. (In most cases you receive only one notice, not hundreds, thank goodness.) You don't have to do anything when you receive a notice that says the e-mail system will keep trying to deliver your letter.

When you get the "User unknown" notice from Post Office, the obvious solution is to check the address and correct any mistakes in it. If you entered the address automatically from your address book (see the instructions for doing so later in this chapter), the recipient probably changed or discontinued the e-mail address since your last communication with that person. In this case, you should get in touch some other way and get an updated address, which you can then add to your address book. If you typed the address manually, however, chances are you made a mistake. Here's how to correct it:

1. **On the Mail List screen, highlight and select the returned e-mail from Post Office.**

2. **On the Message for *YourName* screen, scroll down until you see the** Edit Message **button and then highlight and select it.**

   Another on-screen button, Show Details, displays an incomprehensible screen,

detailing the conversation that took place between two computers as the e-mail delivery was attempted. If only it was translated from computer gibberish, you might see one computer ask, "Doesn't this person live here?", and another answer, "Never heard of her. Humans are always making mistakes — send it back." The message, however, is not nearly so understandable, and you gain very little by selecting the Show Details button.

3. **On the Write a Message screen, change the address listed in the** To: **field.**

   You may also change the body of the e-mail as well as the Subject line on this screen.

4. **Highlight and select the** Send **button.**

Writing and Sending a Letter

All that you need to get started with e-mail is to send a note to someone. If you don't know any e-mail addresses yet, don't worry — you soon will. In the meantime, why not get familiar with the WebTV e-mail system by sending a letter to yourself? Your e-mail name is displayed on the screen when you're in the Mail section. Your address is the name you specified on the Sign-up screen and should look something like yourname@webtv.net. (If you don't see your e-mail address displayed on the screen, consult Chapter 2 for details of signing up with WebTV and creating an e-mail address.)

To write and send an electronic letter, follow these steps:

1. **On the Home screen, highlight and select** Mail.
2. **On the Mail List screen, highlight and select** Write.
3. **On the Write a Message screen, notice the blinking cursor in the** To: **space. In this space, type the recipient's Internet address.**

Figure 6-1 shows the Write a Message screen with a completed message to use as a guide in these steps. The Write a Message screen appears slightly different in WebTV Plus, with more options on the left side of the screen. These options are described later in this chapter.

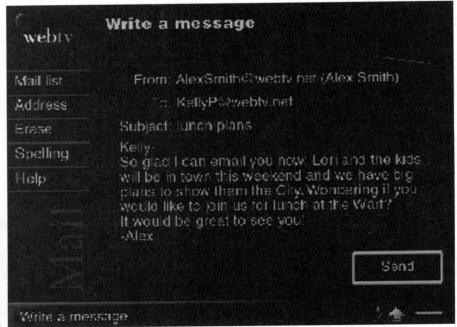

Figure 6-1:
The Write a
Message
screen in
WebTV
Classic.

Press the Select button on the remote (or the Return key of the keyboard) to access your Addresses list. If you don't have the optional keyboard, highlight and select the Keyboard button to use the on-screen keyboard for typing an address manually. To use addresses from your personalized list, just highlight and select them. The correct address zips into the To: field with a satisfying chunk sound. If you want to send a copy of a letter to several people, you don't have to retype the letter. Instead, you simply add multiple names from your Addresses list. (I describe how to add addresses to your Addresses list later in this chapter in the section titled "Using Your WebTV Address Book.")

4. **Still on the Write a Message screen, use the Arrow buttons on the remote to move the blinking cursor down to the** cc: **space and then type the Internet address of the person (or people), if any, whom you want to receive a copy of your outgoing letter.**

Again, you may press the Select button on the remote to view and select a recipient from your Addresses list. The cc: space appears only if you have selected it in your account settings (see Chapter 4).

5. **After you address your e-mail, you're still on the Write a Message screen. Use the Arrow buttons on the remote to move the cursor down to the** Subject: **space, and type a title for your message.**

When choosing an e-mail subject title, be aware of length limitations. The WebTV system has a substantial allowance of 70 characters in the `Subject:` field. When a WebTV subscriber receives a letter, however, only 25 characters appear in the Mail list. (The full title appears when the recipient reads the letter.) E-mail systems other than WebTV have varying limitations on the subject length. The moral: Keep your subject titles short, or put the most important part first. I find it effective (and appreciate it when receiving e-mail) to encapsulate the letter's purpose in the subject line. Subjects such as "Gone for weekend," "Just chatting," and "Urgent question" inform the recipient what to expect before even reading the letter.

6. **Finally, you get to write your letter. Still on the Write a Message screen, move the blinking cursor down to the blank area below the** `Subject:` **space.**

   If you've created a personalized signature, it appears in the blank area, but the cursor squeezes between the subject and the signature. (I describe how to create a signature in Chapter 4 in the section titled "Setting up your mailbox.")

7. **Now, type your letter — it can be as long or short as you want.**

8. **When you're finished, highlight and select the on-screen** Send **button.**

   The e-mail is on its way.

During the process of addressing and writing an e-mail letter, you have the option of using the on-screen `Erase` button lurking to the left of the Write a Message screen. Be careful! The `Erase` button is fierce and irrevocable. Highlight and select it to erase everything you've added to the screen, including all addresses, the subject, and the text of the letter. To erase portions of text or a single address, use the Arrow buttons to position the blinking cursor just past the correction. Then backspace over the part that you want to remove, using the Delete key of the wireless keyboard or the on-screen keyboard.

Checking Your Spelling

WebTV cares about the literacy of its members. Or at least about the appearance of literacy. Well, maybe the service doesn't care at all, but if *you* care, the spell-checking feature of e-mail is handy.

WebTV e-mail has a built-in dictionary, and — on command — checks the spelling of any e-mail you've written, before sending it. You must request the spell check for each and every letter you want to check because there is no way to turn on the feature permanently.

Here's how to use WebTV spell-check:

1. **On the Write a Message screen, compose your e-mail.**

2. **After writing, or at any time while writing, highlight and select** Spelling **from the sidebar on the left of the screen.**

3. **On the Check Your Spelling screen, select one of the words from the** SUGGESTED CORRECTIONS **list to correct the first misspelled word.**

   You can also change the spelling (or the word) manually in the POSSIBLE MISSPELLING field and then select the Change button. If you've used an unusual word that you want unchanged, and furthermore you want WebTV to recognize that word in the future, select the Remember button without changing the word.

4. **Continue in the same fashion for each misspelled word that WebTV puts in the** POSSIBLE MISSPELLING **field.**

5. **When all words have been corrected, changed, or remembered, select the** Done **button.**

Adding Pictures and Sound to Plus E-Mail

WebTV Plus has enhanced e-mail functions that take advantage of certain electronic jacks in the back of the Plus Receiver. (They're not available in the Classic Internet terminal.) These new features are fun, but are not related to the basic functionality of e-mail. In other words, Classic subscribers shouldn't feel that they're missing anything crucial. The Plus enhancements enable you to add pictures (from the TV, VCR, or a camcorder) to an e-mail, and even record an audio greeting. This section is for Plus users, and describes how to use these multimedia e-mail features.

Chapter 13 explains how *any* WebTV subscriber — Classic or Plus — can add pictures and sounds to e-mail by means of HTML tags, which link to multimedia elements stored on the Web. HTML tags are the underlying language of Web pages and can be used in WebTV e-mail to great effect. The HTML process is different from, and unrelated to, the Plus e-mail features I describe in this section.

Clipping an image from TV

I'm about to describe a Plus feature that might not be crucial but sure is cool — way cool. With WebTV Plus, you can view your currently tuned channel on the Write a Message screen in the Mail section, and use a kind of freeze-frame function to clip an image from the TV show, adding it to your e-mail. It's a bit unclear why you'd want to do this, except for the sheer novelty of it, but that might be reason enough. Furthermore, the process I describe can be used to clip a more meaningful or personal image taken from a VCR or camcorder recording.

Weighty e-mail

When sending images and audio greetings to friends using WebTV Plus e-mail, remember that the attached digitized file is of a certain size — sometimes a pretty big size, especially if you're adding both an image *and* an audio greeting. (The added file is called an *attachment*.) The larger the size of the total e-mail package, the longer is takes to receive it. Standard Netiquette, among people who use e-mail a lot, is to avoid sending unsolicited audio or image attachments. It's considered polite to ask before sending.

Among WebTV users, the issue is reduced because e-mail attachments are handled easily within a closed system. Furthermore, WebTVers receive e-mail in the background, while they are surfing the Web, watching TV, or whatever. So delays are not aggravating as they can be for computer users. Accordingly, you should be more cautious about sending image and audio attachments to non-WebTV Internet addresses — in other words, friends who are not on WebTV.

Even if you don't have a VCR or camcorder, you can have fun with e-mail images. Here's how:

1. **On the Web Home screen, highlight and select** Mail.
2. **On the Mail List screen, highlight and select** Write.
3. **On the Write a Message screen, highlight and select** Photo.
4. **When the Add to Message panel appears, move the highlight box down to the** TV/Video **on-screen switch.**

   At first, the image window does not display the television picture. That's because the switch is set to the default Video position, for use with a camcorder. Select the TV/Video switch to change it from Video to TV. You should immediately see the currently tuned television station. (Make sure your TV is turned on!) You can't hear the TV sound no matter what you do, so don't fiddle with the remote trying to hear something. This feature is concerned only with images, so the sound doesn't come through.

   At this point you may also bring your VCR into play, assuming it's connected to your WebTV system as described in Chapter 2. After selecting the TV/Video switch, changing it to TV, simply activate Play on your VCR (if you have a recorded tape inside), and you can see the tape playing in the TV window. Proceed with the following steps.

5. **Highlight and select** Freeze.

   Selecting Freeze is like taking a snapshot of the TV screen. Press it repeatedly to observe what happens. The little green light on the Freeze button illuminates when the picture is frozen. Select Freeze again to turn off the light and unfreeze the TV window. (The program resumes in real-time, not from where you froze it.) Keep selecting the Freeze button until you get an image you want to add to your e-mail.

6. **Highlight and select the** `Add to Message` **button.**

The image attachment is created and added to the bottom of the Write a Message screen. You can scroll down to view it. If you change your mind about sending it, highlight and select the `Remove` button.

7. **Finish addressing and writing your e-mail (as described earlier in this chapter), and then highlight and select the** `Send` **button.**

Your e-mail and attachment are on their way to some lucky recipient.

Clipping an image from a camcorder

You need make only two changes to the instructions in the preceding section to capture an image from a camcorder recording and send it with an e-mail:

1. **First, plug your camcorder into the back of the WebTV Plus Receiver.**

Take the Video Out cable from your camcorder, and plug the free end into the Video In jack of the Plus Receiver. If your camcorder makes VCR-ready tapes, it might be easier to simply pop the tape into your VCR and follow the preceding instructions.

2. **Second, when you reach Step 4 in the preceding section, don't change the** `TV/Video` **switch from its default** `Video` **setting.**

You can see your camcorder's playback only when the switch is set to `Video`. (Look at Figure 6-2 to see the switch in its correct position.)

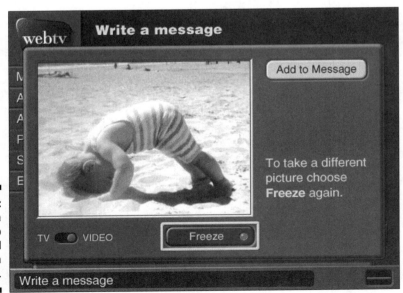

Figure 6-2:
Adding a photo to an e-mail using a camcorder.

Use the Freeze button in the same way as described in the preceding section to capture an image, and then use the Add to Message button to attach the image to your e-mail.

Creating an audio greeting

Making an audio greeting is perhaps more fun than attaching a picture. To use this feature in WebTV Plus, you need a microphone plugged into the Mic jack on the back of the Plus Receiver. You can buy such a microphone at a computer store or a general electronics store such as Radio Shack.

In most cases, you shouldn't think of the audio recording feature as a replacement for typing. For one thing, you're limited to thirty seconds of time — not enough for a longish letter. Even if you had more time, using it would create an enormous attachment to your e-mail, which would be aggravating to the recipient. (Big attachments take longer to receive.) The audio greeting is best used briefly, as a personal touch to a written e-mail.

After you've plugged a microphone into the Mic jack of the Plus Receiver, follow these steps:

1. **On the Web Home screen, highlight and select** Mail.

2. **On the Mail List screen, highlight and select** Write.

3. **On the Write a Message screen, highlight and select** Recording.

4. **When the Add to Message panel appears, get your microphone nearby and then highlight and select the** Record **button.**

   The wavy lines in the little audio window turn from yellow to green or to red if the recording is too loud. Move the microphone away from your mouth until the lines are green.

5. **Speak your message.**

6. **After you've finished recording, highlight and select the** Stop **button.**

7. **Listen to your recording by highlighting and selecting the** Play **button.**

   You may repeat the process as often as you like, until the recording meets your high standards of elocution. Every recording you make erases the previous recording.

8. **When you're satisfied with the recording, highlight and select** Add to Message.

9. **On the Write a Message screen, highlight and select the Recording icon to hear your greeting again.**

   You may change your mind and remove the audio attachment by highlighting and selecting the Remove button.

10. **Address and write the text portion of your e-mail, and then select the Send button.**

WebTV recipients of audio greetings receive a text e-mail with a loudspeaker icon. They can hear your greeting by highlighting and selecting the loudspeaker. Internet recipients who are not on WebTV receive an audio attachment (.wav format) that they must select. Whether they can then hear your greeting depends on the e-mail software they're using and its configuration.

The red light

The Automatic mail-checking feature is terrific. If you've activated it (instructions for doing so are in Chapter 4), WebTV checks your mail once a day at a preset time, even if the system is not logged on. If some e-mail has arrived in your mailbox the next time you log on, the red light on the front of the terminal lights up, just like a telephone answering machine that blinks when someone has left you a phone message. To get your mail, you must log on and visit your mailbox in the Mail area as I outline in the "Checking Your Mail" section.

The red light comes on also when you receive e-mail during a WebTV session. When you're logged on, the system doesn't have to wait until the preset Automatic mail-checking time — the instant you receive an e-mail message, it lets you know with a chirping sound (like an e-mail bird whispering in your ear) and the red light.

For the nifty red light system to work when you're not using WebTV, you must leave the WebTV terminal power on, even when you're not logged on. How? You leave the WebTV power on by logging off with the Hang up button on the Options panel. The Hang up button breaks your connection to WebTV but leaves the terminal power on. (You can always

tell whether the WebTV box is powered on by looking for the green light — if it's lit, you're in business.)

Just follow these steps to log off and leave the WebTV power on:

1. **At any point in your WebTV session, press the Options button on the remote.**

2. **When the Options panel appears on the screen, highlight and select** Hang up.

   See Chapter 4 for information on adding the Hang up option to the Options panel. WebTV hangs up, breaking your phone connection (and freeing your phone line). You can continue watching TV. If you gaze at the WebTV screen long enough, you see it transform into a screen saver — a moving image that bounces around your screen until you log on again.

When logging off in this manner, you may continue using the television normally. Turning off the set does not turn off the power of the WebTV box. And at least once a day, be sure to glance at the WebTV terminal and look for that red light! If it's on, you have mail waiting.

Checking Your Mail

Whether or not you use the Automatic mail-checking feature, you have to go to your mailbox to read your received letters — the Automatic mail check only alerts you to mail; you still have to walk down your electronic driveway to your electronic mailbox and get it. (I go into detail about the Automatic mail-checking feature in "The red light" sidebar.)

You can go to your mailbox at any time. Checking it is a simple matter: On the Home screen, highlight and select Mail. When the Mail List screen appears, your waiting messages are listed.

The Mail List screen shows three columns of information:

- On the left, you see the sender's name. This might not be the sender's real name, but it's the name the sender has chosen for e-mail, just as WebTV enables you to choose an Internet name when you set up your account.

- In the middle is the subject, or title, of the e-mail message. On the Mail List screen, you see only the first 25 characters of the subject. If your correspondent is pithy, 25 characters are enough.

- On the right is the date the e-mail was received. Because e-mail delivery is so fast, the reception date is almost always the same as the sent date, even if the e-mail was sent from someone on another online service.

You have mail — now what?

When you get to the Mail List screen, reading your mail couldn't be easier. Just follow these steps:

1. **Highlight and select the e-mail item that you want to read.**

2. **On the Message for *YourName* screen, read your e-mail.**

   If the message continues past the bottom of your screen, use the Scroll buttons on the remote or the keyboard to scroll down and see the entire letter.

As you read an e-mail message, you have a few choices for what to do next, represented by the list of options on the left side of your screen:

- Highlight and select Mail list to return to your mailbox, where all waiting e-mail is listed.

- Highlight and select Previous to read the previous e-mail on your list without having to return to the Mail List screen. (If you're reading the first letter on your current list, you can still see the Previous option but it appears dimmed, indicating that the option is not available.)

- ✔ Highlight and select Next to view the following e-mail on your list without having to return to the Mail List screen. (If you're reading the last letter on your list, the Next option appears dimmed and is unavailable.)

- ✔ Highlight and select Discard to throw away the letter you're currently reading.

The Discard option is merciless, and no "Are you sure?" message confirms that you really mean it. It just grabs the e-mail and tosses it irretrievably. So make sure, as you're scrolling around those options on the left side of the screen, that you select the correct one.

- ✔ Highlight and select Save to move the e-mail you're reading to the Storage area.

- ✔ Highlight and select Reply to write a response to the recipient of the e-mail you're reading. The Reply to a Message screen appears, looking remarkably similar to the Write a Message screen, except that the To: field is already filled in with the address of the person who wrote you the original message. You can add recipients in the To: and cc: fields just as if you were in the Write a Message screen. Then, as with a normal e-mail, write the message and use the on-screen Send button at the bottom of the screen.

- ✔ Highlight and select Reply all to write a response that's delivered to everyone who received the e-mail you're responding to.

- ✔ Highlight and select Forward to send a copy of the e-mail you're reading to another person. The Forward a Message screen appears; it operates just like the Write a Message screen, only the message text area has a copy of the message you want to forward. Fill in the To: field and the cc: field if you want to send copies to anyone else, and then highlight and select Send. You don't need to write anything in the message text area, although you may if you feel talkative or if the forwarded letter requires some explanation. If you write in the message text area, your addition is placed before the text of the e-mail you're forwarding. If you've created a signature, it's placed at the bottom of the forwarded letter, even if the original letter has someone else's signature.

Forwarding a letter may seem a little tricky, but it's easy. To get the hang of it, try forwarding a couple to yourself. On the Forward a Message screen, type your own WebTV address (or select it from your Addresses list if you've included yourself), and send the letter. Experiment with adding text before the forwarded letter and adding a signature.

Talking to yourself

You can do a lot of things with e-mail you've received. You may be eager to practice your e-mail skills on a voluminous correspondence. Perhaps you're waiting for some letters to arrive. And waiting. Still waiting. (Hey, if I knew your e-mail address, you could practice on me.) Why wait? Just send a few notes to yourself, and try out the features explained in this chapter by reading, discarding, saving, replying to yourself, and forwarding to yourself.

Start by writing yourself a letter or three. They don't have to say much of anything — literary excellence isn't the point here. You can even just put "test" in the body of the messages. Name them differently in the Subject: line,

though, such as "test 1," "test 2," and so on. (I know you must be marveling at the wealth of my imagination right now.) After sending the notes to your own e-mail address, you hear the chirp and see the red light on the set-top box. Go to the Message for *YourName* screen to see your new list of arrived e-mail.

Read the first letter (perhaps called "test 1"). Try discarding it. Now read the second, and practice using the Save feature. With the third self-inflicted letter, forward it to yourself. This exercise is perhaps taking electronic multiple personality disorder to new levels, but it's good practice. Your real correspondents will be glad you did. So will you. And you.

Keeping a neat mailbox

You wouldn't want to invite a friend into your mailbox and have it be all messy, would you? Besides, if you get busy with e-mail, you need a place to store letters you've read but want to save. Often, messages don't need to be saved, and you can use the Discard option on the Message for *YourName* screen. When you do want to save an e-mail message, use the Save option, which moves the message to your personal Storage area.

To see your stored e-mail, follow these steps:

1. **On the Home screen, highlight and select** Mail.
2. **On the Mail List screen, highlight and select** Storage.

The Saved Mail screen displays a list of the e-mail messages you've placed in there using Save. The date in the right column indicates when the message was first received, not when you moved it to storage (although the two momentous events might have occurred on the same day).

On the left of the screen, a few options await you:

Hey, it's a smart system!

WebTV e-mail has some brains to it. You know about Automatic mail checking, which by itself is pretty intelligent. Mail also keeps track of which e-mail messages you've read. New messages in the Mail List screen are displayed in bright blue bold type. After you read a new message and then return to the Mail list, the message is reduced to a nonbold blue listing, indicating that it's no longer new. Furthermore, when all new e-mail messages have been read, the red light on the terminal box goes off.

Not exactly Nobel Prize material, but pretty good for a machine.

✔ Highlight and select `Mail list` to go to your mailbox list of unsaved, undiscarded letters. (If you just came from your mailbox, you can also return to it using the Back button on the remote.)

✔ Highlight and select `Clean up` to see the Clean Up Saved Mail screen. This is where you discard letters from Storage. Highlight and select the check box next to each letter you want to delete from the list. To check them all at once, highlight and select `Check all`. After you've checked all the letters you want to discard, highlight and select `Discard`.

✔ The `Discard` function is no more forgiving than it was on the Message for *YourName* screen, so be careful. Make sure that you've checked the correct disposable messages. The moment you select the `Discard` option, the selected letters are gone.

✔ Using the Clean Up Saved Mail screen is especially useful when you've accumulated lots of unwanted letters in your Storage area. Rather than selecting, viewing, and discarding them one by one, just go to Clean Up Saved Mail and throw out bunches of checked letters all at once.

Using Your WebTV Address Book

E-mail addresses can be complicated, cryptic, and hard to remember. People often don't use their whole, real name as their e-mail name. Sometimes, in fact, they choose a capricious e-mail handle (*handle* is hand-me-down CB radio talk for nickname) that bears no relation to the real moniker. Even if you forget about the name part, there is a long trailer to every e-mail address — the part following the @ symbol. Who wants to be bothered remembering all that gibberish or even writing it down?

WebTV makes it easy to create, maintain, and use an on-screen address book for all your e-mail correspondence. You can add addresses to the address book whenever you want by simply typing them in or effortlessly add them from letters you receive without having to type anything at all.

To view your address book, follow these steps:

1. **On the Home screen, highlight and select** Mail.

2. **On the Mail List screen, highlight and select** Addresses.

3. **On the E-mail addresses for** *YourName* **screen, view the entries you've made so far.**

   Use the Scroll buttons on the remote if the list extends below the bottom of the your TV screen.

On the E-mail Addresses for *YourName* screen, you can make changes to your address book.

Adding an e-mail address to your list

You can add an e-mail address to your list in two ways. The first way involves typing an address for someone who hasn't yet sent you an e-mail message, and the second way uses the return address of a message from your mailbox. The following steps show you the first way, which you should use when you want to add a friend's address before receiving an e-mail message from that person (so you can write first):

1. **On the Home screen, highlight and select** Mail.

2. **On the Mail List screen, highlight and select** Addresses.

3. **On the E-mail Addresses for** *YourName* **screen, highlight and select** Add.

4. **On the Add an E-mail Address screen, highlight the** Name **field and then type the name you want to add.**

   If you need to use the on-screen keyboard, highlight the Name field and press the Select button on the remote. Then, type the name (such as Cousin Billy Bob or Mom) as you want it to appear in your address book — you add the actual e-mail address in the next step.

5. **Highlight the** Address **field and enter the person's e-mail address.**

6. **Highlight and select the** Add **button.**

   The E-mail Addresses for *YourName* screen reappears with your recent addition nestled in the list in alphabetical order.

The second way to add an address is a breeze, but you must have received an e-mail message from the person whose address you want to add to your address book. The following steps show you how:

1. **On the Mail List screen, highlight and select the e-mail message from the person whose address you want to add.**

2. **On the Message for *YourName* screen, highlight and select the blue name on the** From: **line.**

   A box appears asking whether you want to add the name to your Addresses list.

3. **Highlight the box and select** Yes.

   The Add an E-mail Address screen appears, showing the name and e-mail address to be added.

4. **You may highlight and select either the name or address to make changes.**

   Do not make changes to the e-mail address found in the lower of the two boxes, labeled Address. The e-mail address is already accurately copied from the received e-mail. However, you may want to change how the name appears in your address book by highlighting the top box, labeled Name. Using the wireless or on-screen keyboard, type a modified name — you could type a nickname in the case of a friend, for example.

5. **Highlight and select the** Add **button.**

   If you inadvertently try to add a name that already exists in your address book, a window pops up telling you so and offering to replace the previous information with the new address. If the addresses are identical (which is the case most of the time), it doesn't matter whether you replace it in this window.

If the person you're adding has a new e-mail address, you can quickly and easily update your listing with the Replace it function — so highlight and select Replace it. However, the person you're adding may have two e-mail addresses, and if you've received an e-mail from the second address, you can add it to your list under a slightly different name. Just follow these steps:

1. **On the Mail List screen, highlight and select the letter from your friend's second e-mail address.**

2. **On the Message for *YourName* screen, highlight and select the blue address labeled** From.

3. **When the box appears asking whether you'd like to add the address to your Addresses list, highlight and select** Yes.

4. **On the Add an E-mail Address screen, highlight the** Name **box and type your friend's name exactly as you'd like it to appear in your address book.**

   Type something that identifies the second address. For example, if your friend's first e-mail address, which you already have in your address book, is called Bob, you might call the second address Bob's office. (If your friend's name is Frederick, the example doesn't work as well.)

How e-mail addresses work

Even if you've never used a computer or been online, you may have seen an e-mail address in an advertisement or on a business card. They're strange, cryptic things, wouldn't you say (e-mail addresses, not business cards)? To the uninitiated, they appear as unintelligible strings of letters and symbols. In fact, the clusters of letters and punctuation marks have some meaning. Here is your initiation.

All e-mail addresses follow the same basic format. Every e-mail address, whether it's on the WebTV system or an outside system, is divided into two parts, separated by an @ (which most people simply pronounce as "at"). The first part contains the e-mail name of the person who owns the address. The name is usually related to the person's real name but is never identical to the user's whole name for one simple reason: Spaces are not allowed in e-mail addresses. So my e-mail name, for example, could not be `Brad Hill`, but it could be `Brad_Hill` or `BradHill`. Using the underline symbol is common, and so is first initial followed by last name, as in `bhill`. Some people, either through capriciousness or a desire for anonymity, make up an alias totally unrelated to their real name.

Whatever name is chosen, the @ follows. (Again, with no spaces.) The @ indicates — to the computers handling e-mail — that a computer location is about to be spelled out. It's like the street and city address after a person's name on an envelope.

Following the @, you see the domain name. This is just a fancy phrase for the online computer on which the e-mail address and the mailbox itself

reside. It's the computer that stores e-mail letters until the person with the e-mail address retrieves and reads them. For example, in the case of WebTV, the domain name is `webtv`. WebTV's domain name is only one part (followed by an extension that I describe next). Some domain names can have multiple parts to them, each separated by a period, especially in cases in which the e-mail computer is run by a large organization such as a university.

The full name of the WebTV's e-mail computer is `webtv.net`. Notice the `net` part — this is called the *extension*. The extension is usually either `com` or `net`, but can be a variety of other names depending on who uses the computer and where the computer resides. You might see `edu` in an address from someone at a college or a university, `org` from someone at a non-profit organization, or `gov` from a government organization. Countries other than the United States have their own extensions. For example: `jap`, `fin`, `uk`, and `nz` are for addresses from Japan, Finland, United Kingdom, and New Zealand, respectively.

Your complete e-mail address is `yourname@webtv.net`. (Usually, e-mail addresses don't use capital letters.) Your e-mail address identifies you at the WebTV e-mail computer with the extension net, which identifies WebTV as a standard online service.

When exchanging e-mail addresses verbally, you should follow the correct pronunciation: @ is pronounced "at," and people usually say "dot" when referring to any periods in an address. Your e-mail address is pronounced "Yourname at WebTV dot net."

You can save the same address under two (or more) different names. Such duplication could be handy if you know people who share an e-mail account.

Changing an entry in your address book

At some point, you might want to change either the name or e-mail address of a listing in your address book. Changing the name affects only how the listing appears to you. Changing the e-mail address affects the destination of the letters you send when you select the person's name from your address book. Whenever you change a name, be sure that you change the address as well, if necessary. Follow these steps to change an entry in your address book:

1. **On the Mail List screen, highlight and select** Addresses.

2. **On the E-mail Addresses for *YourName* screen, highlight and select the entry you want to change.**

3. **On the Change an E-mail Address screen, highlight the** Name **or** Address **field and type your changes.**

   Use the Delete key on either the wireless keyboard or the on-screen keyboard to backspace over the previous entries. Then type in your corrections or changes.

4. **Highlight and select the** Done **button.**

Discarding an entry from your address book

You say you never want to write another electronic letter to the guy or girl that you met at the last office party? Toss the listing out of your address lineup this way:

1. **On the Mail List screen, highlight and select** Addresses.

2. **On the E-mail Addresses for *YourName* screen, highlight and select the entry you want to discard.**

3. **On the Change an E-mail Address screen, highlight and select** Discard.

Make sure that you have the correct entry selected from your address book! After you've discarded it, you no longer have automatic access to that address. So if your mom thrives on your daily e-mail, be that certain you don't "accidentally" shred her address.

Copying, Cutting, and Pasting

Copying, cutting, and pasting: Sounds like I'm teaching arts and crafts, doesn't it? Thankfully, no. Cutting and pasting refers to removing text from one location on the screen and placing it at another position. Text can also be copied in blocks and placed elsewhere. Cutting, copying, and pasting are *word processing* functions that enhance your e-mail experience, and occasionally come in handy on the Web.

Copying, cutting, and pasting all require the Cmd key on the optional wireless keyboard, a key that doesn't exist on the remote control. For this reason, you need a WebTV keyboard to use this feature.

Cutting and copying text is most flexible when you're viewing a page with standard text. The features don't work on images or on Web pages in which the words are part of images. The best place to get familiar with cutting and copying is in the Mail section. The only place to exercise the paste function is when viewing a text-input screen, such as the Write a Message screen. Cutting, copying, and pasting are most often used when writing e-mail or newsgroup messages.

The following steps lead you through the process of cutting, copying, and pasting. To practice these steps, your Mail settings need to be adjusted to always include the original message when you reply. Here's how to change that setting:

1. **On the Mail List screen, highlight and select** Settings.

2. **On the Mail Settings screen, highlight and select** Extras.

3. **On the Extra Features screen, check** Always include the original message when you reply.

4. **Select the** Done **button.**

To practice cutting, copying, and pasting, it's easiest to select a letter from your mail list and forward it to yourself. Before sending it, you can experiment with your new commands and then view the results when you receive the letter. Here's how to proceed:

1. **On the Mail List screen, select any letter.**

2. **On the Message screen, highlight and select** Forward.

3. **On the Forward a Message screen, enter your WebTV address in the** To: **space.**

4. **Scroll down until you see the text of the letter you're forwarding.**

5. **Hold down the Cmd key on your keyboard, and while continuing to hold it down, press the A key.**

   Cmd+A highlights the entire text of the message you're forwarding, including the address header. *A* stands for *All.*

6. **Hold down the Cmd key and press the C key.**

   Cmd+C copies the entire block of highlighted text. *C* stands for *Copy.*

7. **Still on the Forward a Message screen, scroll back up to the message-writing area and then position the cursor in the text entry space.**

8. **Hold down the Cmd key and press the V key.**

   Cmd+V pastes the copied block of text into the e-mail, including the copied address header. Obscure memory hint: *V* looks like a little wedge that inserts text at a specific screen location.

9. **Position the cursor at the bottom of the header information, just before the text of the letter you're forwarding.**

   You're getting ready to cut the unwanted header text.

10. **Hold down the Shift key and repeatedly press the Left-arrow key.**

    This is a more selective way of highlighting than Cmd+A (which highlights all text on a screen). Notice that each time you press the Left-arrow key, another letter is highlighted. You may also press the Up-arrow key to highlight entire lines above the cursor. In fact, now is a good time to experiment with all the arrow keys, observing how they affect the highlighted text.

11. **When the entire block of unwanted header text is highlighted, hold down the Cmd key and press the X key.**

    Cmd+X performs a cut, deleting the highlighted text from the message box. You may paste it somewhere else or forget about it. (Using the Delete key on the keyboard instead of Cmd+X gets rid of highlighted text, but you can't paste it somewhere else.)

12. **Highlight and select the** Send **button.**

    When the e-mail arrives in your box (about one second later), select it to see the results of your text manipulation.

Here is a review of the cut, copy, and paste keyboard commands:

- ✔ Cmd+A selects all text on a screen, highlighting it.
- ✔ Cmd+C copies all highlighted text, without removing it.
- ✔ Cmd+X cuts all highlighted text, removing it.

- ✔ Cmd+V pastes cut or copied text to a new location defined by the cursor.
- ✔ The Delete key on the keyboard removes highlighted text, making it unavailable for pasting.
- ✔ Shift+Arrow keys highlight text in any direction, one letter at a time (Left- and Right-arrow keys) or one line at a time (Up- and Down-arrow keys).

Things to Do with E-Mail

At first, e-mail seems like an alternative to the telephone. You write, someone receives — it's one-to-one, cheap, and fast (compared to postal mail, not to a telephone conversation). However, the power of e-mail is more than dutifully sending news to family members or trading sports scores with your buddy across the country.

E-mail on Web sites

Web sites often invite e-mail responses from their visitors. The owner or designer of the site may solicit feedback and suggestions about the site or simply provide an e-mail link for any type of visitor contribution. In most cases, the e-mail link is near the bottom of the Web site's home page. It consists of a sentence such as, "To make suggestions about this site, e-mail us at webmaster@oursite.com." (Of course, the address is real.) Follow these steps to take advantage of Web site e-mail:

1. **When you see an e-mail request, highlight and select it.**

   The Write a Message screen appears, with the site's e-mail address automatically inserted in the To: field.

2. **Position the blinking cursor in the message text area and write your letter.**

3. **Highlight and select** Send.

Often, the *Webmaster* (the administrator of the Web site) responds to e-mail letters from visitors, and you might soon have a reply in your mailbox. Such quick response is one of the distinguishing qualities of the Internet, as opposed to the outside world. You may not expect to get a personal response from the vice president of a company, but you can usually count on personal contact with the "president" of a Web site.

E-mail subscriptions

Just as with postal mail, you can receive electronic subscriptions to publications in your WebTV mailbox. Such publications range from newsletters to product updates to delivery of home pages of sites whose content changes often. The best way to find subscription opportunities, which are usually free, is to surf the Web. The following are some of the most common things you can sign up to regularly receive in your e-mail box:

- ✔ **News reports.** Some Web companies provide wire service reports or original journalism in capsule formats on a daily, a weekly, or an irregular basis.

- ✔ **Site updates.** You can enlist your e-mail address to receive periodic updates of a site's content. The update can be in the form of a text summary or the actual home page, complete with links.

- ✔ **Online sales.** Some shopping sites notify their subscribers about special sales or new products.

Mailing lists

Mailing lists, as I describe in thrilling detail in Chapter 8, are basically e-mail party lines. They consist of groups of people who take advantage of automated Internet systems, often called *listservs,* to handle e-mail in such a way that every member receives every other member's post to the mailing list. In this fashion, discussions can take place but without the slick threading features often found on message boards. (*Threading* is a way of organizing discussions held on message boards. See Chapter 8.) Instead, it's up to the users of the mailing list to make sure that the subject header of each post identifies the topic of discussion. Nevertheless, just because *thread* is a cool word, you often see mailing list users refer to a topic of discussion as a thread.

Because mailing lists are closed groups, strangers can't wander by and post messages to the group, as often happens on public message boards. You must subscribe to a mailing list to become a member — don't worry, the mailing list is free and usually open to anyone. The result, however, is a tighter, more close-knit community of people than you usually see on bulletin boards. Mailing lists are usually centered on a shared interest, hobby, or profession.

You can find listservs on all kinds of subjects, and they exist in many sizes from small, cozy groups to large communities trading a hundred or more messages every day. Mailing lists achieve their highest potential when serving as support groups, bringing people together from all over the world who share a difficult life situation, such as an unusual medical disease. In that case, listservs are marvels of grass-roots information distribution, and they demonstrate the value of emotional support, even in the electronic realm. Such groups have bolstered spirits and even saved lives.

Chapter 7

Choosing Favorites

● ●

In This Chapter

▶ Adding a Web page to your collection of Favorites

▶ Accessing the sites you want to revisit

▶ Discovering some tips for managing your Favorites

● ●

*Y*ou can easily get lost browsing the Web. Because the primary means of navigation is following links (highlighting and selecting things on the screen that take you to other screens), a few minutes is all it takes to develop a tangled path you'd never be able to duplicate later. So what do you do when you stumble across a terrific Web site that you want to visit again? Try to retrace your steps? Write down the long, indecipherable URL and type it in again when you want to revisit? Try to outsmart the electronic birds that have eaten your proverbial breadcrumbs?

Retracing steps is usually hopeless, and writing down URLs is inconvenient at best. The solution to the problem of revisiting a far corner of the Web lies in a WebTV feature called Favorites. Any time you view a Web page, you can assign it to your collection of favorite locations and then visit it again with a single click of the remote. Because the Favorites screen is always just one step away from Home, a visit to a saved favorite site is never more than three steps away, no matter where you are on the Web.

Adding a Favorite Page

The Favorites feature is designed to be used on the spur of the moment, any time you're browsing the Web. Saving a Favorite is a good habit to get into — when you see something that you might want to find later, just follow these steps:

1. **While viewing a Web page that you want to add to your Favorites, press the Options button on the remote.**

2. **When the Options panel appears, highlight and select** `Save`.

   A box appears, confirming that you want to save the page as a Favorite and giving you a choice of which Favorites folder to save it in.

3. **Highlight and select the Favorites folder you'd like the page link to reside in.**

4. **Select the already highlighted** `Save Page` **button.**

   The Saving in Favorites window appears briefly (see Figure 7-1), indicating with a glittering treasure chest that your selected page is being saved.

After you save a Web page in this fashion, it's automatically added to your collection of Favorites. After you add the page to your Favorites, you can access a link to it easily at any time, during any future Web session. You don't need to do anything else; you're not taken to the Favorites area — you remain at the Web page you just saved, ready to continue your session.

Keeping a valued site in your Favorites list obviously saves time you would otherwise spend repeatedly searching for the site. Favorites save time in another way, too. Every time you save a site, its contents are saved on WebTV's giant central computer (called a *server*). When you click a Favorite, you are essentially telling the WebTV system to look in its own server computer and display the contents from there. Accessing the site is faster because the system is taking the page's data directly from its own computer, not retrieving it from a remote server (the original host computer for the site).

Figure 7-1:
The Saving in Favorites window.

Save it now!

Most experienced Web surfers fall into a peculiar blithe habit at some point in their travels, causing them to forget about saving Web pages. A certain complacency overcomes all of us at times, making us think we can find a site again if we need to. Regardless of how complex the path may be that brought us to Web site nirvana, it somehow escapes our attention to save it for later retrieval.

The thought often runs like this: "What a great site! I'll just poke around these pages before I save it . . . hey, look at this! Wow, I wonder where this link leads." Before you know it, you're following a path deeper into the Web, and having forgotten to save the ultra-cool site, you might never be able to find it again among the millions of needles in the Web's giant haystack.

The solution: Save it now! Saving to Favorites should be an absolute rule whenever you come across a page you might want to revisit. It's better to save too much than too little. Remember, you can prune your Favorites collection at any time, clearing out the ones you never visited again by using the Organize Favorites feature, as described later in this chapter.

Retrieving pages from remote computers is a process subject to networking and telephone-line delays, but such delays are eliminated when WebTV needs to reach only into its own computer to get your site. The result? The site is displayed on your screen more quickly.

Saving the right page

Remember that most Web sites consist of multiple pages. Every page in a site might be interesting to you, worth visiting again, and therefore worthy of being saved as a Favorite. But saving every page is not practical because your collection of Favorites would quickly become unmanageably large. In most cases, the best strategy is to save the *home page* of a site — the first, main page that links to all the others. The home page is a kind of headquarters for the whole site and should be the page that represents the site in your assortment of Favorites.

Unfortunately, not every home page of a large Web site is clearly labeled as the main page. Some make it clear by splashing a big "Welcome to our site!" across the home page. Even when the welcome carpet isn't rolled out like that, you can figure you're on the home page if an index or a table of contents is displayed for the whole site. Another way to be even surer requires a few steps and a geekish spirit. The trick is to identify a home (main) page by its URL address. Because the URL doesn't appear automatically on the screen when a Web page is displayed, you need to call it up. Here's how:

1. **When viewing any Web page, press the Options button on the remote.**

2. **Highlight and select the Info button on the Options panel that appears.**

   A box appears, displaying the URL.

After following this procedure, you need to use your judgment. Almost all home pages of large Web sites are represented by a short URL with only one (or no) forward slashes in the address. For example, the home page of *The New York Times* Web site is

```
www.nytimes.com
```

Suppose you call up a page's URL and find a lengthy one with a few elements separated by forward slashes like this:

```
www.nytimes.com/subscribe/help/quicktour/jobmarket.html
```

This indicates that you're not at the home page of the site. In that case, you can jot down the URL as it appears before the first single forward slash (in this case, `www.nytimes.com`) and go to that page directly using the `Go To` selection on the Options panel.

You might find exceptions to the rule, however. In some cases, especially for sites that offer some kind of service, you might want to save only the page that offers the specific service you find useful. When the page you want is several links away from the home page, you save time by being able to link directly to the service page from Favorites. Plus, you can usually link backward to the home page from an inner page of the site anyway.

A perfect example is an investment service site that contains many pages of news, information, company evaluations, and stock market updates as well as a stock quote page, where you can look up the price of any security. You might be interested primarily in the stock quote page and intend to visit it several times a day to check your holdings. In that case, you're best off saving the stock quote page in Favorites and occasionally linking from there to other site pages to get more information.

Some sites might hold special interest and value for you and might include one page you want to visit often and a home page that's a hub for the site's many other useful pages. In that case, you might want to save both the home page and the inner page you visit most.

Exploring, searching, and saving

You can build a healthy Favorites area quickly by using it with Search. Browsing randomly can also yield great sites for saving, but searching in a more organized way gets better results. Follow these guidelines:

1. **Select** `Search from Home`, **and type what you're looking for or choose a Search category and browse the directory.**

   Chapter 9 covers the details of using Search.

2. **On the Search Results screen, highlight and select a site that looks promising.**

3. **If the site is worth saving, do so using the Options button on the remote.**

   See the steps at the beginning of the section, "Adding a Favorite Page." Don't look around the site now; save that for later and continue with the Search function.

4. **Use the Back button on the remote to return to the Search results page or the directory page from which you found the site.**

5. **Select another site from the current page of search results, continue to the next page of search results, begin a new search, or continue browsing the directory.**

Your strategy is to collect promising sites quickly: Save sites from Search as soon as you link to them and then return to continue your search. The result is a Favorites area stuffed with links to sites you haven't explored thoroughly but which you know hold promise. The next step is to link directly to those sites from Favorites and check them out. You can later eliminate the ones that aren't worthy of keeping — see the following section for a how-to list.

Organizing Favorites in Folders

Saving sites to Favorites is so easy and such a good idea that it's easy to quickly acquire an overwhelming number of collected sites. Fortunately, organizing them is a breeze using the folder system. The first thing you want to do is create several folders that categorize the types of Web sites you like to save. (See Figure 7-2 for an example of multiple Favorite folders.)

Don't worry about etching your first folder decisions in stone — later, you can change them, create new folders, and move your saved Favorites around from one folder to another.

Follow these steps to create folders:

1. **On the Favorites for *YourName* screen, highlight and select** `Folders`.

   Some WebTV systems come with preset Favorites folders with some recommended sites. Whether you have preset folders or not depends on the manufacturer and version of your set-top box.

Figure 7-2:
You can
organize
your
Favorites
into folders.

2. **On the Favorite Folders for *YourName* screen, highlight and select**
`Add folder`.

3. **On the Add a Folder screen, type a folder name and then highlight**
and select the `Add` **button.**

You may also select the `Samples` button to choose among a handful of
sample folders. Note that each sample folder comes with preselected
Favorites placed in it.

Your new folder is added to the Favorite Folders for *YourName* screen.

Removing a folder is easy, too:

1. **On the Favorite Folders for *YourName* screen, highlight and select**
`Remove`.

2. **On the Remove Folders screen, highlight and select the** `Remove` **button**
that corresponds to the folder you want to delete.

The Remove Folders screen remains visible.

3. **Highlight and select either the** `Done` **button or** `Folders` **to return to**
the Favorite Folders for *YourName* screen.

Note: After you have created at least one folder, the save process looks a
little different when you're surfing the Web. Whenever you use the Save

option, a panel appears asking you which folder you'd like the site saved to. Just highlight and select any of your folders and then highlight and select the Save Page button.

Now comes the organizing part. You can organize your Favorites as you go by saving them to specific folders. Then, at any time, you can rearrange how your Favorites are distributed throughout your folders. Here's how:

1. **On the Favorite Folders for *YourName* screen, highlight and select the folder you want to organize.**

2. **On the Favorites for *YourName* screen, highlight and select** Organize.

3. **On the Organize Favorites in This Folder screen, highlight and select the action you want to take.**

On the Organize Favorites in This Folder screen, you may discard Favorites, change how they're listed, move them to a different folder, rename them, and assign keyboard shortcuts to seven of your favorite Favorites. Here's a detailed rundown on your organizing options:

- ✔ **Discard.** Highlight and select Discard to eliminate any Favorites from a folder. On the Discard Favorites in This Folder screen, select the Discard button next to any item you want to delete.

- ✔ **Listing.** Highlight and select Listing to see the Listing Favorites in Folder screen. This screen lets you select whether you want to see thumbnail pictures of your Favorites or just a listing of names. (A *thumbnail* is just a fancy word for a very small picture.) The pictures are helpful but take up much more screen space. Try the names-only option by unchecking the With pictures selection if your folders get too stuffed with pictures.

- ✔ **Rename.** When you save a Favorite, it has the name of the page. In some cases, a page name bears little relation to its content — the page name might even be just a number. (This confusing phenomenon is especially prevalent with amateur and non-commercial sites.) Use the Rename link to give your Favorites special names that help you remember what they are. Just highlight and select Rename. Then, on the Rename Favorites screen, type a new name for any number of listings in the folder. Highlight and select the Done button when you're . . . well, done.

- ✔ **Shortcuts.** This is one of the coolest features in Favorites. You can assign one of the F keys of the keyboard (they're on the top row) to a Favorite. (Because only seven F keys are available and you probably have more than seven Favorites, you can't assign a key to every Favorite site.) On the Organize Favorites in Folder screen, highlight and select Shortcuts and then highlight and select the picture of a keyboard key next to a site you want to assign. On the Choose Shortcut Label screen, highlight and select the F key you want to assign to that particular Favorite and then scroll down and select the Done button.

The Choose Shortcut Label screen indicates any Favorite sites that are already assigned to F keys. You may override your previous assignments.

✔ **Move to folder.** I habitually save Web sites to my Personal folder, and then every so often create new folders and move Personal favorites to the new folders, clearing out the Personal folder. Highlight and select `Move to folder` and then use the drop-down menus on the Move Favorites in This Folder screen to shift any Favorite to a different folder.

Browsing among Your Favorites

You can access your Favorites from anywhere on the Web. Start by pressing the Home button on the remote to go to the Home screen. Then follow these steps:

1. **On the Home screen, highlight and select** `Favorites`.

2. **On the Favorite Folders for *YourName* screen (refer to Figure 7-2), select a folder.**

   Use the Scroll buttons to see entries hidden below the screen.

3. **On the Favorites for *YourName* screen, view the collection of Favorites.**

4. **Highlight and select any thumbnail image to visit the Web page.**

As you look at the Favorites you've collected, the first thing you notice is that you don't see the sites themselves. When you save a site into Favorites, you really save the site's address (URL) and create a link to it in your Favorites area.

The next thing to notice is that your Favorites list is more than just a list of links. Each item in Favorites has a thumbnail image of the saved page — or, in some cases, a logo of the page. This is a savior when your collection of Favorites grows out of control. The thumbnail or logo can remind you of what the site is about better than just a name can.

You might have more Favorites than you can see on the screen at any one time. Use the Scroll buttons on the remote to get the whole picture.

Chapter 8

Finding and Meeting People

· ·

In This Chapter

▶ Plugging into the Internet community

▶ Making "buddies" with MSN Messenger

▶ Understanding message boards, mailing lists, and online chatting

▶ Joining a newsgroup

· ·

*I*f you spend some time on the Web, it's easy to get the impression that the Internet is just a collection of pages — static, without personality, as though the virtual realm has no scenery, no towns, no life — just billboards.

Actually, a great deal of personality is lurking beneath the surface. If you dig deeper into Web sites, you can often find message boards, e-mail links, and chat rooms that reveal the people behind the scenes. Even more important, you must remember that the Web is only part of the Internet — a relatively new part, at that, and less developed than the Net's community features. Although this book deals mostly with Web access and Web sites and you are accessing the Internet with a product called WebTV, the Internet experience offers more than just the Web. In this chapter, I introduce you to the Internet community.

Accessing the WebTV Community

Underneath the Community icon on the Home screen lie the chatting and bulletin board features built into the WebTV Network service (see Figure 8-1). The Page Builder feature is located in this area too. Instructions for using Page Builder are in Chapter 13. Here we look at the Chat and Discuss sections.

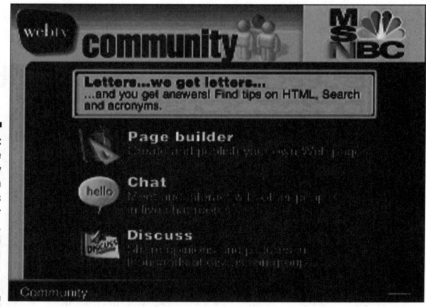

Figure 8-1:
The
Community
screen
contains
links for
chatting,
message
boards, and
Page
Builder.

Live conversations

Chatting, one of the most popular Internet activities, is available through a special WebTV feature. Just select the Chat link on the Community screen to try it out. (Whether the conversations you experience are lively or just live in a pathetically dead kind of way remains to be seen.)

The Chat link takes you to TalkCity, a dedicated chatting location of the Web. The WebTV version of TalkCity is not an exact duplication of the Web site because WebTV automatically edits it somewhat for ease and safety. (In other words, the racy and sexually oriented rooms are removed, but remember that anyone can say anything, in any room, at any time.) WebTV also reformats the chat rooms so they look good and function well through your TV. TalkCity consists of several permanent rooms, plus many temporary rooms that users have created. You can join in any room's discussion or create your own room and wait for people to join you.

Here's the best way to begin chatting:

1. **On the Web Home screen, highlight and select** Community.

2. **On the Community screen, highlight and select** Chat.

3. **On the Chat screen, view one of the featured chat rooms currently open in the What's On Now section or select the** TalkCity **link to see more room selections.**

4. Highlight and select a room that looks interesting.

New2WebTV is almost always available as a gathering place for new WebTV subscribers.

5. In the chat room, participate in the ongoing conversation by using the wireless keyboard or the on-screen keyboard.

Chat conversations scroll up your screen as other people in the room type lines of conversation. Feel free to jump in with your own lines by typing sentences and using the on-screen Send button (or the Return key of the keyboard). Use the Whisper link on the left portion of the screen to send a private line to anyone else in the room. You can even create a new chat room of your own by highlighting and selecting the New link.

Although the on-screen keyboard provides an adequate alternative to the optional keyboard in many Web situations, such as entering a password, chatting is very difficult by that means. Feel free to try it if you don't have the keyboard, but you'll get a lot more out of a chat with the keyboard. Even slow typists are usually faster with the keyboard than with the on-screen letters. Of course, you can observe a chat without saying anything, in which case you don't need any kind of keyboard.

Chatting is an unregulated feature of the Internet, and you never know what you're going to "hear" in a chat room. Most people agree that adult chatting is not for kids. See the sidebar later in this chapter titled "The do's and don'ts of chatting" for more information and tips about online chatting.

Bulletin board postings

The other half of the WebTV Community experience consists of *bulletin boards*, also called *message boards*. WebTV hooks into a portion of the Internet called *Usenet*, which is a system of thousands of message boards (called *newsgroups*, oddly) that let people engage in public discussions of just about any topic. Usenet is a part of the Internet that is much older and more developed than the Web. At least 40,000 Usenet forums exist. Basically, Usenet is the central bulletin board system for the entire Internet.

The division of subjects represented by newsgroups is astonishingly detailed. The basic topic of investment, for example, is splintered into multiple news-groups on technical stock analysis, mutual funds, bonds, options, and many other subdivisions. You can find a newsgroup devoted to almost every popular television show. Many states, cities, and counties throughout the United States have set up newsgroups for Help Wanted and For Sale classified postings. You can find newsgroups about computers, newsgroups about the

Internet, and newsgroups about Usenet newsgroups. Newsgroups saturate the Internet landscape, and each one is a little (or not-so-little) community with a group of people who are familiar with one another and communicate on a daily basis.

When accessing Usenet newsgroups through WebTV, the experience is similar to WebTV's e-mail system. If you're familiar with WebTV e-mail, you should feel right at home using the bulletin boards. You can read, respond to, and forward messages just like in e-mail. The only thing you can't do is store a bulletin board message (called a *post*) directly to your mailbox — but you can forward it to yourself and then store it.

Here's how to get started with message boards:

1. **On the Web Home screen, highlight and select** Community.

2. **On the Community screen, highlight and select** Discuss.

3. **On the Featured Discussions screen, highlight and select any discussion group that interests you.**

   You can also highlight and select All Groups, on the left portion of the screen. The All Groups link displays a list of newsgroup categories with brief descriptions. Highlight and select any one of them to see names of newsgroups, any of which you may select for browsing.

   You may search for newsgroups in a certain topic at the bottom of the Featured Discussions screen. Just type a topic — as general as *sports*, for example, or as specific as *rugby* — and then select the Look for button.

4. **In any newsgroup list, highlight and select a message to read.**

   Reading a newsgroup post is just like reading an e-mail message. (E-mail functions are described in explicit translucency in Chapter 6.) Use the selections on the left portion of the screen to respond to a post, mail a post to an e-mail address, or see the next (or previous) post. No matter how many posts you read using the Next and Previous links, using the Back button on the remote (or keyboard) takes you back to the newsgroup list of posts.

When reading a newsgroup message, the sidebar on the left gives you the following options:

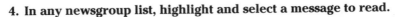

   ✔ **Group** takes you back to the list of messages from which you selected an individual message.

   ✔ **Previous** displays the previous message on the newsgroup list without making you view the list.

   ✔ **Next** displays the next message on the newsgroup list.

- ✔ **Next new** displays the next message that you haven't yet read.

- ✔ **Mail to** puts you on the Write a Message screen, with the `To:` field automatically filled in with the e-mail address of the person who wrote the newsgroup message you're reading. In other words, it's a quick way to respond to a bulletin board message by contacting the author directly through e-mail.

- ✔ **Respond** enables you to respond to a newsgroup message and posts then your response in the group.

You may find a newsgroup that matches one of your interests in two ways:

- ✔ Prowl through the directory displayed when you select `All Groups`.
- ✔ Use a keyword to search from the Featured Discussions screen.

Searching with a keyword is generally faster. As an example, if you want to find newsgroups about *The Late Show with David Letterman*, just type the keyword *letterman*, and three relevant groups appear.

By contrast, without the search feature, you'd be forced to rummage through hundreds of directory pages. Even if you happen to know that all three Letterman groups are in the *.alt* category of newsgroups, you'd have to drill into the directory six screens deep to find them.

On the other hand, browsing the directory is kind of fun, especially if you don't quite know what you're looking for. I've found some gems that way. When you are exploring the directory, a left-hand selection called `Path` displays your past steps in the directory — sort of like a trail of bread crumbs showing how you got to your present location.

After you've found a newsgroup (or three) that you like, don't lose it! Save the main Group page (the list of message titles) to your Favorites. You might want to create a Favorites folder (see Chapter 7 for an unusually compelling description of how to do this) that holds all your newsgroups.

Following are a few useful facts about discussion newsgroups as they are presented through WebTV:

- ✔ Discussions are displayed in *threads*, where responses are indented slightly in relation to the original message. WebTV threads are simplified compared to the way most computers display them, which is both good news and bad. Complex discussions are a little more difficult to follow, but long threads don't take over your screen. It is, unfortunately, impossible to compress threads as most computer programs do to save space and organize the screen.

✔ Each newsgroup page displays 100 message titles. Select the + (plus) and – (minus) signs at the top and bottom of each page to navigate among them.

✔ You can't use the Back button of the remote or keyboard to move from one page of 100 message titles to the previous one. Instead, the Back button yanks you all the way back to the screen displaying the title of the newsgroup. To backtrack by just one screen, use the – (minus) minus sign.

Surviving and thriving in Usenet newsgroups

If the Internet is the gleaming new metropolis of cyberspace, Usenet is the inner city. It's the most unregulated of all online environments. Although it's structurally very organized, with thousands of highly topicalized newsgroups, what goes on within those newsgroups can be pretty wild and woolly. As the portion of the Internet most devoted to community interaction, the Usenet is where Internet culture is most defined, though not necessarily refined or genteel.

The atmosphere of Usenet differs from newsgroup to newsgroup. Some are polite message boards. In others, the protocol is characterized by extreme frankness of expression, whether a participant is writing a respectful note of disagreement or launching a scalding flame war. (*Flames* are vitriolic messages of anger delivered either to a message board or someone's e-mail box; you might call it e-hatemail at times.)

If you don't want to get flamed, it's important to remember that Usenet newsgroups have been around for a long time, and the people who have been using them for years generally cast a leery eye toward the huge influx of newcomers flooding the Net. Everyone is welcome to participate in newsgroup message boards, but you should be aware of the basic unwritten rules of behavior — or risk getting your e-mail box torched with one of those "frank expressions." The basics are as follows:

✔ **Pay attention to the title of the newsgroup,** and don't post anything that's too far outside the topic. You can, however, acceptably ask where your message should be posted, if not in the current newsgroup — doing so shows that you respect the group's topicality and don't want to disrupt it.

✔ **Don't post the same message to multiple newsgroups** — that duplicative practice is known as *spamming,* and spams and spammers are widely despised. If your words are construed as spam, your spam is flamed, and you are forced to eat your words — well, you get the picture.

✔ **Generally, you should keep your responses within the newsgroup.** (When responding to a Usenet message, you have a choice of posting your reply to the newsgroup or the e-mail box of the original author.) If you have something personal to add to the author, however, send a copy to his or her e-mail box also. Remember, though, that some people don't like to receive newsgroup responses through e-mail. On the other side of the coin, some folks ask, in their public messages, that responses be directed to e-mail, not the public group.

✔ **Be careful about showing Usenet to your kids.** It's almost entirely an adult environment. Some newsgroups are devoted to sexual content. Those particular newsgroups are easy enough for an adult to avoid but, by the same token, easy enough for a curious child to find. Furthermore — sexual content aside — newsgroups have no restrictions on spicy language or rude behavior.

✓ **Just as you should practice caution in a chat room, be slow to divulge personal information on any message board**, especially on the Usenet. Your e-mail address is instantly known every time that you post a message, but don't give out your postal address or phone number. Similarly, don't post anyone else's phone number or address, unless it's publicly accessible business contact information.

✓ **Be careful about promoting any business venture in newsgroups.** You see a lot of

people doing it, so it may appear acceptable. In fact, Usenet has only recently attained a somewhat commercial tone, and many old-timers don't like it one bit. You definitely risk incoming flames by posting a promotional announcement in a newsgroup. If you do it tastefully and within the context of an ongoing conversation, however, it's accepted more gracefully. Ideally, you should be a regular contributor to a newsgroup before taking advantage of its advertising potential. If you enter as a stranger and contribute only a commercial announcement, you should insulate your e-mail box with asbestos.

✓ **Don't use all capital letters in a message.** It comes across as SHOUTING!

Chatting with MSN Messenger

Chatting has for many years been a popular way to socialize online. More recently, *instant messaging* has become just as popular, perhaps more so. Whereas the old-style chat rooms let you interact with many individuals in a single place, instant messaging encourages one-to-one chatting. Users can build lists of friends and be notified when those friends come online. Computer users run instant messaging programs all the time, chatting merrily as they move about the Web and write e-mail.

After a couple of years of waiting and pleading, patient WebTV subscribers who wanted instant messaging were rewarded by the May, 2000 service upgrade that delivered MSN Messenger (see Figure 8-2) to Classic and Plus set-top boxes.

Understanding the basics

Following are a few essential facts about WebTV's MSN Messenger to keep in mind. Getting a grip on these basic realities helps you get up to speed with this style of chatting. You need to know these facts to understand the rest of this section:

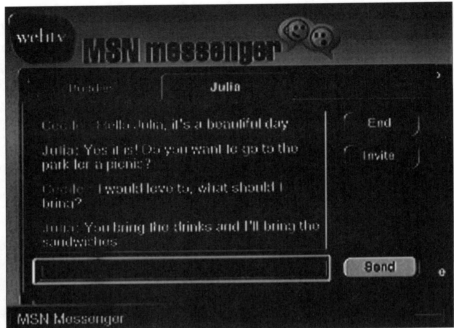

Figure 8-2:
MSN
Messenger
in action.

✔ MSN Messenger is made by Microsoft, the parent company of WebTV Networks, and was first released for computer users. You can use MSN Messenger to chat with any WebTV user and any computer user running the computer version of MSN Messenger.

✔ MSN Messenger does not connect with anyone using AOL Instant Messenger, ICQ, Yahoo! Messenger, or any other instant messaging program on a computer.

✔ MSN Messenger is located on your Options panel (you can also get to it using the big icon on the Home screen). You can use Messenger at any time, no matter what you're currently doing in WebTV.

✔ You may turn MSN Messenger on or off. The default selection is on, so if you've never turned it off, Messenger is on. When Messenger is turned off, it disappears from the Options panel. Messenger must be turned on to receive or send messages.

✔ You must activate MSN Messenger panel to send a message, but you can (and do) receive messages even when you're surfing the Web, posting a message to a newsgroup, working on your Web page, or writing e-mail — as long as Messenger is turned on.

✔ When you activate MSN Messenger, the program appears as a pop-up panel, like the Options panel (but larger and more complicated). You can get rid of the Messenger panel at any time by pressing the Back button on the remote or keyboard. Removing the Messenger panel does not turn Messenger off, discontinue any ongoing chats, or log you off Messenger.

✔ You may conduct up to three Messenger conversations simultaneously.

MSN Messenger uses a system called Buddies to help you keep track of your online friends. Each Buddy is a name plus an e-mail address of someone who uses MSN Messenger. (The e-mail address is just for identification — you don't actually use the e-mail system when chatting.) You are informed when Buddies log on and, in the case of WebTV Buddies, when they log off.

You can have as many Buddies as you please, though you can chat with only three at a time. As a nice touch, MSN Messenger lets you pull those three into the same virtual space so you all see each other's messages. This group chat feature is similar to a chat room (described earlier in this chapter), but strangers can't enter uninvited. I describe how to invite individuals into a group chat a bit later.

When the MSN Messenger panel is on your screen, it uses a system of *tabs* to keep your conversations organized. Each of the three (or fewer) individuals you're chatting with has a tab resembling a file folder, and you can view the conversation in progress by highlighting and selecting that tab. The Buddies tab is a default tab that always appears, giving you a consolidated view of your Buddy list and who is online.

When using the Invite feature to create a group chat (described in a later section), the tabs of your Messenger panel remain unchanged. Suppose you're chatting one-to-one with someone named Joe2354 and also with Betsy657 under another tab. You invite Betsy into your chat with Joe. Both tabs remain, but in the window of Joe's tab you now see messages from both Joe and Betsy.

Creating Buddies

MSN Messenger's essential task is connecting individuals who are on each other's Buddy lists.

The quickest way to get started with MSN Messenger is to fire it up and begin adding friends. Following is one way to add a friend to your Buddy list. Use this method when you have the name and e-mail address of a friend who is either on WebTV or uses MSN Messenger on a computer:

1. **On the Home screen, highlight and select** Messenger.

   Alternatively, you can press the Options key on the keyboard or the remote and then select Messenger.

2. **On the MSN Messenger screen, highlight and select** Use MSN Messenger now.

   The Messenger panel rises up into your screen. Chances are, you don't have any Buddies entered into your Messenger list yet, so the window is blank.

3. **Highlight and select the** Edit Addresses **button.**

   The address book that appears is the very same one used in Mail (see Chapter 6).

4. **On the Addresses for *YourName* screen, highlight and select** Add.

   Don't make the mistake of selecting Messenger, which simply displays the MSN Messenger screen, taking you in a circle.

5. **On the Add an Entry screen, type a name and e-mail address for the person you want to add and then select the** Add **button.**

   It's important to remember that MSN Messenger connects only those individuals (either on computers or on WebTV) using MSN Messenger. The mere fact that someone has an e-mail address doesn't mean that person can be a Messenger Buddy. You can add any e-mail address to your address book, though, whether that person is Messenger-capable or not.

6. **On the Instant Message Settings screen, select the check boxes to put the new address on your Buddy list and, if you desire, to enable that person to send you messages.**

   By leaving that box unchecked, you can place someone on your Buddy list and block that person from sending you messages. But in most cases two-way messaging is best.

7. **Highlight and select the** Continue **button to return to your address book.**

You can also use the Contact feature to add people to your Buddy list on the fly. Contact enables you to send an instant message to a person not yet on your list. If that person is an MSN Messenger computer user (or WebTV user) *and* if that person is currently logged on, the message is received and a conversation may be initiated. From that point on, the person is added to your Buddy list and your address book. The Contact system is useful when adding new acquaintances to your Buddy list from chat rooms.

Follow these steps to use the Contact feature in a chat room:

1. **In any chat room, make a note of the screen name of any individual you'd like as a Buddy.**

2. **Press the Options key on the remote or the keyboard and then select** `Messenger`.

3. **Highlight and select the** `Buddies` **tab if it's not already selected.**

4. **Highlight and select the** `Contact` **button.**

5. **In the highlighted window, type the screen name.**

   The check box must be checked to make this person a Buddy. Or, if you prefer to chat without making that person a buddy, highlight and select the check box to uncheck it.

6. **Highlight and select the** `Continue` **button.**

   If you've chosen a computer user not registered with MSN Messenger, the system notifies you that your message can't be delivered. If you've selected a WebTV user — or a computer user currently running MSN Messenger — the message is delivered. The person may or may not answer you — there's never an obligation to chat. Whether a conversation develops or not, that person is now on your Buddy list.

Removing people from your Buddy list

Alas, disagreements arise, resentments simmer, friendships die. Actually, there's no need to be that dramatic; many reasons exist for removing a name from your Buddy list. It's so easy to add names, in fact, that occasionally cleaning out your list is recommended. Here's how to do it:

1. **On any screen, press the Options key and select** `Messenger`.

2. **Highlight and select the** `Buddies` **tab if it's not already selected.**

3. **Highlight and select the** `Edit Addresses` **button.**

4. **On the Addresses for** *YourName* **screen, highlight and select the** `Change` **link next to any name you want to remove from your Buddy list.**

5. **On the Change Entry for** *BuddyName* **screen, highlight and select the** `Instant message settings` **link, below the e-mail address.**

6. **On the Instant Message Settings screen, highlight and select the check box next to** `BuddyName` `is your buddy.`

   A new check box quickly appears, checked to allow your ex-Buddy to continue to send you instant messages.

7. **If you'd rather not hear from your ex-Buddy, highlight and select the check box to uncheck it.**

8. **When finished, highlight and select the** `Continue` **button.**

After removing a person from your Buddy list, your log ons and log offs are invisible to that person, and likewise, you can't know when that person comes and goes.

Receiving messages and chatting

Receiving instant messages is the easiest part of this whole MSN Messenger business. You must do absolutely nothing, besides making sure that Messenger is turned on. The Messenger panel doesn't need to be displayed on your screen to receive messages, so go about your online business as usual; incoming messages are displayed across the bottom of your screen.

When a WebTV Buddy logs onto WebTV or when a computer Buddy activates MSN Messenger, a short musical sound notifies you that someone has logged on. Nothing visual happens on your screen until a Buddy sends you a message.

When a Buddy sends you a message, one of three things happens, depending on how you're using the service:

✔ If the MSN Messenger panel is not on your screen, you receive a musical sound and the message scrolls across the bottom of your screen.

✔ If the MSN Messenger panel is on your screen and you're currently viewing any tab besides the tab for the Buddy sending you a message, you hear a musical sound. You must highlight and select your Buddy's tab to see the message.

✔ If the MSN Messenger panel is on your screen and you're currently viewing your Buddy's tab, you hear the sound and see the message added to the dialog window.

In all cases, MSN Messenger must be on to receive and send messages. If you turned Messenger off in the past, these steps turn it on again:

1. **On the Home screen, highlight and select** Messenger.

   You can't access Messenger through the Options panel when Messenger is turned off.

2. **On the MSN Messenger screen, highlight and select** Turn MSN Messenger **on.**

   All your Buddies receive notification that you are now logged on.

   You were logged on previously, of course, but when Messenger is turned off your Buddies show you as logged off. In this context, _logged on_ and _logged off_ refer to your use of MSN Messenger, not your use of WebTV.

When a message comes to you while you're surfing, with the Messenger panel hidden, you may or may not want to respond. You can continue doing what you're doing without responding. If you would like to chat, however, follow these steps:

1. **On any screen, press the Options key on the remote or the keyboard and select** Messenger.

    The MSN Messenger panel slides up onto your screen, with the tab of the person who just messaged you selected by default.

2. **Highlight the small window next to the** Send **button, below the main window.**

3. **Type your response.**

4. **Press the Return key on the keyboard or highlight and select the** Send **button.**

    Pressing the Return key is always easier, and a good habit to get into when chatting.

After you have begun chatting, you may choose to keep the Messenger panel on your screen to follow the conversation. If your input is sporadic, you can get rid of the Messenger panel by pressing the Back key on the keyboard or the remote. When you're ready to say something again, repeat the preceding steps.

Group chatting

You can gather multiple Buddies in a single Messenger chat. Such impromptu "rooms" have a privacy advantage over general chat rooms. Your gathering is invisible to all other Messenger users, and no other Buddies can get in without an invitation. After you have three Buddies chatting with you, no one else can get in by any means.

When chatting with one person through Messenger, follow these steps to bring another person into the conversation:

1. **On the MSN Messenger panel, highlight and select the** Invite **button.**

2. **On the Buddies tab of the Messenger panel, highlight and select a name from your Buddies list.**

Bingo. That's all there is to it. The invited person is automatically included in the discussion, provided that person is logged on to WebTV with Messenger turned on or — if that person is a computer user — both logged on and using MSN Messenger.

If you invite a Buddy with whom you're currently chatting one-to-one, the appearance of your tabs on the Messenger panel doesn't change. Suppose you're chatting separately with two Buddies named A and B. (First of all, tell them to get better screen names.) You invite B into your chat with A. On your Messenger panel, both the A and B tabs remain, but now you see messages from you, A, and B in the chat window under the A tab. You can still talk privately with B under the B tab.

Ending a conversation

For one reason or another, you may want to end one of your individual Messenger conversations. Perhaps your chatting partner is rambling on endlessly about barley prices in Poland, and you can't stand the tedium any longer. More likely, you have three chats going on at once, and you can't start another without closing one.

Ending a conversation is easy. Here's how:

1. **On the Messenger panel, highlight and select the tab of the conversation you want to end.**

2. **Highlight and select the** End **button.**

   Nothing more to it than that. That person's tab disappears immediately, so make sure you say your goodbyes before selecting the End button.

If you use the End button for a group chat, it removes you from the group and closes that tab on your Messenger panel. The others in the group continue chatting — probably about you.

The End button is how you leave a group chat. Each group chat counts as a single Buddy toward your limit of three simultaneous chats. Extracting yourself from a group chat is one way to free up space for another individual or group chat.

Accessing the Internet Community

A community is on the Internet — somewhere. Real people are hiding behind all those Web pages, like actors awaiting their cue behind storefronts of a Hollywood set. You can find these real people in several ways.

Message boards

Online message boards are almost as old as computer networking, and they're a big part of the appeal of cyberspace for many people. Message boards helped fuel the popularity of online services throughout the 1980s and early 1990s. I know that you might be wondering why message boards are such a big deal, if *you* haven't heard of them, or why they aren't heavily promoted as part of the contemporary Internet experience. The reason is mostly due to the blinding glare of the Web and its attendant frantic publicity. The rest of the Internet, including message boards, is sometimes lost in the Web's hype. But it's still there, waiting to be explored.

Sometimes called bulletin boards, *message boards* are computer versions of public bulletin boards, like the type you see in supermarkets or on college campuses. Supermarket bulletin boards don't provide a very communal experience and are usually full of notices from people who want to give away kittens, mow your lawn, or sell you services of one kind or another. Well, the Internet bulletin boards are enhanced in ways that emphasize the personal aspect of written correspondence, while maintaining the communal quality of a public forum. Although classified advertisement bulletin boards do exist in cyberspace, Internet bulletin boards usually serve as a forum for discussion rather than as a place to post offers of services or notices of items for sale.

The following items show you how online message boards differ from physical bulletin boards:

- **Personal responses.** When you see a message posted on an Internet bulletin board, you can reply to it directly. Your return message is posted on the same board, in close proximity to the original message. The idea behind online boards, unlike physical public bulletin boards, is that conversations develop when the person who posted an original message returns later to check for responses, to which he or she might write additional responses. In this way, ongoing group discussion begins and flourishes, with more people joining in as time goes on. (You wouldn't even think of responding to the offer of free kittens on the supermarket bulletin board with a post of your own — nothing would come of it.)

- **Threading.** Personal responses to bulletin board messages are even more effective with a system known as threading. *Threading* connects messages to each other by topic, the order in which they were posted, and which message is addressed to whom. When people respond to each other's written posts, the messages are displayed in such a way that you can follow the thread that weaves the discussion together.

For example, suppose someone starts by posting an opinion of the new John Travolta movie on an entertainment bulletin board. (This could happen any minute because there's always bound to be a new John

Travolta movie in the theaters.) Maybe two people respond to the initial message, one agreeing and one disagreeing with its content. Five more people read the young discussion; three respond to the agreeing message, and two reply to the disagreeing message. The next day, the original writer revisits the board and replies to six of the eight accumulated messages, and soon people respond to those posts. You can see how a thread can develop into a message tree after only a few days.

✔ **The e-mail connection.** Many online bulletin boards incorporate a feature that allows you to send your response to any message either to the bulletin board for the good of the discussion or to the author's e-mail address. You can use the e-mail feature to extend a message board acquaintance into an e-mail friendship.

Basic rules of message boards

Message boards that you run across on the Web may not have written rules like a municipal swimming pool that posts its rules at the gate. If you do a lot of swimming at different pools, you get a feel for what is generally allowed and not allowed — no running along the side of the pool, no splashing, and so on — and you probably don't stop to read the rules carefully at each visit. Public swimming has a culture that you understand and are part of. In the same way, online message boards have a culture. It's not arcane or complicated, and understanding it helps you participate more quickly and without hesitation.

First, remember that message boards are public discussions and everyone is welcome to join in. When you see a string of messages between only two people, it may seem rude to interject your own post into the conversation. But it's a universally understood convention that anyone can jump in at any time. If you want to be polite about it, start your message with, "Pardon me for jumping in" and then proceed.

Second, when jumping in as a newcomer, be sensitive to the fact that you may have missed an earlier part of the conversation. Not all message boards keep a backlog of all previous messages. A common practice is to start a contribution to the discussion this way: "I'm new to this thread, so pardon me if you've gone over this already" and then proceed with a question or comment.

Your contributions to a message thread don't have to be long or of professional writing caliber — far from it. Just get your point across, and you fit right in. You see all levels of expressive skill on message boards, from erudite statements of expertise to humble opinions with cracked spelling. Messages are mostly written by regular folks, eager to talk about a shared interest.

Finally, keep in mind that message boards are, by and large, adult places that sometimes display adult language. I don't mean to encourage unnecessary swearing, but I do mean to caution you against sharing message boards with your kids.

Using message boards on Web sites

It used to be that the only message boards on the Internet were in the Usenet system. Usenet is still the main bulletin board network on the Internet. The Web initially contained no message boards. But as the Web becomes more personable, the individuals and companies that design Web sites are increasingly incorporating more of a community atmosphere in their sites. One of the best ways to incorporate a community atmosphere is — you guessed it — to put in message boards.

You've probably visited Web sites without realizing that message boards are available on those sites. Bulletin boards are usually not promoted as a site's main feature. You can find them, though, by looking carefully at the home page for links to forums or discussion groups. Also, any link that invites you to contribute your opinion on a topic is likely to lead to a message board. (But don't get confused by *feedback links,* which are usually simple e-mail opportunities to praise or criticize a site.)

Message boards on Web sites often function nearly identically to Usenet newsgroups. They're not part of the Usenet system, but that has no bearing on your enjoyment of them.

Recently, some trends have developed in how message boards are being used within Web sites. The following are some of the types of sites in which you can expect to find bulletin boards:

- **Search engines.** It used to be that *search engines* (which I describe in Chapter 9) were useful but modest sites that helped you find things on the Web. Now, some of the major search engines, such as Yahoo!, Excite, and Lycos, have built message boards into their sites to encourage a sense of community. Search-engine message boards are among the biggest Internet trends these days.

- **News sites.** Delivering news is perhaps the driest of all reasons for a Web site's existence. But some of the prominent news sites are capitalizing on the universal desire to comment about the news by providing a bulletin board platform to do just that. I guess it's the digital version of the old soapbox. In some cases, a separate message board is dedicated to each feature story from the day's news.

- **Entertainment sites.** Movie, music, and TV boards are popular. They were located primarily in online services and Usenet, but they are now appearing in Web sites. I discuss entertainment sites in Chapter 11.

- **Special interest sites.** Bulletin boards are wonderful for connecting people who have unusual interests but who don't often meet like-minded folks in daily life. Because the Internet knows no geographic borders, message boards work perfectly to bring people together over shared passions. As you seek out Web sites related to a special interest, be sure to check for links to message areas within those sites.

When you follow a link to a Web message board, you often see a list of message topics. Highlighting and selecting a topic displays a list of message headers, which may be displayed to show how the thread has developed. (I discuss threads at the beginning of this chapter if you're wondering what one is.) Usually, the message headers of responses to one message are indented beneath the original message, and responses to the responses are further indented beneath them. Such graphical representations of a thread make who is talking to whom clearer. Highlighting and selecting one of the message's headers displays the individual message. As you read the message, you have the choice of responding to it or going on to the next message in the thread.

Mailing lists

Mailing lists are not what you may think. Also sometimes known as listservs, *mailing lists* are e-mail communities that operate like an e-mail version of telephone party lines. When a group of people wants to communicate through e-mail on a certain topic, an automated system can be set up that distributes each e-mail message sent to the mailing list to every member of the mailing list. Everyone reads what everyone else has to say, and anyone can respond, knowing that all the others are going to receive the reply.

Listservs abound, covering all kinds of subjects from cancer support groups to TV-show fan clubs. You can find listservs for people who want to practice their Esperanto and others for the discussion of lucid dreaming. But for all their proliferation, listservs are harder to locate than Web sites. They're promoted through word of mouth, and you can also find references to them on some Web pages. Another tactic, if you're hankering for the mailing list experience, is to type **listserv** on the Search screen. (Search is described in exquisite detail in Chapter 9.)

You join a listserv by subscribing to it. Subscription instructions are provided by the group and whatever promotion the group puts out on the Internet. In all cases, subscribing is a simple matter of sending an e-mail message to the listserv address (you're writing to the computer, not an actual person), in most cases with the word *subscribe* either in the message body or the subject line. Getting off the list is usually a repeat of the subscription process but with the word *unsubscribe*.

Mailing lists can be tremendously rewarding and worthwhile. They're a great way to meet people with whom you have something in common, and you can learn a great deal. So why the warning? Because joining a mailing list invariably increases your e-mail load, sometimes drastically. Getting into a Star Trek listserv community might seem like a great idea until you're suddenly receiving 75 e-mail messages every day, all debating which Enterprise crewmember is the best.

The birth of a listserv

Listservs — also called mailing lists or e-mail discussion groups — are a great idea. E-mail communities provide a more private alternative to electronic message boards. So how are listservs created? Do groups of people plan and create them, like planned residential communities? Sometimes, but not usually.

A mailing list is usually created by an individual, who becomes the listserv administrator. Although the computer automatically handles the mail-forwarding chores and distribution of a mailing list, a human administrator is needed to answer questions and smack the computer when it's misbehaving. In some cases, a small group of people share the leadership of a listserv, and the group grows from a small nucleus.

Creating listservs requires a fair amount of computer savvy, not to mention access to an Internet computer, or server. Mailing lists are perfectly accessible to WebTV users, but WebTV does not provide the means to create a listserv. I should note, though, that informal mailing list discussion groups can be set up spontaneously by any number of people who share an interest and know each other's e-mail addresses. Instead of being an automated system like a true listserv, each person in the group must manually copy all e-mail contributions to each member of the group. All that copying might sound like a tremendous hassle, but it's only a slight hassle. (Hey — small hassles are better than big ones in my book.) Here's how it works:

1. **Make sure that your** `Reply to All` **feature is activated in Setup, as I describe in Chapter 4.**

2. **When you reply to an e-mail from someone in the group, highlight and select** `Reply`.

3. **On the Reply to a Message screen, highlight and select** `Reply All`.

    The Reply to a Message screen appears, with several e-mail addresses in the `cc:` line.

A couple of good Web-based services allow you to set up mailing lists. The technical listserv functions are handled by the service, leaving you free to decide on the topic. You don't need any special knowledge besides an ability to navigate around a Web site. Try these two sites:

- Topica, at `www.topica.com`
- eGroups, at `www.egroups.com`

You say you're impatient to try a mailing list? You don't want to wait until you stumble across a random reference to one on the Web? There are Web sites where you can search for a mailing list groups that match your interest. The Web addresses are

```
www.liszt.com
www.onelist.com
www.topica.com
```

Listserv tips

Many people have discovered not only the joy but also the overwhelming aspects of being on a mailing list. It's great to share a common interest with people all over the world but not always so great to trudge through piles of e-mail each day (in some cases). And although it's a wonderful system, it doesn't seem so terrific when it doesn't work correctly and you don't know where to turn for help. Here are some survival tips:

✒ Write down (or save to your address book) the e-mail address of the listserv. The listserv's e-mail address is the location to which you sent your initial subscription request.

✒ Listservs usually work flawlessly, but glitches can develop. For example, you might suddenly stop receiving the group's letters or start receiving duplicates. (I'm not sure which is worse.) Whenever you encounter trouble, send a note to that address with the word *help* in both the subject field and the body of the note. You might get an automated response or a letter from the human listserv administrator.

✒ If you want to leave the group and stop receiving all group e-mails, send a note to the listserv address with the word *unsubscribe* in both the subject field and the message body.

✒ Some listservs are available in digest form. A *listserv digest* consists of one large daily e-mail instead of many. The large digest has every message of the day compacted into it.

✒ Remember that you can always reply privately to the person who wrote a letter. Mailing list members commonly engage in private discussions in the background of the group. In fact, it's viewed as considerate and polite to respond privately when discussing something off-topic from the group's stated purpose. To respond privately when using the `Reply` feature, just don't add other members of the group to the `To:` field.

✒ Stay reasonably on-topic at all times when making group-wide messages. It's best to participate quietly for a while to get the flow of the group and to learn the extent to which miscellaneous e-mail chatter is tolerated.

Chatting

Message boards and mailing lists both exist outside real time, which is to say that you can participate even if no one else is. When you read messages on an Internet bulletin board, for example, you have no idea who else is reading the same messages at the same time. You might write a few replies or post an original message and then return the next day to see what has been posted in response. This might be a daily routine you enjoy just before bedtime or in the middle of the night. Even if most of the others post messages during the daytime, that action doesn't affect your participation.

The do's and don'ts of chatting

Chatting has become one of the most popular online activities. It has been around for a long time, first in the online services, and more recently spreading to the Internet. Chatting's reputation as a fun activity is balanced by widespread stories of the hazards of meeting people in Internet chat rooms; although such stories are often blown out of proportion, you shouldn't disregard them. You meet a lot of strangers while chatting, and the encounters are more immediate than meeting people on a message board or through e-mail. As with mailing lists, e-mail, and other forms of Internet direct communication, a popular protocol has developed over the years that provides everyone with an unwritten code of behavior in chat environments. The following are the high points:

✔ **Don't give personal information — including your e-mail address — to a stranger in a chat room.** Most people don't even use their true names when chatting. Certainly, giving out your phone number or address is very unwise and has been deeply regretted by people in a few well-publicized cases.

✔ **Never feel that you must talk to any individual.** If somebody appears on your screen with words that are disagreeable to you in any way, simply excuse yourself and leave. Remember — you hold all the power in any chat encounter because you can always leave or simply turn WebTV off.

✔ **Say hello when you enter a chat area.** Sitting quietly in a chat room is called *lurking,* and nothing is wrong with it. (Reading a message board without participating is also called lurking and is likewise accepted.) But it's generally considered polite to offer a general "Hi, all" when first entering, if only to assure everyone present that you're a genial sort.

✔ **Many chat areas are used for sexual conversations.** This fact is increasingly well known, and there's no point glossing over it. Web-based chat pages are usually devoted to just one subject, and you can find plenty that have nothing to do with sex if that's your preference. But Java-based chat locations often provide a choice of virtual rooms, and some are overtly sexual.

In Java chat environments, you sometimes find sexual prowlers — people who cruise Internet chat environments in search of sexual conversations. (Sexual prowlers can't hurt or hassle you in the real world as long as you don't divulge your address, phone number, or e-mail address.)

You or your kids might find that some chat rooms can be unsavory environments, no question about it. If you're uninterested in sexual chatting, always remember your power to leave. At the same time, remember that online sexual chatting is not illegal, and it's accepted within Internet culture even by those who don't engage in it. Refrain from expressing any indignation that you may feel toward those engaging in sexual chats. Honor their right to an undisrupted experience, just as you should insist on that right yourself. For Internet speech to be truly free, it must be allowed to include language that some consider offensive.

Chatting, however, is a real-time Internet activity. You can chat only when someone else (or a group of people) is at a chat site, or in a *chat room* as chat sites are sometimes called, at the same time you are. At a chat site, an

Internet system is set up to display messages as they are written — your words appear on the screen of the person you're talking to, and the other chatters' words appear on your screen. You type one sentence at a time and then "send" the words; likewise, you receive incoming conversation a sentence at a time. You can chat in a couple of Internet environments:

- ✔ **Web chatting.** When I refer to Web chatting, I mean Web sites that incorporate chatting environments right in the site's pages. Web chatting usually takes place on screens that look like text-based Web site pages. When someone in the chat room types and sends a sentence, it either appears at the top of the screen or causes the whole page to reload, showing the new sentence in the fresh version.

- ✔ **Java chatting.** Java is a multimedia enhancement to the Web that has been available to computers for some time but isn't available to WebTV. You don't need to know anything to use Java. But if you're curious, read on. Java is a language used to create small *applets* (miniature computer programs) and larger, task-oriented programs that automatically spring into action when called upon by a Web site that incorporates Java elements. One such Java applet could be a chatting program that downloads automatically and appears on your screen.

How well can you really know someone online?

Can you form an online friendship that's anywhere near the depth of a friendship that you can form in person? Good question. I can say without hesitation that, in my years of online experience, I have made friendships that would be considered legitimate and close by most criteria. Most of them started on message boards, others in e-mail, and a very few in chat rooms. (I don't spend that much time in chat rooms, but I still love message boards as much as I did when I first found them many years ago.)

I admit that an online friendship has a different quality than a face-to-face friendship. (When people speak on the Internet of offline, or face-to-face, encounters, the abbreviation FTF is often used.) When you get to know someone in person, FTF, you receive a multitude of clues about that person, starting with his or her (whether he or she is even a he or she, for example) general appearance and extending all the way to the subtle clues you get from such details as wardrobe and mannerisms. Unconsciously, evaluations are made in both directions that help form the FTF relationship right from the beginning.

Online relationships are quite different. When you engage in a long-lasting discussion on a message board or talk with a new acquaintance for an hour in a chat room, you get only one clue: that person's words. It's a realm of thought, idea, and typed expression. It has often occurred to me that, online, people get to know each other from the inside out, without the distraction of the external clues that color our impressions in person.

Believe it or not, I know married couples who met each other in cyberspace. In fact, you might know of at least one couple (whether you like them or not) who met this way: Rush Limbaugh and his wife, who met in the CompuServe online service. Very often, an intimate online relationship begins on a message board and proceeds to real-time chatting, and then the two people take the plunge of meeting in person.

On the other hand, people can take on different personas online, and if the online personality differs too much from the real personality, it can be a jarring — and occasionally dangerous — experience. The obvious risks are ones that are the most easily avoided. More subtle risks have to do with getting comfortable with the online world. For many people, the from-the-inside-out way of getting acquainted online is a heady and intoxicating experience, and it can cloud a person's judgment. I've talked to many people who have fallen in love online and then been disappointed by the real goods when the relationship moves to an FTF meeting. Always remember that you see only half of a person online — and the other half is just as important.

Using Newsgroups on the Web

As described earlier in this chapter, Usenet is a distinct part of the Internet, separate from the Web. Usenet is divided into thousands of bulletin boards called *newsgroups,* each devoted to a particular subject. Newsgroups range from online support groups to fan clubs, from medical information centers to classified ad sections. They all share the same design and bulletin board functions. Usenet is basically the central bulletin board system for the Internet.

You can access newsgroup discussion using WebTV's special Discuss section, as explained earlier in this chapter. In addition, you always have the option of reading Usenet newsgroups through two specialized Web sites:

- ✔ **Deja.com.** The original Web-based newsgroup site, Deja.com (www.deja.com) has evolved into a consumer products reporting site but still carries Usenet newsgroups.

- ✔ **Remarq.** A relative newcomer, Remarq (www.remarq.com) is popular among people using America Online and WebTV to access the Internet.

Both these sites allow you to browse the newsgroup directory and search for newsgroups by keyword, just like in WebTV.

Chapter 9

Searching and Browsing

• •

In This Chapter

▶ Using WebTV Search

▶ Choosing good keywords

▶ Using the Search directory

▶ Discovering other search directories

▶ Checking out other search engines

• •

*T*he Web is less than ten years old, but already it has a distinct history, and its history can be divided into two periods. In the first period, the Web was mostly a browser's paradise. It was a place where you could get happily lost. It took a while for the Web to become commercial, and in the early days (pardon me while the mist of nostalgia glazes my eyes), it consisted primarily of personal home pages placed by individuals wanting to share with the world their likes, dislikes, passions, quirks, and favorite hyperlinks.

Nobody was serious about trying to find anything useful on the Web during its young period. Instead, everyone was delighting in the sudden ease of navigating the Internet with hyperlinks and enjoying the rudimentary graphics and home page designs. The early days established a culture of online browsing that is still going strong today. Even though the quality of the Web has changed drastically, it's still a great place to get lost, wandering with blissful aimlessness from one link to the next.

As the Web matured, however, it became more useful — meatier, you could say. Web sites appeared that were worth locating in a determined fashion. The Web became a research tool, a shopping mall, and a service center, among other things. Suddenly, Netizens could shop on it, look up a movie, learn about a composer — all the uses and activities described in this book became available seemingly overnight. The Web entered the second period of its young history.

Ironically, after the Web became useful, it also became too complex to find anything easily! The hyperlinked quality of the Web capitalizes on disorganization by connecting the millions of pages without forethought, planning, or any intelligent structure. A site links only to pages determined by the creator of that site. What the Internet community needed was a service that could find Web pages on certain subjects, cutting through the tangled maze of interconnected links. Following the true character of the Internet, when the need arose, solutions started springing up to fill it. Specifically, things called *search engines* and *directories* began appearing.

Search engines allow Netizens to enter keywords indicating what they're looking for. If you're searching for information about the actor Anthony Hopkins, for example (who I think is wonderful, and if you want to argue the point, please e-mail me), you simply go to one of the Web search engines and type his name as your keywords. The search engine then finds sites related to Anthony the Great (as I like to call him) and displays a list of links to those sites.

Directories don't use keywords — rather, they're like big menus. A good Web directory serves as a sort of table of contents to the Web, letting you see the big picture at a glance and encouraging further exploration into increasingly defined topics. WebTV's directory, included in the Search portion of the service, moves you easily from general topics to specific topics, recommending sites along the way.

This chapter explains how to search the Internet through WebTV using keywords and then describes how to use the WebTV directory included in Search. To get on the right page for using this chapter, go to the Home screen (the Web Home screen for Plus users) and select Search.

How do search engines really work?

When you enter a keyword in a search engine, you may imagine the industrious engine scouring the Web to find relevant sites. You also probably imagine it taking quite a long time, given the sprawling enormity of the Web. In fact, the search results usually come back within a few seconds, which brings up the question: How in the World Wide Web do they do it?

The truth is, search engines shortcut the process to save you time. Search engines do most of their work before you even show up. They are constantly engaged in searching the Web automatically with software devices called *search robots,* or *bots* for short. These industrious creatures are programmed to roam the entire Web and collect information about sites.

The information they gather is collected and organized into an index, which is the search engine's main commodity. Each search engine has its own bots and its own index, differing from the others depending on how the bots are programmed to search.

When you use a search engine and enter your keywords, you are really searching the index, not the Web itself. This is not a problem because the indexes are kept very up-to-date — the bots are working and updating all the time. Because the index is located on one computer, it can be searched much more quickly than the Web, which is spread out over millions of computers, and the search results come flying to you.

Searching with WebTV

WebTV has its own search engine. Actually, the WebTV search engine is an adaptation of one of the best and most popular search engines that computer users have been enjoying for a few years. It's called Infoseek, and it makes basic searching very easy.

Infoseek exists as a Web search engine and directory for computer users, but the WebTV version of Infoseek is not a direct import of the computer version. Infoseek has worked with WebTV Networks to develop a WebTV-specific search engine and directory.

Getting started right away doesn't take any special knowledge — just be aware of what you want Search to find and give it a whirl. Your target subject can be as general (such as television) or as specific (such as *Twilight Zone* episode titles) as you want. Figure 9-1 shows you what the WebTV Search screen looks like.

To start your first search, just follow these steps:

1. **On the Home screen, highlight and select** Search.

Figure 9-1: The Search screen, where you type a keyword (or several keywords).

2. **On the Search screen, highlight the** Search **field (if it's not already highlighted). Then, using either the wireless keyboard or the on-screen keyboard, type what you're looking for.**

3. **Highlight and select the** Search **button or press the Return key on the keyboard.**

   The "Contacting service" notice appears for a few seconds at the top left of your screen. The notice shouldn't stay there long, but some searches take a bit more time than others. If you submit an especially puzzling string of keywords, you might have time to feed your cat while waiting for a response. Actually, other factors can influence how long the wait is, and you can't do much to shorten it. Most searches happen quickly, though, giving you the results in no more time than it takes to load any other Web page.

4. **On the next screen, view the *hits* (Web sites that match your keywords) of your search.**

Interpreting search results

The Search Results page tells you where to go. Oops — that sounds insulting. Try this: The Search Results page presents the results of its search, based on your keywords, in a format that enables you to follow its leads. (That's better.) Basically a simple list, the Search Results page displays several elements, as I poetically describe in the following sections.

Titles of Web sites

The titles of Web sites show up as bold blue words running down the left of your screen. Beneath many of the titles are summaries. If you use the Arrow buttons, you can see that each title is a link to a Web site. You can highlight and select links from the Search Results page as you would do to any other link on WebTV and jump straight to the corresponding Web site.

Some titles seem cryptic at best. For example, in a search for chocolate dessert, one of the many links in the list of results is called Chocolates + la Carte - v3i1 New products. What on earth does v3i1 mean? Probably nothing more than a bit of miscellaneous word-processing code that snuck into the page title. Number strings and other clusters of unintelligible syllables that you may encounter make up the computer title given to the page after it was created. Web page designers have the option of presenting an official page title that supersedes the computer title, which then remains invisibly in the background. But if the page's creator didn't assign a specific title to the page, the computer name rises to the surface.

In a typical search, the results have similar titles, whether completely intelligible or not. With the keywords *american history,* for example, the Search results page displays many sites that predictably include the words *american* and *history* in the title. In other words, the title doesn't tell you a heck of a lot about the site, which is why a brief summary is (sometimes) useful. By the way, you don't have to worry about using capital letters when typing keywords. Search doesn't distinguish between uppercase and lowercase letters when processing your search request, although it displays search results with the capitalization provided by the Web site.

Short descriptions of Web sites

Below each title link, in green characters, is a short description of what awaits you if you link to that location. You might notice that the summaries are incomplete and brief. They don't tell you much, but of course you can always visit the site itself to see what's there. The summaries are provided by the creators of the sites (not by the WebTV staff), and they're sometimes cut off in mid-explanation simply because the summary is longer than the space allotted on the hit list. The following is an example from a search on the keywords *chocolate dessert*:

```
BAKE AND FREEZE CHOCOLATE DESSERTS contains over 120 do-ahead
    desserts with recipes for cakes, pies, cookies,
    brownies, bars, ice creams, terrines and sorbets.
    Included on this home page are freezing . . .
```

Freezing hints? Freezing toes? Now, sometimes a summary doesn't seem to have enough to say. This example of the Reviews in American History site came up in a search of the keywords *american history*:

```
REVIEWS IN AMERICAN HISTORY. REVIEWS IN AMERICAN HISTORY.
```

What do you suppose that site could be about? Just guessing, I think it has to do with reviews in American history, although I have no idea what a review contains. The point of all this is to say that the summary description below each link of a Search Results page is only marginally useful, but it sometimes gives you a little more to go on than the mere title of the Web site.

The summaries, which are displayed in black, unbolded characters, are not links. (In other words, you can't click them to jump anywhere.) The summaries refer to the blue-worded titles directly above them, which *are* links. Each title and summary together represents a site that matches your search request.

Best Bets

On the right side of each Search Results screen resides the Best Bets sidebar with suggested selections. Note that some of the Best Bets lists are divided into two sections: WebTV and Infoseek. Most links, except those under the WebTV heading, don't lead to Web sites, but do lead to directory pages within the Search directory.

Links under the WebTV heading are basically advertisements, and they *do* lead to Web sites. In the *chocolate dessert* search, a WebTV Best Bet led to Hickory Farms, an online food retailer that sells many gourmet items, some more chocolatey than others. Following that site suggestion, the Infoseek links lead to directory pages such as Desserts, Brownies, and Chocolate Pie recipes, any of which could be found by prowling through the Search directory. (This chapter explains such prowlings later.)

Best Bets is a handy little tool, all too easily taken for granted. Of course, you can always start out searching for topics found in the Best Bets list, such as *chocolate pie recipes*. In that case, you wouldn't need the Best Bets link with the same keywords. But that search yields a different Best Bets list that includes Rhubarb pie recipes, Pumpkin pie recipes, and Pie & pastry recipes. In this case, you might find your imagination sparked by ideas you didn't have when you started searching. Best Bets helps broaden your ideas while narrowing down your search results.

Revising your search

For the final element of the results screen, scroll down to the bottom. Below the next 10 link, you can see the Search banner and another keyword entry space, as well as another Search button. Essentially, this setup is the same as you find on the original Search screen. Having the keyword entry opportunity on every screen throughout the Search system is great — you can revise your search words or scrap them in favor of new ones without having to return to the Search screen where you started. Returning to the Search screen wouldn't require hard labor, but all the little conveniences are appreciated.

Look at the section "Getting precise in your searching" later in this chapter for tips about refining your keywords.

Getting More and Getting Less

Most keyword searches generate a huge number of results. Just how huge? Well, the number of results you get depends partly on how general your keywords are and how many keywords you type. But in most cases, no matter what you enter, you get more results than you can handle. The WebTV Search system spares you the shock of being deluged with thousands or millions (literally) of Web links by presenting only ten at a time. At the bottom of the page (scroll down by using the Scroll buttons on your remote), look for the next 10 link. Highlight and select it to display the next screen of ten results. At the bottom of the screen, Search doesn't tell you how many results screens lie ahead of you, which is probably just as well. (The total number of matched sites is listed at the top of the results screen.) In most cases, Search returns more results than you want see. Results of a typical search can easily number in the hundreds of thousands. Did I tell you that the Web is a big place?

At the bottom of each results screen, Search reminds you, `For best results, be specific.` That's one way of saying that you can narrow down your results by using several keywords instead of just one or two.

When it comes to searching the Web, more is not necessarily better. Knowing that the Web has so much to choose from is gratifying, but to think of browsing through it all can be intimidating. Furthermore, many search results aren't exactly what you're looking for — sometimes not even close to what you're looking for. An example: If you enter *movie stars* as your keywords in Search, the system returns links to astronomy sites (stars in the sky, get it?) in addition to movie-related sites. (I show you a trick to avoid that kind of irrelevant search result just a bit further in this chapter.) Most people who search the Web place a value on getting fewer (and more accurate) results, which is what this section is all about.

Knowing what's good

Obviously, if you could get to one site that you really want to see by browsing only ten possibilities, you would be better off than if you had to scour through hundreds (never mind thousands) of potential links to locate the one site with the good stuff. Granted, you may not know exactly what you're looking for or even what a good site is in the first place. Even Web veterans usually feel like they're searching in the dark, not knowing exactly what they're looking for, but knowing that they will recognize it when they find it.

The reason for vagueness when it comes to search goals is simply that the Web is a huge and unpredictable place, with quite a bit of varied quality among its millions of sites. But part of its appeal is the surprise of bumping into things you don't expect, so you should feel comfortable searching with a naive spirit toward what you may find. Getting there is more than half the fun. I find that keeping an open mind enhances the experience.

Nevertheless, good Web sites, generally speaking, share certain characteristics regardless of subject matter. Following are the characteristics that I find indicative of high quality on the Web:

✔ **Speedy.** Web devotees are always gossiping about the speed of a site. If you have a few Web-browsing sessions under your belt, you might have noticed that some pages display more quickly than others. Any one of several factors can be blamed for sluggish displays, and any Web page can deliver itself slowly to your screen from time to time, even if it's normally quick. Some pages, however, are chronically slow, and the blame lies with the computer where the page resides, the geographic location of the host computer (a European location might perform more slowly to an American user than to a European user), or a graphics-heavy (lots of pictures) design because graphics take longer to load than text.

Therefore, sites that always display with molasses-like speed either have too many graphics or reside on a laggard computer. Whatever the specific reason, such sites are frustrating. I have a blacklist of sites I avoid for this reason, and you might develop one over time, too. Contrarily, speedy sites are gratifying and immediately make a good first impression when you encounter them.

✔ **Well organized.** Almost all modern Web sites consist of multiple pages (unlike the Web in its infancy, when it was primarily a collection of single home pages). Many sites embody hundreds, even thousands, of pages, all hyperlinked. As you can imagine, finding your way around some megasites can be as daunting as navigating the New York City subway system.

The first page you see when exploring a big Web site (which in this book, I call the *home page* or *front page*) ideally presents a coherent overview of the site's main sections and prominently offers links to each section. From there, each section's front page should have a clearly organized set of links to take you deeper into the site. You can find all sorts of bewildering sites out there that might have good content, but that content is so hard to dig out that doing so is hardly worth the effort. Sometimes, thankfully, a map is provided, each point on which is a link. A well-organized site, whose content is outlined from the beginning, wins points with me.

✔ **Attractive.** Beauty may be only skin deep, and being pretty is not a site's first priority, but seeing something pleasing on the screen is nice. Some sites are purely informational and present only text, though text-only sites are increasingly rare. If you're out to find pure information, an all-text site is not a problem; but most people want a good package of engaging information and graphics, perhaps with some whiz-bang animation or music thrown in.

✔ **User searchable.** Gigantic sites with large amounts of information sometimes provide keyword-entry forms for searching within the site. This feature is always welcome, especially in a Web publication such as the online edition of a newspaper. Using the keyword form, you can quickly find subjects without ransacking the whole site, which can take forever and still get you nowhere. I don't mean to say that the lack of a keyword search form indicates a bad site; but when you have the capability to search at the home page, you know that the designers of the site have your best interests in mind and respect your time.

✔ **Up to date.** Nothing splashes cold water on my enthusiasm for a site more than noticing that all its content is out of date, such as a movie database that hasn't yet included movies released in the last two months or a sports scoreboard site that doesn't stay on top of the game. Such "lazy" sites might have great peripheral or background content and be packaged in beautiful graphics and multimedia bells 'n' whistles, but all that's for naught if the sites aren't current. Look for sites regularly maintained by organizations that are taking advantage of the cutting-edge immediacy of the Internet.

Getting precise in your searching

Unfortunately, you can't limit the results of a search to only good sites that are fast, well organized, attractive, and searchable. You can search only by topic, and you must ultimately take the bad results with the good. Searching with keywords rarely delivers you to the perfect site immediately, so don't set your hopes too high! On the upside, a few tricks can help you zoom in on sites that have the specific content you're looking for.

Choosing good keywords

Keeping in mind that Search is going to give you more than you can look at, you should make your keywords as specific as possible. If you have only a general idea of what you want to find on the Web, you might be better off browsing through the Search directory rather than using keywords. Use keywords in Search to find items of specific interest. For example, if you want to browse through movie sites, go to the Entertainment portion of the directory; but if you want to find sites about a particular actor, enter the actor's name into Search.

You can type more than one keyword in Search. The question naturally arises: When given a choice, is it better to use one keyword or more than one? There's no simple answer for all situations, sorry to say. You might think that entering one keyword brings up more results than using two or three because one word is more general. But the fact is, Search automatically assumes that you want results on each word you enter, so you might get two or three times as many results that way. On the other hand, if you type two or three very specific keywords, such as *beagle labrador collie* (for dog lovers), your results are more fine-tuned than if you enter the single word *dog*. In that example, Search returns links to sites with some content about beagles or Labradors or collies, but not necessarily all three or even two. Such a search might result in a big selection, but it's still more manageable than the mountain of selections you would face by using *dog* as a keyword.

Search might be a little indiscriminate in how it handles multiple keywords because it's automatically set to treat them separately, returning sites that match any keywords you enter. The good news, though, is that Search recognizes when a site matches both (or all) your keywords. It assumes that the site is more important to you and places it at the top of the Search Results list. When more than one such site is found, they're all piled near the top of the list. This means the first sites you're likely to explore are probably the most useful and relevant sites.

When looking for information about a famous person (or even a semi-famous one), enter both first and last names as keywords. You might still run into trouble if one name is shared by someone else (for example, another actor or the creator of a personal home page) or if the name is also a real word, such as *Bob Hope*. But because sites returned from double keywords are listed with double matches first, you can probably spot the irrelevant Search results and avoid them.

Ideally, one perfect, highly specific keyword can summarize your search need, but coming up with such a keyword is not too likely. Don't despair! A way to turn multiple keywords into an effective tool that can zoom you to the most appropriate sites *is* available. Just keep reading.

Using the plus and minus signs

No, I'm not going to teach you basic math. But I am going to tell you about something called search operators. You don't need to remember what they're called, but remembering how they work is useful. With these operators, you can tell Search to view multiple keywords as inseparable or even to eliminate one keyword from consideration.

The three search operators you want to remember are AND, NOT, and the quotation operator. But instead of the words, just remember their symbols, which are + (a plus sign), – (a minus sign), and " " (quotation marks). Plus for AND, minus for NOT, and quote marks for the quotation operator. The following points show you how the search operators work:

✔ AND (+) tells Search that you want links to sites that contain only both (or all) keywords. Going back to the previous dog example, perhaps you want to see sites that talk about Labradors AND collies, and you want to eliminate sites that discuss only one or the other. Enter the keywords as follows:

```
labrador +collie
```

The Search results from `labrador +collie` contain only sites that make some reference to both Labradors and collies. (The sites might also have content about other types of dogs, of course, and even canaries for all you know.)

✔ NOT (–) tells Search that you want links only to sites that don't contain a certain keyword. For example, if you decide to search for sites that contain information about Labradors and you specifically don't want to see anything about collies (maybe Lassie bit you once), enter the following:

```
labrador -collie
```

The Search results contain sites that are all blissfully collie-free.

✔ QUOTES (" ") tell Search to treat your keywords literally, as an explicit phrase that must be matched exactly. Using quotes ensures that all your keywords will be matched in each result in the exact order that you submitted them. For example, if you want to glean further information about the lethal collie, enter this:

```
"Lassie Come Home"
```

What you must remember about the quotation operator is that it's absolutely literal about spelling and capitalization. It's very useful for finding Web sites that refer to titles of books, movies, or names of famous people.

When using the AND (+) and NOT (–) symbols, attach the one you're using directly to the front of the word that it applies to, as in the previous examples. The temptation to space the operators between two keywords with a nudge of the spacebar both before and after the symbol is overwhelming (if you ever took a typing class), but resist temptation — otherwise, the symbol might not have effect. Type the first keyword, type a space, type the symbol, and then immediately follow with the second keyword.

So you ask, "How complicated can you get with search operators?" (Didn't know I had such good hearing, did you?) You can get as complex as you want, although beyond a certain point you go through more trouble than it's worth. The two main ways to complicate your search string *usefully* are as follows:

✔ Use both AND and NOT in the same search string. Sure, go ahead! You can tell Search to include one keyword in the results list while eliminating another. Use dogs again for an example. Perhaps now you want to get sites about Labradors and beagles, but definitely not collies. (You still hold a grudge against Lassie.) You want Search to know that you won't accept sites that refer to Labradors without beagles (you want them together), and you also can't accept any mention of collies. Type the following search string:

```
labrador +beagle -collie
```

Snoopy is in; Lassie is left out in the cold to contemplate her behavior.

✔ Use either AND or NOT multiple times. This can be quite useful. You can tell Search to include one keyword in the results list but not any of several others. Pretend for a moment that you've finally forgiven Lassie (perhaps you remember that you bit her first), and now you want as much information about collies as you can find. In your newfound enthusiasm for reddish, long-haired dogs with graceful noses, you don't want to even see any mention of the breeds you previously found compelling. Enter the following:

```
collie -labrador -beagle
```

Or, if your reconciliation with the heroine dog has put you in an egalitarian mood, you might want to wallow in information about all three breeds but want to see only sites that refer to all three. In that case, enter this search string:

```
collie +labrador +beagle
```

Experiment! Don't waste too much of your time drowning in screen after screen of search results that don't look promising. Chances are good that if you don't find something that looks useful within the first 30 links and summaries (that's the first three Search results screens), you aren't going to find anything better in the next 300. (For goodness sake, don't ever investigate 300 links on the same subject. I would fear for your sanity.)

The following is an example of quick, resourceful searching — using the dog example for what we all, no doubt, hope is the last time:

1. **Type** labrador +collie **in the keyword entry form of Search.**

   At first glance over the titles and summaries, the results seem to be too specific.

2. **Wanting more general-purpose dog sites, scroll down to the bottom of the Search Results page (or use the Back button to return to the main Search form) and enter one simple keyword:** dogs.

   You get lots of results, but the first two Search Results screens don't look promising. Maybe you link to one or two sites but quickly retreat into Search when you see that they don't have the pet-oriented information you want.

3. **Finding the nearest keyword-entry form, enter your next attempt:** pets.

4. **From the resulting Search Results screen, link to the first site listed, which might be a great one.**

   Although generally devoted to all pets, the hypothetical site in this example has an excellent dog section that tells you how to home-groom your Labrador and collie, which you now remember you had been wondering about last week. Bingo! This is a perfect example of finding exactly what you didn't know you were looking for, all because you kept an open, flexible mind while searching and didn't get bogged down in the first set of results.

Searching for names

WebTV's Search is smart in one particular way: It recognizes uppercase letters (capital letters) at the beginning of names, and realizes you're searching for a person when using those capitals.

Normally, you don't need to worry about uppercase typing — just type your keywords in lowercase letters even if they contain proper nouns, as in this example:

```
Luxury hotels paris
```

When searching for Web information about a person, though, it's a good idea to use uppercase letters to avoid confusion, especially if the person's name contains words with other meanings. Here's an example:

```
Jack London
```

Both *jack* and *london* have meanings unrelated to the author. Using capitals for the first and last names tells Search that you aren't interested in the city.

Browsing in the Search Directory

The Web is many things to many people, but if there's one descriptor that anyone would agree to, it's *big. Vast.* (Okay, two words.) At the time of this writing, the Web contained somewhere between 800 million and 1 billion Web pages.

Now, big is good. Part of the Web's unique value and attraction is that you can find so many different things on it. It has awesome variety, but with that variety comes tremendous duplication. Are you hoping to find a Web site with information about *Star Trek?* You can find dozens, maybe even hundreds of them. Each is different; some are good, and others are not worth the pixels they're displayed on. Some sites may list only every other site related to *Star Trek* (often called a *links page*); other sites may collect only the musings of anyone who wants to voice an opinion on why *Star Trek* is the silliest thing they have ever seen. Whatever the case, the site you want is probably out there — you just need to find it.

To a newcomer, venturing into such virtual bounty might be exciting and is bound to be a bit bewildering. For the old hand, the Web experience can still be sort of like being a good swimmer and getting dropped into the middle of the ocean. Browsing the Web is a fun pastime, but even experienced Netizens, who have identified their personal watering holes, find the endless maze of sites and links overwhelming at times.

WebTV does a good job of easing the Internet beginner into the sprawling online culture of the Web. Instead of just throwing you into the ocean, it provides a map. This map, or *directory,* is part of Search; it functions as a table of contents for the entire Web. Now, don't take me literally; the directory doesn't contain every site on the Web — that would hardly be useful. Instead, it offers selected sites chosen by a team of reviewers and also dishes up unreviewed sites. The selections are divided into categories and updated continually.

How the directory works

Using the Search directory is good practice for making the most of other Web directories should you decide to venture outside the friendly confines of WebTV's suggestions. (I show you how to go outside Search later in this chapter.) All Web directories use a multilevel system for narrowing in on topics that interest you. The Search directory is no exception, providing as many as six directory levels in some topics.

The main menu, on the Search page, is a grand overview of the Web as the specialists at WebTV see it. At the top level of the directory, the Web is divided into broad categories of subjects such as Money, News, Games, and Sports (look back at Figure 9-1). Selecting any category takes you to the second directory level (see Figure 9-2), from which you can visit a Web site or try links in various subcategories.

Suppose you want to visit a music-trivia site site. Glancing over the Main menu list of topics, you correctly assume that such a site would fall under the Trivia category. Highlighting and selecting the Trivia category takes you to the directory's second level, where you see a variety of trivia topics (not to be confused with trivial topics).

Entering the second level

Follow these steps to proceed to the second level from the main Search directory screen:

1. **On the main Search screen, highlight and select any level-one topic.**

2. **On the next screen, highlight and select either a subtopic from the top of the screen or one of the featured sites lower down.**

   If necessary, use the Scroll buttons on the remote to view the Web sites below the screen.

Figure 9-2:
A second directory level, showing subcategories of the Games topic.

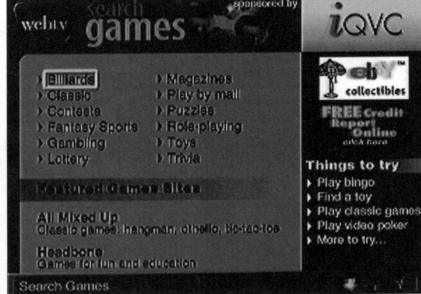

The second level of the Search directory is where the action is, and you always have two options: choosing a subtopic or choosing a Web site. (Some deeper levels of the directory offer only Web sites, no further subtopics. It stands to reason that eventually you reach topics so well defined that they can't be usefully divided any further.)

Choosing a subtopic from the top list displays a new list of related sites, all organized under the main menu topic you originally selected — kind of like moving sideways through the rooms on the second story of a house. For example, if you select the Entertainment topic on the Main menu (the house) and in the second level you select News (the floor), you stay in the general Entertainment area as a new list of Web sites (the rooms on the floor of the house) appears on the screen. Each Main menu subject has several second-level subtopics to check out.

Choosing a Web site from the display of featured sites of any second-level screen takes you directly to that site. When you click a Web site link, you leave the Search directory entirely, but that's not a big deal because you can easily get back to the point from which you left — just use the Back button on the remote or the keyboard to retrace your steps. If you wander far away from the directory by selecting several links, you might find it easier to press the Home button on the remote and then highlight and select Explore on the Home screen. Or use the Recent button on the remote or the keyboard to find a previous screen up to twelve screens back.

The Search directory doesn't contain actual Web sites; it offers only links to sites. You must highlight and select an item to visit the site. The link then takes you to the site's home page, which usually has links to other pages within the site. The only way to check whether a site meets your interests and needs is to visit it and poke around.

Working with the Search directory

The Search directory is a launch pad for your forays into the Web. To make the best use of the directory, you must constantly leave it. Directory-based Web browsing is best performed by bouncing back and forth between the directory and a Web site. A typical browsing session runs along these lines:

1. **On the directory's main menu, highlight and select any subject category.**

2. **On the second level, highlight and select the subtopic closest to your interest.**

3. On the next screen, highlight and select a particular Web site you'd like to visit.

Use the Scroll buttons to view links further down on the page.

Use the brief descriptions beneath each link to help you decide in advance whether the site is right. The descriptions are short, though, so you can't get too much information from them. The only way to tell about a site for sure is to jump over to it.

4. Look at the home page of the site and try out a few of its links.

When you're ready to leave the site and return to the directory, use the Back button on the remote to retrace your steps to the Explore page from which you left.

If you selected several links within the Web site and visited many of its pages, using the Back button is a cumbersome way to return. You must press it repeatedly to trudge your way through the pages you've already seen, this time in reverse order. A better solution is to use the Recent button on the remote. A panel displaying your last 12 screens is displayed. From this panel, you can highlight and select the Explore screen to jump straight to it.

Remember to save the Web site to your Favorites collection if you want to revisit it easily. When on the site's home page (or a particularly useful inner page), press the Options button on the remote and then select Save.

5. Back on the directory page from which you left, highlight and select another link and repeat the process.

You can bounce back and forth dozens of times during a typical directory browsing session. (Like you need my permission, right?) The important thing to remember is to save sites to Favorites before returning to Explore. The rule is: It's better to save too many than too few. The reason? It's easier to erase items from your Favorites collection than it is to find the sites you forgot to save.

If you do forget to save a good Web site (for shame) and you remember (with embarrassment) after you've returned to Explore, there's an easy way to correct the oversight (and redeem yourself):

1. Press the Recent button on the remote.

2. Highlight and select the Web page you want to save.

3. When the page appears on your screen, press the Options button on the remote.

4. Highlight and select Save.

Not the Only Directory in Town

The Search directory is a fine, upstanding directory of the Web. It's worth remembering, however, that it's not complete. If the directory were complete, it would be far less useful. Imagine finding sites among a directory of approximately 100 million Web pages! It would give *couch potato* a new meaning. The Search directory does a wonderful job of editing the possibilities and presenting a wide range of good Web sites.

Other directories abound on the Web. Some attempt to represent a thorough view of the Web by presenting almost all current Web pages. Other directories are more modest, like WebTV's directory, offering links to sites that have been checked and approved by the editors of the directory. The upshot is that you have choices in how you browse the Web. In this section, I describe two of the main choices: the very popular Yahoo! and Lycos Web directories.

The Yahoo! Web directory

If you want to get a gigantic overview of the entire Web, you'll agree with the name of the Yahoo! directory. It's big. It's glorious. And, believe it or not, Yahoo! is easy to use. You can try it out by highlighting and selecting the Go to option and then typing this URL:

```
www.yahoo.com
```

The Yahoo! home page (see Figure 9-3) looks like a typical Web directory and even bears a similarity to Explore (although it's not as pretty, you've got to admit). Figure 9-3 shows only a portion of the home page; you must scroll down to see the rest of the main subject areas.

Each main subject area shows a few subtopics immediately beneath it — for example, Reference contains the subtopics Libraries, Dictionaries, and Quotations beneath it. Any topic, either a main topic or a subtopic, is a link, and may be highlighted and selected to view another directory page. Like all Web directories, each time you select a link, a more detailed page is displayed, showing more specific topic divisions within the main subject category. You continue this process until you find specific Web pages that seem worth visiting. In Yahoo!, you have a vast choice.

The best way to become familiar with a big directory is to go on a browsing expedition. Suppose you want to survey how the Web covers karate, one of the martial arts. Here's how you would bore down through the Yahoo! directory to find karate sites:

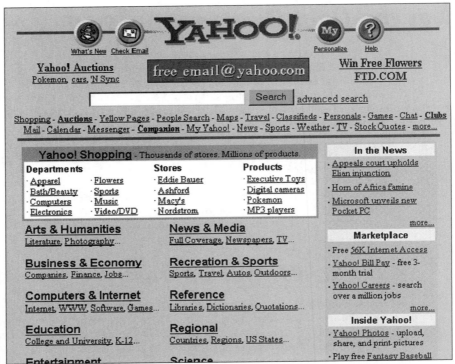

Figure 9-3:
The home
page of the
Yahoo!
directory.

1. **On the Yahoo! directory home page, highlight and select** Recreation
   & Sports.

   Karate may be more than recreational for you, and you might not regard
   it exactly as a sport. But very often when dealing with large directories,
   you must take your best guess as to what subject area a specific topic
   lies in. This guess works — trust me.

2. **On the Recreation screen, highlight and select** Sports.

   Check out the Recreation screen in Figure 9-4. On this second-level directory page, you have several recreational subtopics from which you must
   guess where karate sites probably lie. Sports seems like the best bet.
   (Don't worry, I've been down this path before.)

3. **On the Home>Recreation>Sports screen, highlight and select**
   Martial Arts.

   The Home>Recreation>Sports screen is a third-level page of the Yahoo!
   directory. As you can see in Figure 9-5, it offers further subtopics, and
   we haven't reached any links to actual Web sites yet. This is an indication of how big the Yahoo! directory is — you must drill down several
   levels to increasingly specific pages before getting to any site links.

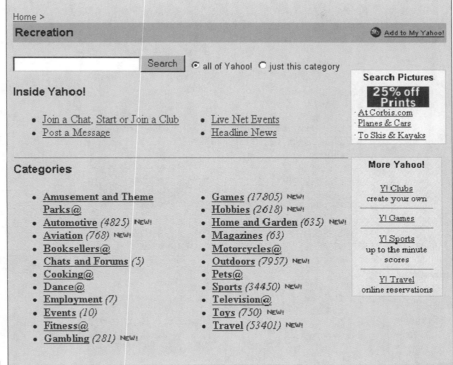

Home >
Recreation   Add to My Yahoo!

[   ] Search   ⊙ all of Yahoo! ○ just this category

Search Pictures

Inside Yahoo!

25% off Prints
· At Corbis.com
· Planes & Cars
· To Skis & Kayaks

- Join a Chat, Start or Join a Club   • Live Net Events
- Post a Message   • Headline News

More Yahoo!

Y! Clubs
create your own

Categories

Y! Games

- **Amusement and Theme Parks@**   • **Games** *(17805)* NEW!
- **Automotive** *(4825)* NEW!   • **Hobbies** *(2618)* NEW!
- **Aviation** *(768)* NEW!   • **Home and Garden** *(635)* NEW!
- **Booksellers@**   • **Magazines** *(63)*
- **Chats and Forums** *(5)*   • **Motorcycles@**
- **Cooking@**   • **Outdoors** *(7957)* NEW!
- **Dance@**   • **Pets@**
- **Employment** *(7)*   • **Sports** *(34450)* NEW!
- **Events** *(10)*   • **Television@**
- **Fitness@**   • **Toys** *(750)* NEW!
- **Gambling** *(281)* NEW!   • **Travel** *(53401)* NEW!

Y! Sports
up to the minute scores

Y! Travel
online reservations

Figure 9-4:
A second-level directory page in Yahoo!

4. **On the Home>Recreation>Sports>Martial Arts screen, highlight and select** Karate.

The Home>Recreation>Sports>Martial Arts page is shown in Figure 9-6. This fourth level of the Yahoo! directory contains both subtopics and links to Web sites. (Finally!) The site links deal with martial arts generally, and not necessarily with karate to the degree you want. You can certainly browse them and link to any interesting looking sites, but if you're really focused on karate, it makes more sense to go for the Karate subtopic link, which leads to the fifth-level screen.

5. **On the Home>Recreation>Sports>Martial Arts>Karate screen, browse through the site links and visit any Web sites that look interesting.**

You've arrived! This fifth-level directory page gives you the overview of karate you were looking for. Scroll down the page to see all the site links it offers. The Organizations links in the Categories list (above the Most Popular Sites list) leads to yet a deeper directory level — the sixth — devoted to listing links to karate schools, clubs, and other organizations.

- Curling *(70)*
- Cycling *(1537)* NEW!
- Danball *(3)*
- Dog Racing *(9)*
- Dogsledding@
- Equestrian *(335)*
- Extreme Sports *(54)*
- Fencing *(152)*
- Fishing@
- Flying Discs *(165)* NEW!
- Footbag (Hacky Sack) *(16)*
- Football (American) *(3028)* NEW!
- Football (Australian) *(44)*
- Football (Gaelic) *(19)*
- Golf *(1206)* NEW!
- Gymnastics *(247)*
- Handball *(26)*
- Hockey *(3176)* NEW!
- Horse Racing@
- Hurling *(9)*
- Jai-Alai *(7)*
- Korfball *(19)*
- Lacrosse *(186)*
- Luge *(13)*
- Lumbering *(5)*
- Martial Arts *(824)* NEW!
- Motorcycle Racing *(163)*

- Skeleton *(10)*
- Skiing, Snow *(553)* NEW!
- Skydiving@
- Snowboarding *(169)*
- Snowmobiling@
- Soccer *(1604)* NEW!
- Softball *(372)*
- Squash *(46)* NEW!
- Surfing *(220)* NEW!
- Swimming and Diving *(477)* NEW!
- Table Tennis *(40)* NEW!
- Tchoukball *(4)*
- Tennis *(642)* NEW!
- Track and Field *(257)*
- Triathlon *(153)* NEW!
- Tug-of-War *(6)*
- Twirling *(6)*
- Volleyball *(346)* NEW!
- Wakeboarding@
- Walking@
- Water Polo *(53)*
- Waterskiing *(75)* NEW!
- Weightlifting *(243)*
- Windsurfing *(108)*
- Winter Sports *(315)*
- Wrestling *(839)* NEW!

Figure 9-5:
A third-level directory page in Yahoo!

You can see from this expedition that Yahoo! is a deep and detailed directory. It might seem overwhelming. But it's a heck of a fun place to browse and it's easy to get delightfully lost in, if getting lost in the Web is your idea of a good time. (There's nothing quite like it, in my opinion.)

The Lycos Web directory

Lycos is a different directory experience than Yahoo!, which is described in the preceding section. You might compare it to the difference between a professor and a chatty neighbor. Yahoo! is massive; Lycos is edited down to a manageable size. Yahoo! is thorough to the point of exhaustion in cataloging the Web; Lycos is satisfied to hit the high points.

Start your Lycos investigation at the home page, at this URL:

```
www.lycos.com
```

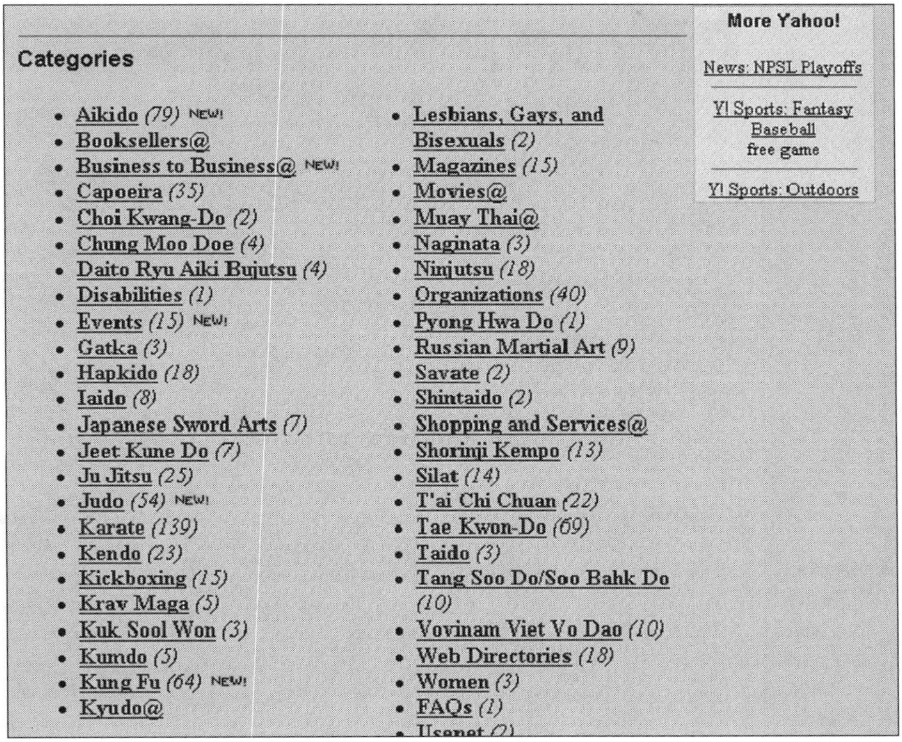

More Yahoo!

News: NPSL Playoffs

Y! Sports: Fantasy
Baseball
free game

Y! Sports: Outdoors

Categories

- Aikido *(79)* NEW!
- Booksellers@
- Business to Business@ NEW!
- Capoeira *(35)*
- Choi Kwang-Do *(2)*
- Chung Moo Doe *(4)*
- Daito Ryu Aiki Bujutsu *(4)*
- Disabilities *(1)*
- Events *(15)* NEW!
- Gatka *(3)*
- Hapkido *(18)*
- Iaido *(8)*
- Japanese Sword Arts *(7)*
- Jeet Kune Do *(7)*
- Ju Jitsu *(25)*
- Judo *(54)* NEW!
- Karate *(139)*
- Kendo *(23)*
- Kickboxing *(15)*
- Krav Maga *(5)*
- Kuk Sool Won *(3)*
- Kumdo *(5)*
- Kung Fu *(64)* NEW!
- Kyudo@

- Lesbians, Gays, and Bisexuals *(2)*
- Magazines *(15)*
- Movies@
- Muay Thai@
- Naginata *(3)*
- Ninjutsu *(18)*
- Organizations *(40)*
- Pyong Hwa Do *(1)*
- Russian Martial Art *(9)*
- Savate *(2)*
- Shintaido *(2)*
- Shopping and Services@
- Shorinji Kempo *(13)*
- Silat *(14)*
- T'ai Chi Chuan *(22)*
- Tae Kwon-Do *(69)*
- Taido *(3)*
- Tang Soo Do/Soo Bahk Do *(10)*
- Vovinam Viet Vo Dao *(10)*
- Web Directories *(18)*
- Women *(3)*
- FAQs *(1)*
- Usenet *(2)*

Figure 9-6:
A fourth-level
directory
page in
Yahoo!

As you can see in Figure 9-7, the Lycos home page is somewhat more colorful than the sparse (yet useful) Yahoo! interface. That doesn't mean it's better, necessarily. Actually, besides the cosmetic differences, Lycos works pretty much the same as Yahoo! and every other Web directory. On the home page is the top level with the most basic subjects, each of which leads to underlying directory levels with more detailed topics and links to Web sites related to those topics. The home page, as shown in Figure 9-7, displays the main subject links in the center of the page.

Here's how to explore the Lycos directory:

1. **On the Lycos home page, highlight and select a subject, such as Computers & Internet.**

   The second level of the directory appears. In Figure 9-8, you can see the top portion of a second-level screen.

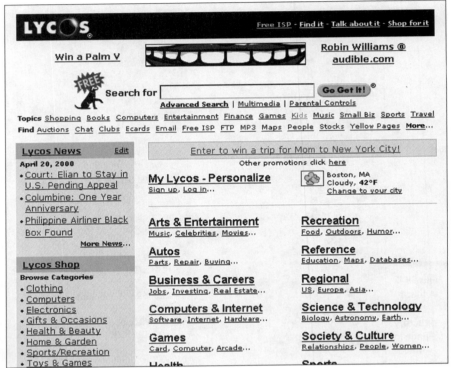

Figure 9-7:
The Lycos
directory
home page.

2. **Scroll down the page to see a list of subtopic links and then highlight
   and select one of the subtopic links. I chose** Games.

   The third-level directory screen appears. Figure 9-9 shows an area of the
   screen after I scrolled down a bit.

   Unlike the Yahoo! directory, which can take you to the fourth level
   before showing you any links to Web sites, Lycos puts out some good
   stuff at the third level. The screen layout isn't as compact as it could be,
   so you have a chance to exercise your Scroll button technique with the
   remote as you plunge down, down, and further down, and then down
   some more — and then still further down — on very long third-level
   pages. All the sites are selected by the Lycos staff and described in a
   single brief sentence next to the link.

3. **Highlight and select a Web site link.**

Lycos is an easy, friendly environment. You can save a lot of time finding
good Web locations, if you're not interested in wading through the exhaust-
ingly thorough map of the Web provided by Yahoo!

Lycos Home > **Computers**

- **Lycos Computers** – Computers from A-Z; all the information you need.

- **Algorithms** *(218)*
- **Artificial Intelligence** *(818)*
- **Artificial Life** *(236)*
- **Bulletin Board Systems** *(368)*
- **CAD** *(644)*
- **Companies** *(546)*
- **Computer Science** *(1,706)*
- **Consultants** *(2,100)*
- **Data Communications** *(1,158)*
- **Data Formats** *(1,084)*
- **Desk_Customization** *(540)*
- **Desk_Publishing** *(73)*
- **DSP** *(39)*
- **E-Books** *(180)*
- **Education** *(595)* NEW!
- **Emulators** *(340)*
- **Ethics** *(53)*
- **Fonts** *(325)** NEW!
- **Games** *(13,701)**
- **Graphics** *(2,414)*
- **Hacking** *(559)*
- **Hardware** *(5,890)*
- **History** *(180)*
- **Home Automation** *(136)*

- **Internet** *(63,024)*
- **Intranet** *(124)*
- **Jobs** *(387)**
- **MIS** *(79)**
- **Mobile Computing** *(320)*
- **Multimedia** *(1,101)*
- **News** *(176)*
- **Newsgroups** *(157)** NEW!
- **Open Source** *(195)*
- **Operating Systems** *(6,063)**
- **Organizations** *(281)*
- **Parallel Computing** *(410)*
- **Performance and Capacity** *(57)*
- **Product Support** *(303)**
- **Programming** *(9,169)*
- **Robotics** *(176)*
- **Security** *(1,866)*
- **Shopping** *(88)*
- **Software** *(23,241)*
- **Speech Technology** *(133)*
- **Supercomputing** *(49)*

Figure 9-8: A second-level page of the Lycos directory. You must scroll down to see all the subtopics.

Other Web Directories

This book doesn't have enough room to describe fully every Web directory. In fact, five books wouldn't have enough room. Instead, I've created a brief list of all-star Web directories for you to try the next time you get stricken with virtual wanderlust.

If you get *really* interested in Web directories, you might want to look at my *Internet Searching For Dummies* (published by IDG Books Worldwide, Inc.), in which I describe how Web directories work in greater detail than I can here.

Excite

```
www.excite.com/
```

Excite is a major league Web directory with a multitude of additional features.

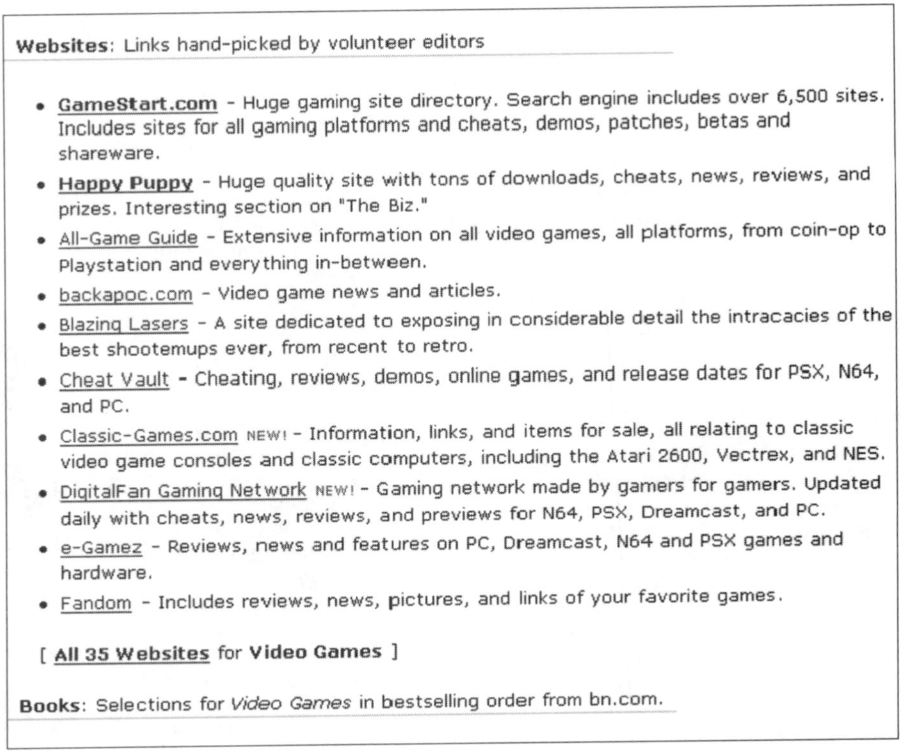

Websites: Links hand-picked by volunteer editors

- **GameStart.com** - Huge gaming site directory. Search engine includes over 6,500 sites. Includes sites for all gaming platforms and cheats, demos, patches, betas and shareware.
- **Happy Puppy** - Huge quality site with tons of downloads, cheats, news, reviews, and prizes. Interesting section on "The Biz."
- All-Game Guide - Extensive information on all video games, all platforms, from coin-op to Playstation and everything in-between.
- backapoc.com - Video game news and articles.
- Blazing Lasers - A site dedicated to exposing in considerable detail the intracacies of the best shootemups ever, from recent to retro.
- Cheat Vault - Cheating, reviews, demos, online games, and release dates for PSX, N64, and PC.
- Classic-Games.com NEW! - Information, links, and items for sale, all relating to classic video game consoles and classic computers, including the Atari 2600, Vectrex, and NES.
- DigitalFan Gaming Network NEW! - Gaming network made by gamers for gamers. Updated daily with cheats, news, reviews, and previews for N64, PSX, Dreamcast, and PC.
- e-Gamez - Reviews, news and features on PC, Dreamcast, N64 and PSX games and hardware.
- Fandom - Includes reviews, news, pictures, and links of your favorite games.

[**All 35 Websites** for **Video Games**]

Books: Selections for *Video Games* in bestselling order from bn.com.

Figure 9-9:
The third
level of the
Lycos
directory,
showing
links to
Web sites.

InfoSeek

www.infoseek.com

InfoSeek is a popular directory with a notable Kids and Family section.

The BigHub

www.thebighub.com

A fantastic research tool, The BigHub is a directory to databases where you can get specialized information.

LookSmart

www.looksmart.com/

LookSmart is distinguished by an intelligent and easy-to-use interface that makes it easy to backtrack when you get lost in the directory.

About.com

```
www.about.com
```

About.com is a huge directory of Web sites on hundreds of topics, operated by expert Guides. A unique and popular resource.

Web Crawler

```
www.webcrawler.com/
```

Web Crawler has been around forever and is still going strong. It's one of the most-used Web directories.

Other Search Engines on the Web

Search is a great tool; it's well-designed and simple to use. It's modeled on Infoseek, a Web search tool that has been around since before WebTV and is one of the most popular and impressive search tools. (Notice the Infoseek logo that's sprinkled throughout Search.) Infoseek is only one of several *search engines* (as they're called) on the Web, and they're all available to you through WebTV. You're not limited to using only Search, although you might not want to try another if you're happy with the results you get from Search. If you seek better or different results or are simply curious, read on to find out how to use other Web search engines.

Note: Search engines are different from Web directories. Search engines let you find explicit subjects by keyword; directories let you browse menus of subjects. In WebTV, Search is the search engine, and it contains a directory. In the same fashion, some Web sites, including some of the sites described in this section, contain both a search engine and a directory.

Why use any other search engine?

Curiosity is one reason to try another search engine. You might want to simply try something new or see how Web search tools designed for computer users work. By and large, these search engines don't contain any features that you can't easily use through WebTV.

A larger reason to use another search engine has to do with the enormity of the Web and the varied results you get from one search engine to the next. Each search engine not only has a unique design and user interface but is different in how it operates and obtains its search results. Deeper differences are invisible to you when visiting different engines' Web sites but become apparent in better, worse, or different search results.

In each of the sites listed in this section, you don't need to know anything special to start a basic search of the Web. The interfaces are more cluttered and complex than WebTV's elegantly simple Search, but the only thing you really need to see is the keyword-entry form. In each case, just follow the same basic routine:

1. **Highlight the keyword-entry form.**

2. **Use either the wireless keyboard or the on-screen keyboard to type your keyword(s) with any operator(s).**

   Yep. The search operators + and – or the words AND and NOT work with most other search engines as well. Try them out and see what you get. If you use AND or NOT, type them in capitals and leave a space between the operator and your keywords. For example:

   ```
   labrador AND collie NOT beagle
   ```

3. **Find the Search or Go button next to the keyword-entry form and select it.**

   Sometimes, using the Enter key on the wireless keyboard works.

So many search engines are on the Web that I could write an entire book about them. Come to think of it, I did! Check out *Internet Searching For Dummies* (published by IDG Books Worldwide, Inc.) for an elaborate rundown on how to search for darn near anything on the Web. More briefly, here are a few other search engines for you to try. They each have advantages and disadvantages, and each is yet another fascinating way to angle into the incredible resources of the Web.

Furthermore, some search engines contain advanced searching features not found in WebTV's Search. Fancy search operators and other ways of limiting or defining a search might be too esoteric for the average user, but if you are someone who enjoys virtual gadgetry and to whom the challenge of a perfect search is appealing, the advanced search engines may be right up your alley.

Yahoo!

www.yahoo.com

The most famous of them all, Yahoo! performs keyword searches of its own massive index.

AltaVista

www.altavista.com

For years a search engine for sophisticated Web users, AltaVista has over-hauled its service and is now easier to use.

Excite

```
www.excite.com
```

One of the best, Excite delivers edited search results that cut through mediocrity.

Lycos

```
www.lycos.com
```

Lycos reinvents itself almost every year, but the search engine remains consistently fast and useful.

HotBot

```
www.hotbot.com
```

HotBot searches one of the largest and most complete indexes on the planet. It certainly has one of the hippest design interfaces, and it gives you tons of complicated search options. Check it out if you want to get serious about searching.

Part III
Cruising with WebTV

The 5th Wave — By Rich Tennant

The 500 channel multimedia future

The Dental Network is starting a 10-hour, 3-day, 16-part miniseries on gum disease. Wanna watch?

In this part . . .

Here, I show you some of the slightly more advanced fun stuff you can do with WebTV and the Internet. From using TV commercials imaginatively to creating multimedia e-mail and Web pages, the chapters in this part get you cruising on the WebTV fast lane. Be sure to look at Chapter 13, which describes the Page Builder feature, an important upgrade since this book's last edition.

Chapter 10

Around Town and WebTV Today

. . . .

In This Chapter

▶ Finding your way Around Town

▶ Exploring the Yellow and White Pages of WebTV

▶ Getting local movie listings through your TV

▶ Finding out how to use the Classifieds

▶ Dining out, finding a job, and a smorgasbord of other activities

▶ Using WebTV Today

. . . .

*T*he World Wide Web is, as the name implies, a global phenomenon. It's thoroughly decentralized, unorganized, and unlocalized. But being global doesn't mean that the Web doesn't have local information for you. No matter where you live, you can find information specific to your area — and it's the mission of the Around Town section to help you find it. Around Town is divided into several main areas that can help you find a local business phone number, look up a long-lost friend, browse classified ads, check out movie schedules, and get a weather forecast.

In addition to Around Town, a Home-screen feature called WebTV Today displays a selection of headlines, local weather summaries, money and sports news, health information, shopping ideas, and links to Web locations. This chapter shows you how to navigate Around Town and WebTV Today.

Getting Around Town

Around Town is identical on the Classic and Plus systems. You can get to Around Town easily from anywhere on the Web by following these steps:

1. **Press the Home button on the remote.**

2. **Near the bottom of the Home screen, highlight and select** Around Town.

   The Around Town screen (see Figure 10-1) is automatically optimized for your local area, based on the ZIP code you entered when signing up.

Figure 10-1:
The Around
Town
screen is
optimized to
your logon
location.

Around Town starts by giving you the weather, according to the principle that you shouldn't wear sandals in a snowstorm. The capsule five-day summary gives you the quick picture, and that five-day graphic is a linked item that you can highlight and select to get a more detailed forecast from The Weather Channel on the Web. (Don't expect to see The Weather Channel cable station.)

If you ever want to see the weather of a different city, highlight and select change city near the top of the screen, just to the right of your current city. Or scroll down to the bottom of the screen to the Change City area where you can type a new town or zip code.

Yellow Pages

The Yellow Pages section of Around Town has been much simplified since the early days of WebTV. Any long-time users who were put off might want to try it again.

WebTV's Yellow Pages are provided by Microsoft Network (MSN) and operate in directory style. You select categories, just as if you were opening a Yellow Pages phone book, but you zero in on your topic of choice in a different fashion. Here's how to get started:

1. **On the Around Town screen, scroll down to the Yellow Pages section.**

2. **Highlight and select any category — for this example, select** Home & Garden.

3. **On the Home & Garden screen, highlight and select any subcategory — in this case,** Hardware & tools.

4. **On the MSN Yellow Pages screen, scroll down to see all local listings in your chosen category.**

At the bottom of each MSN Yellow Pages screen you may start a more detailed search is your category is still too broad or if you know the name of a store you're trying to find. In the Refine Search area of the screen, fill in the blanks and select the Go button to begin a new search. You can repeat the process as often as you want.

Some listings on the MSN Yellow Pages screen include a small map link next to the address. Highlight and select that link to see a local map of the neighborhood in which the store is located. If a printer is attached to WebTV, this is a handy time to use it. You can change the scale of the map before printing it by using the ZOOM LEVEL tool, located to the right of the map. Highlight and select the ZOOM LEVEL graphic, and then select either the plus (+) or minus (–) sign to zoom in and out. Each one causes the screen to reload with a new map. Specifically, here's what the plus and minus signs do:

✔ The plus sign (+) zooms in, so the map becomes more detailed. Use this selection to see small streets.

✔ The minus sign (–) zooms out, so the map becomes less detailed. Use this selection to see a larger view of the neighborhood.

Another customization feature for the MSN Yellow Pages maps is called the MAP MOVER. Use the arrows to skid the map up and down or side to side. Each time you select an arrow the screen must reload, so the process can take a bit of time if you make several adjustments. Use MAP MOVER and ZOOM LEVEL in tandem to get the map to encompass both your starting point and your destination. Or if all this seems ridiculously complicated and uselessly technical, just call up the darn store and ask for directions.

Finding People

The White Pages of Around Town are provided by a popular Web-searching service called InfoSpace. InfoSpace is a free registration service on the Web that has customized its directory and search engine for WebTV users. Through InfoSpace, you can search for individuals, in many cases getting their home addresses, phone numbers, and e-mail addresses.

Here's how to get started with InfoSpace:

1. **On the Around Town screen, scroll down and then highlight and select** People.

2. **On the White Pages screen, enter the name, city, state, and country of the person you're looking for.**

   The last name is crucial, but the first name can be left blank. Remember, the listing corresponds to the person's phone-book entry, so an initial in the First Name field might get results when a full name doesn't. Leaving the First Name field blank expands the results considerably, as does leaving the City field blank. You must choose a state from the drop-down list.

3. **Highlight and select the** Find **button.**

4. **On the Listings screen, highlight and select the individual whose listing seems to match your search (if more than one listing appears).**

   The Detail screen appears, showing (in most cases) the person's address and phone number.

After you get to the Detail screen, you can initiate a search for the person's e-mail address by selecting the Email Search link beneath the person's name and address. Email Search, however, is much less reliable and generally less rewarding compared to searching for a phone number.

Finding Flicks

Around Town enables you to check movie times for local theaters and even buy tickets in some cases. The provider of this service is MovieQuest, a Web service well known for its excellent database of movie showings and locations. In MovieQuest, you can search for a theater, a movie, or a time of day that you want to watch a movie. Follow these steps to get there:

1. **From anywhere on the Web, press the Home button on the remote.**

2. **On the Home screen, highlight and select** Around Town.

3. **On the Around Town screen, highlight and select** Movies.

The MovieQuest screen appears with your local information loaded and ready to go. Featured movie selections are presented first; scroll down past them to get to some movie theaters in and around your town. At this point, you can do one of a few things:

 ✔ Highlight and select any movie theater to see a complete rundown of its show times.

 ✔ Highlight and select `more theaters at MovieQuest` to see all theaters in the MovieQuest database associated with your town and the surrounding area.

 ✔ Scroll down to the Search area at the bottom of the screen to locate show times for a particular movie. Just type the movie name and select the `Find` button.

MovieQuest is nicely presented — it's clear and looks good through WebTV — and the facility with which you can search by movie title or by theater makes the service really useful. MovieQuest merges the best features of newspaper listings and theater phone recordings.

For Sale

Around Town features an electronic classified ad system called Classifieds2000. You can use it to find used cars, rental apartments, personal ads, pre-owned computer equipment, job listings, and miscellaneous used merchandise. Classifieds2000 is set up as an interactive directory in which you first browse within a category and then select detailed specifications before seeing ads that match your needs. Here's how it works:

1. **On the Home screen, highlight and select** `Around Town`.

2. **On the Around Town screen, highlight and select** `For Sale`.

3. **On the Free Classifieds screen, highlight and select any category of ads.**

   For this example, select `Vehicles`.

4. **On the Search Ads screen, highlight and select the subcategory you're looking for.**

   The Vehicles subcategories include Cars, Trucks, Vans, Motorcycles, RVs, Snowmobiles, and a few other choices. For the sake of this example, pretend you're looking for a used car. Highlight and select `Cars`.

5. **On the next Search Ads screen, make any specific selections that define what you're looking for.**

   This screen offers pull-down selection lists and radio buttons for specifying the make of car, the state the vehicle currently resides in, the price range, the model year, the mileage, and a variety of auto features. The default settings are for the widest possible selection of features and characteristics, so if you want to get a sample of available used cars anywhere in the United States, just leave all the settings as they are.

Perhaps the most important setting is the box labeled Show Me the Newest Ads First. I always highlight and select that box because it sorts the results with new ads first. The Classifieds2000 system never displays more than 200 results.

6. **Highlight and select the** Search Current Ads **button at the bottom of the screen.**

   Selecting the Search Current Ads button displays yet another Search Ads screen, this one containing a list of items (or people, in the case of personal ads) that match your search selections. Click any item to see a description, which sometimes includes a photograph and always includes information for contacting the person or store selling the item.

In some categories (including Vehicles used in the preceding example), a detailed search query form exists way down at the bottom of the screen, below the Search Current Ads button. This is where you can (in the case of the Vehicles category) specify a mileage range for the car, how many doors it must have, whether it's a sedan or a hatchback, and more.

Classifieds2000 is a two-way street. You can browse the ads, and you can place your own classified. The service is free, whether you're hoping to sell a car or find a soul mate. (A word to the wise: Never try to sell your soul mate or marry your car.) Here's how to place a Classifieds2000 ad:

1. **On the Around Town screen, highlight and select** For Sale.

2. **On the Free Classifieds screen, highlight and select** Place Ads **on the left sidebar.**

3. **On the Place Ad screen, highlight and select a category for your ad.**

   This is where you choose whether you're selling an item or looking for love. If you have a job available, there's a category for that, too.

4. **On the next Place Ad screen, choose a subcategory in which your ad will appear.**

5. **On the next Place Ad screen, highlight and select the** New User **button.**

   I'm assuming you haven't used Classifieds2000 before. The New User button displays a screen on which you choose a member name and a password. Use this information on future visits to skip over the New User procedure. When you get to this screen on subsequent visits, scroll down and enter your phone number, e-mail address, and password, and then highlight and select the Continue button.

6. **On the next series of Place Ad screens (don't you think they could have come up with other screen names?), use the drop-down selection lists and check boxes to describe your item.**

7. **At the end of the selection and description process, highlight and select the** `Preview Ad` **button at the bottom of the screen.**

   The `Preview Ad` button enables you to take a final look at your ad before posting it. It also tells you whether you made any mistakes or omissions when filling out the information.

8. **Highlight and select the** `Place My Ad` **button.**

Other Strolls around Town

Around Town, besides searching Yellow Pages, White Pages, and Classifieds, dishes up some features that are useful and possibly exciting to some users but less tailored to the look and feel of WebTV. Following are the features rounding out the Around Town experience. In each case, you access the feature by highlighting and selecting the service's name — you might need to scroll down the Around Town screen a bit.

- ✔ **Dining out.** WebTV links to CitySearch for restaurant reviews, recommendations, and plentiful listings related to your location. Searching works much better than browsing the directory in this section. I've been puzzled many a time to find restaurants located two hundred miles away appear in my directory. But searching with a keyword seems to work pretty well.

- ✔ **Events.** This CitySearch feature uses the database provided by Ticketmaster, a business partner of CitySearch. Browse or search for concerts, sports, and other live events in your area. The Events screen is like a digital magazine of art and culture. Scroll down to the directory and search engine to find specific venues and attractions.

- ✔ **Auctions.** Highlight and select this feature to be whisked off to eBay, the gigantic online marketplace for buying and selling Stuff (with a capital *S*). You may have heard of eBay — it's more than an auction site; it's a lifestyle. An addiction. A marvel of the virtual realm. Millions of items both rare and trivial are up for grabs on eBay.

- ✔ **Careers.** Supplementing the Classifieds section is this link to Monster.com, one of the big online employment databases. This customizable service helps folks of every stripe find a first job or trade up to a better job.

- ✔ **Directions.** This feature is supposed to be a mapping service. Provided by Zip2, the site is, in fact, more of an information portal with a Yellow Pages search engine attached. Maps play a minor part in the scheme of things at Zip2; if you're looking for a map, you might just get frustrated here. Instead, try the fine mapping service provided by Yahoo! at the following URL:

  `maps.yahoo.com`

Just type the URL into the `Go to` selection of the Options panel.

Around Town isn't limited to your town. Two scenarios come to mind in which you might want to change the town of Around Town:

 ✔ You're going to visit a city.
 ✔ You're in another city, and you brought your WebTV box with you.

Changing the locality is easy:

1. **Highlight and select** change city **next to your town name.**

2. **In the provided field, type a city, a state, or a ZIP code.**

   Each time you change cities, WebTV keeps track of the change and displays previously selected cities whenever you reach this step.

3. **Highlight and select the** Change **button.**

WebTV Today

If you've spent any time gazing at the Web Home screen (and who wouldn't, considering it's more lovely than the most dazzling sunset), you've noticed the ever-changing display of headlines and attractions in the center Today In section of the screen. That center portion can always be highlighted and selected, taking you to WebTV Today (see Figure 10-2). The Today In display is basically an on-screen billboard for WebTV Today.

Adventurous surfers wouldn't think of limiting their Web viewing to WebTV Today suggestions, but the service does provide a nice starting point for important, broad topics. Every day, WebTV Today provides selections related to sports, entertainment, general news, money and finance, health, and shopping.

Here's how to reach WebTV Today:

1. **From anywhere on the Web, press the Home button on the remote or keyboard.**

2. **On the Home screen (called Web Home in WebTV Plus), highlight and select the large central portion of the screen or the** WebTV Today **link beneath it.**

If the central portion of the Home screen happens to be displaying today in around town when you select it, you're taken to Around Town, not WebTV Today. Rather than attempt to synchronize your selection to that changing portion of the screen, just use the WebTV Today link beneath the center banner.

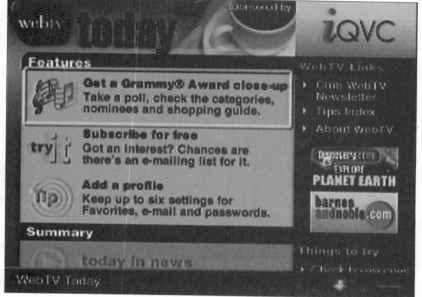

Figure 10-2:
WebTV
Today
features
different
destinations
every day.

WebTV Today is self-explanatory — simply scroll down the page to see your choices. Each topic area (sports, health, news, and so on) leads to another WebTV screen containing feature stories. When you select any link on one of these topic-specific pages, you're taken to the Web site providing news on that subject. In this fashion, WebTV Today functions as a well-designed directory for content from around the Web.

Along the right side of the WebTV Today screen are some intriguing links that, for some users, provide the best part of WebTV Today:

- ✔ **Club WebTV Newsletter.** Club WebTV is an electronic, on-screen monthly publication that gives subscribers a certain sense of community and a way of getting in touch with WebTV management. Each Club WebTV newsletter contains news, editorials, answers to reader questions, news about the service, technical tutorials, a few features, and an archive of past issues.

- ✔ **Tips Index.** The Tips Index is basically a big list of ideas and little tutorials. The items on this list remind you of little service features and help you accomplish tasks — all of which is, of course, covered in this book.

- ✔ **About WebTV.** This section provides a tour of the WebTV service and gives basic, clear information about its main functions.

- ✔ **Things to try.** All the "things" in this list link to Around Town features covered earlier in this chapter.

Chapter 11

Using Interactive Television

*W*hy has the Internet become so popular? The answer can be summed up in a single word, one of the most important words of our information age: *plastics*. No, not plastics — I meant to say *interactivity*. As a WebTV user, you have a great chance to understand interactivity from a hands-on perspective and to push it right up against the *passivity* of television. Okay, fine. Now what on earth is interactivity?

Interactive entertainment is the opposite of passive entertainment in that it invites the viewer to participate. Television is passive entertainment because it requires nothing besides a couch and a well-stocked refrigerator. You can do nothing to affect the course of a TV drama — a frustrating predicament in many cases. Although passive television entertainment has a selection of channels and programs, no menu of selections exists within a program. You are force-fed.

Imagine if the television were a different sort of device, one that accepted input from you, the viewer, to determine the course of the programming. Well, in a sense, the fantasy has become reality. WebTV doesn't affect the passivity of television programs, but it turns the television itself into an interactive device. No longer is the "boob tube" just a passive viewer for scripted programs; with WebTV, it's also an interactive Web surfer. Best of all, you can make this transformation happen while you're watching TV, without disrupting the programming the set was originally made for.

The Web and TV — Joined at the Hip

WebTV is designed to be used with television, not to replace it. Good thing, because the programming on the Web can't compete with television programming — the Web is great in its own way, but it's different from television. The Web's strong points are as follows:

- **Information.** The Internet began as a way to exchange information, and though it has evolved considerably since the early days, it's still an unparalleled way of simply finding things out. The Web, which was invented only a few years ago, has made it even easier to get news, do research, and ferret out hard-to-find information about almost any topic.

- **Personal contact.** You won't find a better way to meet people with shared interests than going online. Of course, meeting someone over an electronic device isn't quite the same as meeting in person. Nevertheless, the interactive nature of cyberspace is partly a result of the fact that millions of people are plugged into it and can all talk to each other.

- **Products and services.** The commercial nature of the Internet has grown dramatically. Not only is it a shopper's haven, but some services, such as online stockbrokers, offer features you can't find offline.

Now compare how television differs in these areas:

- **Information on TV?** Well, TV does have news, newsmagazines, sports, and many other informational programs. No doubt about it, television always had information delivery as part of its mandate in our homes. How much choice do you, the viewer, have over the quality of information you receive over the tube? Aha! That's the difference between TV information and Web information. Watching TV, you get only the news — and the depth of that news — that a particular channel deems important for you to know. On the Web, you get exactly what you're looking for, as shallow as a headline or as deep as a current-events research project.

- **Personal contact on TV?** Unless you build personal relationships with your favorite soap opera characters or forge close friendships with the smiling anchor of the evening news, you don't get a lot of personal interaction through the TV. You and your sister in the next state may both be watching David Letterman at the same time, but the TV doesn't give you a way to share the experience.

- **Products and services on TV?** Well, there's always the Home Shopping Channel, if you have cable. Here again, the rigidity of television, compared to the Internet, comes through loud and clear. You are offered only what "they" think you want. This, as we all know, is rarely accurate — are you one of us or are you one of them? And if you don't have cable, what are you left with? Infomercials — 30-minute hard sells to buy one product. On the Web, you could use that same time to research the entire history of a product, order five versions of it, and still have a few minutes left over to send an e-mail message to your sister.

You might think from this rant that I am against TV, but that's far from the truth. My goal is to point out the differences between television and the Web. The Web's strengths are weaknesses on TV, but television runs circles around the Web in the following crucial ways:

- ✔ **Self-contained entertainment.** Passive entertainment has its benefits. Most of us enjoy sitting back and being told a story or watching a talk-show host fawn over a celebrity, without having to interact (or even really pay attention, for that matter). On the Web, if you don't interact, nothing happens.

- ✔ **Movies.** Although the Web is a multimedia environment, it doesn't display moving pictures with the fluidity of television. The typical Web experience is based on pages, not moving scenes. This limitation will change in the future, but for now, the Internet is relatively static compared to TV.

So the big point is that TV and the Web are meant for each other. It's a perfect marriage. The Web's informational, personal, and service-oriented strengths mesh with TV's complete, fluid entertainment. When joined at the hip, as they are with WebTV, they act together to transform your TV from a passive device into an interactive multimedia powerhouse. It's twice as fun as it was before.

Logging on during a TV Program

WebTV is modest in its requirements: You don't even need to turn your attention away from the television to get it started. It would be awkward indeed if you had to always choose between being logged on to the Web and watching a program in progress. The system is designed to work *with* the television, and it reaches its full potential when used simultaneously with TV.

Logging on to the Web while watching TV could hardly be easier. Just follow these steps (unless your Web TV Classic is hooked up through your VCR, in which case you should skip down to the next set of steps):

1. **Press the Web button on the remote at any time.**

2. **If you want to watch the logon process, press the TV button of WebTV Classic or the View button of WebTV Plus.**

   The logon process probably isn't as interesting as something you could watch on TV. Whether or not you watch the logon, the system enters the Web and waits for you at the Home screen.

WebTV doesn't wait for you forever. If it doesn't receive a selection from you in ten minutes, it automatically logs off so that your phone line isn't occupied unnecessarily. You may log on during a TV show and then get so absorbed in watching the show that you forget to use the Web. (Of course, this has never happened to me. At least, not very often. Well, not in the last day or two.) If you're automatically logged off, you need to log on again when you're finally ready to do something on the Web.

After logging on, you can switch back and forth between the television and the Web without limitation. Doing so is a one-step process: Simply press the TV/Video button on the remote or the View button on WebTV Plus. It toggles to the mode that's not currently on your screen.

If a WebTV Classic set-top box is connected to a VCR instead of to the TV directly, you need to make a few more button-pushes to switch back and forth:

1. **Press the Web button on the remote to log on to WebTV.**

2. **To view the Web, press the TV/VCR button on your VCR remote.**

   The button on your VCR might be labeled slightly differently. In any case, press the button that switches your screen from television broadcast input to VCR input.

3. **With the television remote, change the channel to that required to view input from the VCR.**

   It's the same channel you use to watch movies — usually channel 3 or 4.

With WebTV Plus, even if the set-top box is connected to the VCR as described in Chapter 2, you need to use only the single WebTV remote control to switch back and forth between Web viewing and TV viewing. This added convenience is courtesy of the fact that a WebTV Plus set-top box is a broadcast and cable receiver in its own right, just like your television. It's one of the big differences between WebTV Classic and Plus, and it makes navigation between the Web and TV simpler.

WebTV turns the television into a new interactive device. The enhancement is drastic, not to mention very cool, and can be explored in many ways. You'll find that sometimes you just want to use WebTV by itself — the Internet without television enhancement. And of course everyone still likes to just watch TV at times without Internet enhancement. But when the two are brought together, the sparks fly. (That's a metaphor. If sparks really fly, yell loudly and unplug everything.)

Using WebTV Plus Crossover Links

WebTV Plus takes a step forward in the integration of television programming and Internet programming. In both Classic and Plus, your WebTV experience is essentially divided: You're either watching TV or viewing Web pages. (I'm not counting picture-in-picture capabilities. Classic users with PIP television sets can have the Internet and TV on the same screen, and all Plus users, regardless of their TV models, can place a TV window on the same screen as a Web page.) This division between the Web and TV is bridged by WebTV Plus to a greater degree than by WebTV Classic. And that bridge is built with TV Crossover Links.

TV Crossover Links are little icons that appear on your screen in different places, at different times, to different ends. Figure 11-1 illustrates a Crossover Link as it appears during a broadcast of the TV show *Baywatch*. These links all share one function: to send you to a particular place on the Web that relates to what you're watching on TV. And the Crossover Links all share the same basic *i* appearance.

Figure 11-1:
A TV Crossover Link as it appears when watching TV through WebTV Plus.

In their most prevalent manifestation, TV Crossover Links appear on the TV Home screen next to a program title, when you're watching that program. For example, they appear next to almost all movies broadcast on cable or satellite TV. Here's how to use them:

1. **On the TV Home screen, highlight and select the program title, if it includes a TV Crossover Link.**

   Not all shows have Crossover Links. Find a movie playing on some channel, and you'll probably see a Crossover Link.

2. **On the Program Info screen, highlight and select the Web site link.**

   You can see the *i* Crossover Link next to the movie (or program) title.

3. **Wait for WebTV to log on to the Internet.**

   While WebTV is logging on, you can continue watching the program. After logging on, and while you continue watching TV, WebTV goes to the Web site related to the program. Then, after the site is located, your screen switches automatically to the Web, leaving a picture-in-picture TV window on your screen so you can still watch the program.

A less-frequent version of TV Crossover Links appears on the TV screen, even when the TV image is at full size. (Refer to Figure 11-1.) It appears for only a brief time — not during the entire program. Here's how to take advantage of these fleeting Crossover Links:

1. **When you see a Crossover Link on the TV screen, press the Select button on the remote (in the middle of the Arrow buttons) or the Return key on the keyboard.**

   A panel appears at the top of your TV screen (see Figure 11-2). The panel has two on-screen buttons. If you change your mind about using the link, highlight and select the `Watch TV` button. If you want to see the link, continue to Step 2.

Figure 11-2: When you click a TV Crossover Link during a program, you see this panel.

2. On the Crossover Link panel, highlight and select the Go to Web Page **button.**

At this point, WebTV logs on to the Internet (if it's not already logged on) and goes to the Web page associated with the link. (See Figure 11-3.) During the log on, you can continue to watch TV. When the Web page is located and displayed, your screen automatically switches to the Web, shows the page, and puts a picture-in-picture TV window in the lower corner.

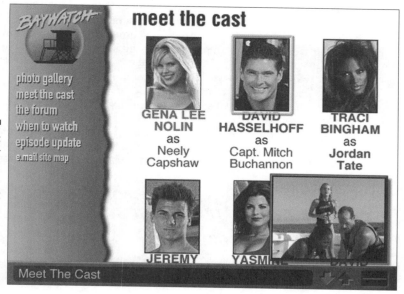

Figure 11-3: Crossover Links lead to Web-relevant Web pages and place a PIP TV window on the screen.

3. View the Web page while continuing to watch the program.

The Web page has some information relating to the program or the movie. WebTV Network has developed some special Web sites about certain popular TV shows, and you might be taken to one of them. Or the site might be produced by another company or individual and selected by WebTV for its relevant content. As of this writing, most movie Crossover Links take you to the Internet Movie Database, where you can look up cast members, read reviews of that movie, and gather other information about the film.

Playing Along with Game Shows

WebTV Plus takes interactive TV further than WebTV Classic. The Plus service is definitely for people interested in the convergence of TV and the Internet. In addition to the television browsing, planning, and recording features described in Chapter 5, WebTV has partnered with some TV shows to bring specific interactive experiences into the living room.

Have you ever thought it would be fun to play along with TV game shows from home? Of course, many of us do to some extent; I humiliate myself in front of friends and family on a nightly basis when *Jeopardy* is broadcast. But that kind of shout-at-the-TV participation seems removed, somehow, like the difference between watching a play and acting in it. WebTV Plus can't put you in front of the cameras, but it does give you a truly interactive TV experience with at least two shows: *Jeopardy* and *Wheel of Fortune*.

Other television shows — *Judge Judy, Dateline, Newshour with Jim Lehrer,* to name a few — provide WebTV Plus crossover features. I'm including instructions for playing *Jeopardy* and *Wheel of Fortune* in this section because they're (at this writing) the most involved WebTV Plus crossover programming ventures and, frankly, my favorites of the available interactive TV shows.

Registering for Jeopardy and Wheel of Fortune

Jeopardy and *Wheel of Fortune* are affiliated, and that affiliation saves you some time. Register to play either game through WebTV Plus (it's free), and you're registered to play both. Here's what you need to do before you first play one of the games:

1. **At the beginning of either show, look for the WebTV Interactive *i* icon in the upper-right of the TV screen, and press the Go button on the remote or the Return key on the keyboard.**

   If the Web side of WebTV Plus is not logged on, it connects now and automatically takes you to the player panel of whichever game is showing on TV. After the connection is made, you see the TV show in the center of your screen, with panels on the left and bottom of the image reserved for instructions and game selections. You can see and hear the show at all times.

   The interactive *i* icon might appear during the show, not only at the beginning. Frankly, it would be better if it appeared more often. I once missed it at the start of *Wheel of Fortune,* and waited for twenty minutes before seeing it again. I'm easily disappointed.

2. **Highlight and select the** `Sign Me Up` **button.**

3. **Enter your name in the field as indicated.**

4. **Enter your address and phone number in the fields as indicated.**

5. **Enter your age and gender as indicated.**

6. **Choose a player name — it can be any name or group of letters — and enter it as indicated.**

7. **Enter your e-mail address as indicated.**

Shortly, you receive an e-mail with your player name and password. You need them to play future games, so it's a good idea to save this e-mail in case you forget those crucial bits of information.

The optional keyboard is not essential for playing either game, but it's useful, especially in *Wheel of Fortune*. *Jeopardy* is rather simple to play with just the remote. (It's still easy to get answers wrong, though.)

Playing Jeopardy through WebTV Plus

Jeopardy is a fast-moving game. It would be impossible for most people (certainly me) to type answers before the on-air contestants speak them. So, the online version of the game has been transformed into a multiple-choice contest. You may play with other people in the room but not against them. The idea is to pit your speed against the contestants on the show.

You remember how *Jeopardy* works — each clue is an answer to a question you must provide. The WebTV game provides you with three solutions to each clue, one of which is always `None of the above`. (See Figure 11-4.) Using the arrow buttons of the remote or the keyboard, highlight and select one of the three choices (the middle choice is always highlighted first). You can't change your mind. When one of the show's contestants responds to the clue, correctly or wrongly, your time is up and WebTV tells you (immediately beneath the TV picture) whether you're right or wrong.

Your score adds up (or spirals downward) exactly as on TV — each clue is worth to you what it's worth in the show. What about Daily Doubles, which occur three times during the course of the game? You may wager all your points, half their value, or no points. Same deal for Final Jeopardy.

Don't change channels at any time during the show! You lose the game panel and your score-in-progress.

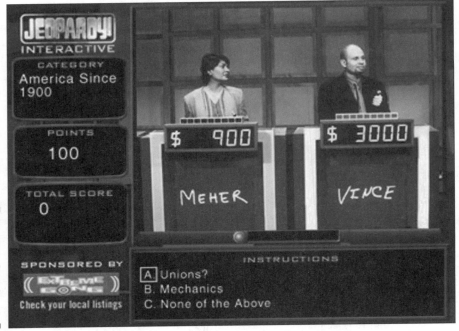

Figure 11-4:
Playing along with Jeopardy through WebTV Interactive.

Playing Wheel of Fortune through WebTV Plus

There's no practical way to spin the big wheel when using WebTV Interactive. Nor can Pat Sajak hear you when you talk back to him. These breaches of reality aside, interactive *Wheel of Fortune* is fun to play.

The entire goal of the WebTV game is to solve the puzzle — and quickly. No need to wait for your turn to spin — you never spin, and it's always your turn. Just concentrate on solving the puzzle. (See Figure 11-5.) A ticker counts down your points, second by second, and the only way to stop it and retrieve the remaining points is to solve the puzzle. The money values of the wheel have no bearing on your game.

If you've registered for *Jeopardy,* use that user name and password to play *Wheel of Fortune.* If not, follow the instructions previously listed to register for both games.

Figure 11-5:
Playing
Wheel of
Fortune
through
WebTV.

After you cross over to the Web side for an interactive game, you must wait for a new puzzle to begin — no jumping in mid-puzzle. One advantage to playing the interactive game is that the puzzle board, partly filled in with letters, remains visible on your game panel at all times. You know how annoying it is during the TV show to wait for the camera to show the board? That's never a problem with the WebTV version.

During commercials, the TV image expands to fill the entire screen and then contracts within the game screen when the show resumes. As with *Jeopardy,* don't change channels. If you do, you lose your score.

One final hint when playing *Wheel of Fortune.* Watch your spelling! If you mistype a word when solving the puzzle, you lose all your points for the current puzzle. After you enter a solution, you can't change or correct it.

Making Use of Commercials

Commercials — the bane of TV addicts everywhere. Of course, these breaks are sometimes opportunities for the time-honored refrigerator raid or the quickie phone call. But you haven't seen real opportunity until you've had the Internet one button-click away. Commercial breaks may no longer seem long enough when you get into the habit of flipping to the Web during them. Short as they are, commercials enable you to stay in touch with your widespread e-mail friends or look up the cast of a Sunday-afternoon movie.

Before long, jotting e-mail might replace snacking as the traditional commercial-break activity. Even on computers, the availability of e-mail has transformative properties on people who normally don't like to write letters. Now that you don't even have to leave the couch, you might end up being a more diligent correspondent than ever before.

Follow these steps to optimize those precious two or three minutes of commercial time:

1. **When a commercial starts, use the TV/Video button of the WebTV Classic remote (or the View button of Plus) to switch to WebTV.**

   If a WebTV Classic set-top box is connected to your VCR — not directly to your television — use the TV/VCR button of the VCR remote to switch to WebTV viewing.

2. **Grab the keyboard and press the Mail key.**

3. **On the Mail list screen, highlight and select** Write.

4. **Type the address and begin writing your e-mail.**

   See Chapter 6 for breathtaking details about e-mail.

Unless you're jotting down a short note, you probably aren't going to finish your masterful epistle before switching back to the TV show in progress. No problem. Just leave WebTV parked at the Write a Message screen. At the next commercial break, press the TV/Video button on the Classic remote (or the View button on the Plus remote) to return directly to the letter. If you've been gone longer than 10 minutes, you must highlight and select the on-screen Reconnect button to get back online. Your unfinished letter awaits you.

Watch your phone calls!

As I describe in Chapter 2, logging on to WebTV is normally a free phone call that doesn't even appear on your phone bill. However, you might want to check what kind of phone service you have. Some telephone plans allow you to make a certain number of local calls without charge, and then a per-call fee kicks in. Others allow unlimited local calling for a basic monthly cost.

It's important to know what kind of phone service you have when we're talking about writing e-mail during commercials. Because commercials show up every 10 or 15 minutes, and WebTV automatically logs off after 10 minutes of inactivity (called the *timeout* period), chances are you'll be knocked offline quite often. It's only a slight inconvenience because logging back on requires a simple button-push on the remote and takes a few seconds. But if you have the type of phone service with limited free local calls, you could have an unpleasant surprise waiting on your next phone bill. If you plan on logging on often, call your local phone company to determine what kind of local service you have.

One nifty possibility of writing e-mail during commercials occurs when you correspond with someone who also has WebTV and who is watching the same program you are. In that situation, the potentials of WebTV meet the unique features of e-mail for a fun digital-age communication. If you and your friend each shoot notes back and forth during the commercials, it amounts to a conversation about the TV show — or about anything else, for that matter — across the digital couch. Every time you switch to WebTV during a break, a note is waiting for you, and you have a chance to respond to it. This kind of rapid-fire correspondence is sometimes called interactive e-mail.

You can take rapid-fire digital communication a step further by chatting on the Web with other people watching the same program. During the 1999 Academy Awards, I was glued to the TV set, movie addict that I am, with my WebTV keyboard on my lap. I logged into a chat room about movies (see Chapter 8 to find out about chatting through WebTV) that was filled with other digitized souls simultaneously watching the awards and rooting for their favorite movies. (Not all of them were using WebTV, but that doesn't matter. When it comes to criticizing hairstyles and wardrobes, WebTVers and computer users are brethren.) It was easy to flip back and forth between the Oscars and the chat room, and it enhanced the fun of the evening tremendously.

Writing e-mail and chatting are just two ways to while away those empty minutes during commercial breaks. Any of the online activities described in Parts II and III can be applied, if briefly, to commercial breaks.

Chapter 12

The Multimedia Web

*W*hen it comes to the Internet, two buzzwords pop up all the time. One is *interactivity,* which simply means that you, the viewer, can participate in the experience. The Internet is strong on interactivity; in fact, it relies on it. The Web sits there as limp as an overcooked noodle until you interact with it — and then it becomes a spicy pasta marinara. Selecting a link gets the ball rolling, but until you make a selection, the Internet just stares at you blankly.

The other buzzword everyone associates with the Web is multimedia. *Multimedia* refers to everything in addition to text (writing) that you see on your screen. Big deal, right? We see multimedia every day. Well, remember that the Internet used to be located exclusively in a far-off place known as computerland, and not too long ago, computers displayed only text. Anything more exciting than a screen full of flickering words seemed like a rarefied glimpse of the digital Promised Land. Besides, computer users, being innocent, sensitive souls (occasionally mischaracterized as geeks), are easily thrilled.

In any event, multimedia consists of things like these:

- **Pictures.** Gather 'round kids, and let Uncle Web tell you of the days when pictures were never seen on the Internet. Well, never mind about that. Suffice it to say, the Web is full of pictures. Some even move.

- **Moving pictures.** These include movie clips, videos, and animations.

- **Audio.** Music, sound effects, soundtracks, and radio broadcasts can be found on the multimedia Web.

The Web is struggling to get up to television's speed in the multimedia department. Today's cutting-edge technology, however, is tomorrow's mature technology, and the day when the Web does sound and video as well as TV does it now can't be too far off. In the meantime, the Web has a lot going for it besides its early attempts at multimedia.

Pictures and Sound on the Web

Multimedia isn't the same on the Web as it is on TV. You don't see an integrated package of sight and sound fly out at you from the screen as soon as you turn on the WebTV box and log on. Remember, the Web is an interactive environment as opposed to the passive television environment; in many cases, you have to do something to enjoy moving pictures and sounds — not that it's difficult. In most cases, you need only to highlight and select a link to be rewarded with a song or an animated dance. The following sections describe the types of multimedia found on the Web and what you can expect when you view them through WebTV.

Untangling multimedia formats

Over the few years that WebTV has been around, some confusion has developed about what audio and video formats can be played through the service. If anything, that confusion has intensified as time has passed. Although the formats themselves continue to develop and evolve, WebTV is sporadic at updating its capacity to play new versions of those formats. The result is erratic performance and widespread head-scratching. Not to mention some annoyance. WebTV subscribers voice their desires clearly and articulately, and the subject of multimedia capability is continually a hot topic.

Much of the controversy and desire for better performance centers around RealAudio, described later in this chapter. RealAudio was invented by a company that continues to improve the product. WebTV built a business partnership with RealAudio right from the start but has failed to keep pace with improvements. As a result, much of the audio programming available on the Web works inconsistently through WebTV.

Of all the questions I receive from WebTV users, the confusing RealAudio situation is perhaps the most frequent. So, expanding on that topic, here's a rundown of several multimedia formats and how they behave through WebTV as of this book's publication. Remember, the service periodically upgrades its playback capacity, so the programming available to you might be improved by the time you read this.

MIDI. MIDI hasn't changed much during the past decade, and no upgrades to WebTV's basic MIDI capacity have been necessary. You can still listen to any MIDI file on the Web, if it's properly encoded and presented. If a MIDI file doesn't work for you, it's not your fault or, most likely, WebTV's fault.

Audio. WebTV supports several audio files as described next:

- **WAV.** WAV files are a type of audio files found on CDs, and they're sometimes used on the Web. Because WAVs are larger in size (not necessarily in song length, but in data size), they're not as popular as certain other formats. Still, it's good to have them.

- **MP3.** MP3 is an extremely popular music format that some Web programmers make available for downloading and streaming. MP3 capability is built into WebTV Classic and Plus, but there are problems sometimes. Remember that downloads are not possible on WebTV as they are on computers. However, streaming MP3 is possible, and short downloads that can be stored in your box's limited memory also work nicely. The upshot is unpredictability. You can't tell in advance whether an MP3 link on a Web page is going to work — you have to try it.

- **RealAudio.** This is the controversial one. Most radio stations simulcasting on the Internet use RealAudio. WebTV supports playback of RealAudio up to Version G2 (as of the publication of this book). RealAudio has evolved to version 7, one step beyond G2. By the time you read this, both systems might have moved forward, but the ongoing fact of WebTV life is that RealAudio is unpredictable. Some broadcasts encoded in version 7 don't work through WebTV.

- **Windows Media.** Windows Media is a high-quality format that competes with MP3. The May, 2000 upgrade brought Windows Media compatibility to WebTV.

- **Liquid Audio.** Nope. A competitor to MP3 and Microsoft, Liquid Audio programming requires a downloaded player.

- **Other audio formats.** WebTV supports AU, AIFF, and QuickTime audio formats, none of which is particularly important in the large Net-audio landscape.

Video and Animation. Smooth video is difficult to deliver from online sources even in the best conditions and even through computers. Following is the status of WebTV and various video formats:

- **VideoFlash.** This format was invented by WebTV and is rarely used on the Internet.

- **MPEG-1.** A fairly common format for delivering video clips. But they don't look too good over any kind of telephone modem, including those built into Classic and Plus units.

- **Macromedia Flash.** A format for delivering Web-site animations, Flash is important to the multimedia Web experience. WebTV has no problem with Flash versions 1.0 and 2.0, but Flash itself (as of this book's deadline) is up to version 4. Content produced with later Flash versions might not work through WebTV. However, some of those Flash-enhanced pages still display on WebTV but without the animations.

- **Macromedia Shockwave.** This format is the heavy-duty sibling of Flash. WebTV doesn't support it. Shockwave delivers some interactive games and sophisticated animation and video content.

Pictures. WebTV doesn't generally have trouble with still pictures. The system displays the four most common Internet graphics formats: JPEG, PNG, GIF (including GIF animations), and TIFF.

Fun with MIDI

Remember when a certain mid-length type of woman's skirt was called a midi? If you do remember, please forget it now because it has nothing to do with the kind of MIDI that you get on the Web. *MIDI* stands for Musical Instrument Digital Interface. Now that you know the definition, you have another good thing to forget.

Here's what you really need to know: MIDI creates music. It uses electronic keyboards, computers, and other digital music equipment, and one of its many uses is to provide a musical soundtrack to certain Web sites.

MIDI is best compared to the piano rolls on an old player piano or the cylinder with little spikes in a music box. That is, it's not like an audio recording of a real sound or performance, such as a flute playing. A MIDI recording is just a sequence of digital commands that's turned into music only when run through a device that creates digital sounds, such as a computer sound card. The commands get turned into notes played in prearranged patterns, rhythms, and melodies by the built-in sound card in your WebTV set-top box. Likewise, a player piano roll is not a recording, but it does contain sequences of notes that, when run through the piano, cause the piano to play a song.

When a MIDI composition is playing, you don't hear the same consistent result that you would if you were playing a compact disc. Take that compact disc from one CD player to another, and it sounds the same each time. But when you play a MIDI recording on different computer systems, it's likely to sound quite different — the piano roll is the same, but the player piano might be made by a different manufacturer and have a different sound.

The way that music plays is a major difference between computers and WebTV. In both cases, an audio circuit board, called a *sound card,* is needed. In a computer, that sound card can be removed and replaced, whereas in the WebTV box, it's there to stay. Because the WebTV audio hardware is installed for the long run and can't be upgraded, special care has gone into its design, especially when it comes to the playback of MIDI. This is fortunate because MIDI music is a big part of the WebTV experience — in fact, the WebTV soundtrack is in the MIDI format. If it didn't sound good, we'd all get tired of WebTV's soundtrack in a hurry.

When you listen to a MIDI song (or a song in any other audio format), you must remain on the page from which you started playback to continue listening. In other words, if you continue surfing the Web, even using the Back or Home buttons, the audio stops. This abrupt characteristic differs from audio on a computer, which continues as you surf around. On WebTV, if you want background surfing music, you must be satisfied with the built-in surfing soundtrack described in Chapter 4.

Some Excellent MIDI Sites

Many informational sites exist about MIDI technology, mostly designed for people who produce music with MIDI equipment, but that's not what I'm interested in here. For most people, the most fun MIDI sites are the ones that actually *play* music. They, in turn, lead to other sites you might prefer, and you might stumble across still others in your Web travels. I describe a few of my favorites in the following paragraphs. This list is hardly complete, but it can get you started. If you've already started, it will urge you on.

MIDI files are presented in two ways to WebTV users and computer users alike. Commonly, you access them by means of a link that reads "Play the MIDI piece" or words to that effect. You don't need to know the actual *file-name* (the computer name of the piece as it is stored on the host Internet computer) and never even see it. Sometimes, though, you're confronted with the actual file in hyperlink format. It's no harder to access when you see the filename — just highlight and select it as usual. What you do need to know is the file extension of MIDI files, so you can recognize them. MIDI files always have the *.mid* file extension. (A *file extension* is the last three letters of a file-name — the three letters following the period.) Any .mid file that has been created and stored properly and is presented as a hyperlink can be high-lighted, selected, and heard through WebTV.

When listening to MIDI through WebTV Plus, you may switch back to televi-sion viewing (or the TV Home screen) by pressing the View button (or the TV/Video button in WebTV Classic). What happens to the MIDI music you were listening to? Don't worry — it doesn't keep playing as you try to watch a TV show. The music remains suspended in pause mode, and you may resume listening to it at any time by pressing the View button again. If you log off the Web or let your Web session time out, the MIDI playback is disconnected.

The MIDI Farm

www.midifarm.com

The monster MIDI site on the Web. Much of the MIDI Farm appeals to musi-cians involved with MIDI production but everyone can enjoy the MIDI files sprinkled liberally about. Highlight and select any item to see another screen displaying the songs of that artist that are available for listening. Have a blast! I'm always impressed by the electronic interpretations of some songs, and I fall on the floor laughing at others.

Classical MIDI Archives

www.prs.net/midi.html#index

Being a sort of synthesizer jukebox of classical music, the Classical MIDI Archives site is worth a whirl. Its alphabetical linking scheme makes it easy to find composers. Classical music loses some of its sublimity when played with the synthetic sounds available with MIDI, but in some cases the sounds make the music more fun. Music of Bach comes across pretty well in MIDI format.

Standard MIDI Files on the Net

www.aitech.ac.jp/~ckelly/SMF.html

A great starting point for finding other sites with MIDI files, this page contains more than 40,000 links to sites related to MIDI. A search engine helps you find playable files in other locations. The URL is on the complicated side, so after you get to this page, add it to your Favorites if you want to return easily.

MIDICITY

www.midicity.com

When you get to MIDI City, the first thing to do is highlight and select ARTISTS and MUSIC, the default selection at the top of the page. That takes you to a small directory from which you can select collections of MIDI song archives. Much of the material connected to this site is located on other pages, so MIDI City acts as a directory. The Original Artists collection is my favorite — by and large, music composed specifically for the MIDI format sounds better than transcriptions of pop songs and classical music.

Ragtimers

www.ragtimers.org/midi/

This directory is all about ragtime in MIDI format, which sounds pretty good. This page presents a list of about two dozen sites featuring MIDI files.

Why RealAudio is a big deal

Internet veterans make a big deal out of RealAudio. Yet to a WebTV subscriber, it's just sound over the television. So what's all the fuss about? To understand the hype surrounding RealAudio, you must remember that the Internet, and computers in general, have been capable of multimedia for only a short time. Television has been numbing our minds — I mean, stimulating our cultural sensibilities — for decades. But even a few years ago, it was impossible to get sound over the Internet through a computer without going through an arduous process of downloading sound files and playing them through special software. Compared to flipping on a TV or radio, the process was about as rewarding as planting tomatoes to make a pizza.

Like the cavalry appearing on the horizon, a new process called audio streaming arrived to save the day. *Audio streaming* feeds audio from the Internet to your personal computer (or to WebTV) in a constant stream of tiny chunks. Each chunk is stored while the previous chunk finishes playing, and in this way, you avoid the odious process of downloading an entire piece of music (or other audio programming). The program is played in real time (no waiting), not later, not tomorrow, not when the software is configured and feels like it wants to play. RealAudio is a tremendous increase in convenience, and it makes surfing the Web a much happier experience for your ears.

RealAudio requires a few seconds to load the first small chunks of streaming sound. Keep your eye on the status box in the lower-right corner of the TV screen. While the beginning of the audio program is loading, the jagged line is activated, exactly as if you were loading a new Web page. Just before the audio begins playing, the line flattens. That's when you should perk up your ears.

Even More Fun with RealAudio

MIDI is a fun and easy way to get music over the Web and through your TV, but it has limitations. Here's what MIDI can't deliver:

- Real music, played on real instruments, as heard on real albums
- Audio programming that isn't musical, such as news broadcasts, talk shows, and radio stations

RealAudio is an Internet system that delivers all kinds of good audio stuff. It's not the only system of its kind, but it has established itself among computer users as the most popular and prevalent system, and it's incorporated in WebTV. You don't need to know anything to use RealAudio, and — because this is WebTV — you don't need to buy anything extra. As you cruise around the Web, just notice the references to RealAudio that appear on some Web pages. (Also, check the high-intensity RealAudio that I describe a bit later in this section.) When you see a link offering a RealAudio presentation, just highlight and select it to hear it.

On some Web pages, you might see a choice of RealAudio links labeled 14.4K, 28.8K, 56K, and high speed. Those numbers refer to computer modem and digital connection speeds. Faster speed results in better audio quality. All WebTV users, Classic and Plus, should click the 28K or 56K options (select the former if you have an older Classic box), avoiding high-speed options such as DSL and cable modems.

RealAudio is a great addition for computer-based Web users, but getting it sometimes involves hassles. If the computer's browser isn't preloaded with RealAudio, you need to surf to the RealAudio Web site and download a special RealAudio program that plugs into the computer's Web browser. Then the computer-savvy Netizen must configure the Web browser to recognize the newly installed program and use it whenever a RealAudio sound file is selected. With WebTV, by contrast, you must follow this step:

1. Do nothing.

RealAudio is built into the system. Any time you highlight and select a RealAudio music selection or other audio item, RealAudio simply plays it. (See the sidebar describing audio formats presented previously in this chapter to find out more about RealAudio formats that WebTV supports.)

I've been using the word *program* when referring to something you hear with RealAudio. This might be overstating the case a bit. RealAudio presentations aren't the same as television programs and aren't always similar to radio programs. (You can, however, find radio stations on the Internet, as I describe a bit later in this chapter.) A RealAudio presentation can be as short as a small excerpt of music or as long as a continuous broadcast. Here are some examples of the kinds of RealAudio goodies you can expect to find on the Web:

- ✔ Selections from music albums
- ✔ Entire songs or albums — RealAudio jukeboxes
- ✔ Recorded interviews
- ✔ Prerecorded news reports
- ✔ Radio broadcasts
- ✔ Audio portions of television programs
- ✔ Concert broadcasts
- ✔ Sporting events
- ✔ Specialty programming, such as movie reviews, comedy shows, past-generation radio, and syndicated programs

RealAudio works only while using the Web, and it shuts off automatically if you press the TV/Video button (or the View button for WebTV Plus users) to switch to a TV show. Similarly, any RealAudio program stops playing if you move to a different Web page (as does MIDI music). This is something of a disadvantage in comparison to computer systems, in which RealAudio continues playing its program as the user continues to surf the Web.

RealAudio Sites Worth Visiting

Some Web sites incorporate RealAudio to such a prominent degree that the audio capability is the site's primary attraction. Because RealAudio is such a fun feature on the Web, some people (like me) become RealAudio fans and go out of the way to save such sites to Favorites for frequent visits. This section describes some of the best sites.

RealGuide

www.realguide.com/

Created by the company that developed RealAudio, RealGuide is the RealAudio program guide on the Web, as shown in Figure 12-1. Be sure to try the Daily Briefing link, a customizable audio newsmagazine.

Figure 12-1: The RealGuide home page links to the best RealAudio directories on the Web.

RealGuide is the essential Favorites addition for RealAudio. (See Chapter 7 if you're unsure how to create Favorites.) From the RealGuide page, you can link to some of the best RealAudio attractions on the Web. As you find RealAudio pages and shows worth saving and revisiting, be sure to add them to your Favorites also.

RealGuide has expanded by leaps and bounds in the past two years, and now covers non-RealAudio types of programming, such as streaming MP3 and song downloads. Some of this expanded coverage can't be accessed by WebTV, but much of it can. There's no effective way to guide WebTV users through the rich resources of this site. Your best bet is to explore and try links that seem interesting. Avoid links that say "Download Music," and go for the Radio and Music directories.

Shadow RealAudio Radio Theater

`www.shadowradio.org`

Nostalgia buffs love this site. Here (see Figure 12-2) you can listen to old *The Shadow* radio broadcasts from the golden, pre-television age. (Maybe it was golden only in our imaginations.) The site works well through WebTV; for best results, choose the `28.8` option.

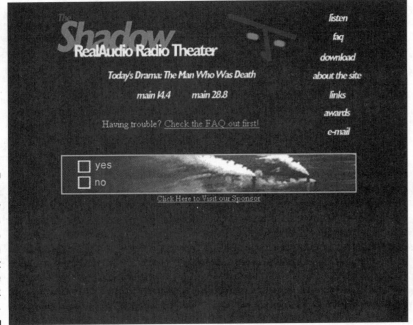

Figure 12-2:
The Shadow
RealAudio
Radio
Theater site
is a blast
from the
way-back
past.

RadioTower.com

`www.radiotower.com`

RadioTower (see Figure 12-3) is an online guide to Web radio stations from around the world. Search the database by country or broadcasting category, using drop-down menus. When you arrive at the home page, scroll down and select the `Enter No Frames` link for easiest navigation. This site doesn't host any original programming, but links you to radio sites around the Web. Accordingly, WebTV's response to the stations is uneven — some work and others don't. But overall I've had good success finding broadcasts through this directory.

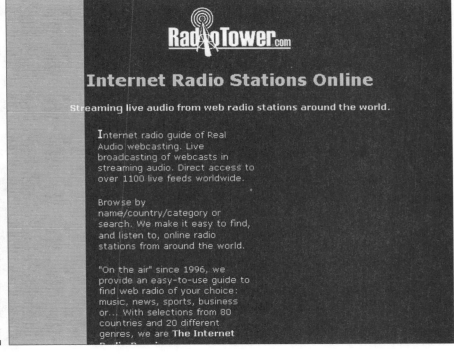

Figure 12-3:
The RadioTower directory of Internet radio stations netcasting with RealAudio.

Artist Underground

www.aumusic.com/m1.shtml

Artist Underground is one of the most famous musical sites among those "in the know." Shown in Figure 12-4, Artist Underground is a famous Web location for hearing unsigned bands who place recordings of their songs here. From the beautiful home page, highlight and select `view the artist list` to begin your adventure. If you're looking for a particular artist or group, be sure to check the `Artist List` link near the bottom of the map page. Needless to say in this commercial age, you can buy compact discs of the musical artists you hear directly from the site.

Figure 12-4:
Artist
Under-
ground is
famous
among
musicians
and music
lovers.

Video through WebTV

For technical reasons far too boring to elucidate, video streaming through the Internet is far more difficult than audio streaming. In most cases, video comes through in a halting, jerky fashion. Imagine a movie projector with the hiccups, and you get the gist of streaming video. WebTV, however, has developed a new technology called VideoFlash that customizes video transmission to the specifications of the WebTV Internet terminals.

Before you get too excited, you should know that VideoFlash won't make you give up TV programming. There isn't much VideoFlash content, as they say in showbiz. As more Internet programmers produce content for VideoFlash, it will become more useful to WebTV users.

Chapter 13

Creating Web Pages with WebTV

● ●

● ●

*H*TML is an acronym that stands for one of the following things. Guess which.

✔ HyperText Markup Language

✔ Helen Tells Margaret Lies

✔ Hideous Trolls Molest Latvians

✔ Help! Ten Malicious Lemmings!

It stands for HyperText Markup Language. My apologies to Helen and all trolls. *Hypertext* is the defining feature of the Web. The Internet existed long before the Web, but it lacked an easy navigational system. Hypertext, which is a fancy word for *link*, makes surfing the Web possible. *Markup Language* is the underlying code, or computer language, that makes hypertext possible.

This is probably sounding more technical than you would like. But HTML is not that difficult. HTML is a system of tags you can type. When those tags are inserted into text, they tell WebTV (or the Web browsing program of a computer) how to format the text so that it looks like a nice Web page. HTML can make words big or small, center lines on the screen or push them to the right or left, and change the color of the words or the color of the background beneath the words. HTML is responsible for displaying pictures and playing sounds.

Every Web screen you see through WebTV has underlying HTML tags. The tags themselves remain invisible, but they're at work formatting and displaying the words and images on your screen.

Three items of good news are associated with HTML:

✔ HTML is fairly easy to learn.

✔ You can learn just what you want to and forget the rest.

✔ I show you the basics in this chapter.

Things to Do with HTML

HTML is typically used to create Web pages. In addition, WebTV understands HTML when its tags are embedded into e-mail messages, e-mail signatures, and newsgroup bulletin board postings. Many of the more adventurous WebTV members delight in creating elaborate backgrounds for their e-mails or e-mail signature files.

To HTML or not to HTML?

One of the most important upgrades to WebTV (Classic and Plus) has been the addition of Page Builder, which is explained later in this chapter. Page Builder lets you create HTML pages (Web pages) without knowing a scrap of HTML or ever seeing HTML tags in the process.

WebTV subscribers were making Web pages before Page Builder came along by learning HTML and using free page-hosting services on the Web. Page Builder gives you a choice:

✔ Learn enough HTML to create your page manually

✔ Use Page Builder and let WebTV handle the background code for you

Clearly, using Page Builder is easier for anyone with little or no experience with HTML. The advantage to creating your own HTML code outside Page Builder is that you begin with a clean slate. Page Builder uses templates within which you place text, pictures, and links. Those templates make life easy, but they predetermine

some choices. Although it's possible to override those choices and enter your own HTML in Page Builder, the program is generally for those who don't care to learn HTML.

Page Builder has many templates from which to choose, but they're all on the simple side, designed to deliver basic text-plus-pictures pages with no tables, frames, or many other formatting elements. For many users, that's just fine! Page Builder is a beautiful tool for quickly assembling and publishing pages with family photos and descriptions, for example.

To HTML or not to HTML? The answer lies in how ambitious and technically minded you are. One solution is to start with Page Builder and then see whether, over time, you develop a hankering for a more complex page. If you do become motivated to learning a bit of HTML, this chapter isn't going anywhere. (As long as you don't rip it out of the book and leave it on a plane.)

Here are a few things you can do with HTML:

- ✔ Make a piece of music play whenever anyone gets e-mail from you
- ✔ Make a starry background appear behind your e-mail letters
- ✔ Create an e-mail signature with large, colored letters
- ✔ Using a free home-page hosting service (see the *WebTV For Dummies Online Directory*), create a Web page for the world to see

Many people are satisfied in creating just a touch of pizzazz for their e-mail and don't bother with the larger project of making a whole Web page. You can get as involved as you like in creating Web material. But when creating HTML for e-mail, keep in mind a few points:

- ✔ HTML in e-mail is interpreted differently by various computer e-mail programs. If you're sending to a WebTV address (webtv.net), there's no problem. But your careful HTML creation might appear as gibberish code to someone reading it on a computer. America Online (aol.com) and CompuServe (compuserve.com) recipients will definitely not see what you want them to see.

- ✔ For the same reason, be careful when posting messages to general newsgroups outside WebTV. Computer users might not see exactly what you intended.

- ✔ Not everyone enjoys receiving highly formatted e-mail with pictures and sounds. For one thing, those pictures and sounds take time to load, and e-mail is supposed to be a fast experience. If you put HTML in your e-mail signature, you always have the option of removing the signature when you write an e-mail.

- ✔ Page Builder, described later in this chapter, is for only full-fledged Web pages. You can't transfer your Page Builder creations to e-mail or e-mail signatures.

A Shockingly Brief HTML Tutorial

HTML is not a difficult thing, but it's a big thing. It started out as a small system of basic codes that enabled early Web page creators to format text with **bold**, *italic*, and <u>underlined</u> styles, plus various heading sizes, bulleted lists, and other design elements. At the beginning, nothing was too fancy, but that changed quickly. Through continual developments and additions, HTML has grown to sizable complexity.

Calling all keyboards

You can do many things with WebTV sans the optional keyboard. You may have put off buying one, satisfied with the on-screen keyboard for entering bits of text required by some Web pages.

If you're interested in creating HTML documents of any sort — whether they be e-mail signatures

or full-fledged Web pages — you need that keyboard. Well, *need* might be too strong a word. Suffice it to say that you will probably be driven beyond the realm of sanity should you attempt to create HTML code with the on-screen keyboard.

Most computer users create their Web pages with the assistance of HTML editors (like specialized word processors) that automate the creation of tags. Such programs allow them to manufacture tables, frames, style sheets, and other evolved formatting entities with complicated tag structures. You can't use these HTML editors with WebTV, but WebTV does provide its own editing tool called Page Builder, which I describe later in this chapter.

Most WebTV members create Web pages either with Page Builder or with the online wizards provided by the service that hosts the Web site. (I describe several such hosting services in the Online Directory.) When making an e-mail signature (and in some cases when creating a whole Web page), most WebTVers do it the old-fashioned way, by writing the HTML codes manually.

This section is an overview and tutorial of basic HTML tags, plus some tags that work *only* in WebTV. In the following sections, I describe the tags, show you what they look like when you type them, and explain what they do. I can't demonstrate what they look like on the screen, translated into beautiful formatting. For that, you need to refer to some of the HTML help sites I list in the Directory.

The best way to test your understanding of HTML tags and try out the fun formatting I describe in this chapter is to create an e-mail message and send it to yourself. When you receive your own e-mail, you can see whether the tags are creating the results you hoped for. In this fashion, with repeated experiments, you can refine your use of the tags until you feel comfortable enough to create an HTML e-mail signature or a Web page. (See Chapter 6 for details about using e-mail and Chapter 4 to find out how to create an e-mail signature.)

Getting started with HTML tags

HTML is a system of tags that tell WebTV how to interpret and format your text. The tags are always enclosed in the < and > brackets like this:

```
<tag>
```

Find those brackets now on the keyboard, and get used to typing them; you'll be using them a lot. The two basic kinds of HTML tags are

- ✔ **Opening tags.** Opening tags tell WebTV that a certain type of formatting should begin. They look like this:

  ```
  <tag>
  ```

- ✔ **Closing tags.** Closing tags tell WebTV that the formatting currently in effect should end. Note the forward slash in the closing tag:

  ```
  </tag>
  ```

The forward slash, placed just after the first bracket and before the tag, is the only thing that distinguishes a closing tag from an opening tag. The tag itself, representing a formatting command, remains the same. Here's an example of the opening and closing tags that turn plain text into **bold** text:

```
<b> </b>
```

To make text bold, you place the opening tag before and the closing tag after the text that you want to appear bold. The bolded text might be a single word in a sentence, an entire sentence, a paragraph, or a page. For example, I might want to create the following sentence:

This sentence contains a single **bold** word.

To make that sentence appear correctly formatted in HTML, I type this:

```
This sentence contains a single <b>bold</b> word.
```

Here are two basic details to remember about HTML tags:

- ✔ You don't need to type any spaces between the tags and the word, the sentence, or the text block that they affect.
- ✔ An opening tag remains in effect until a closing tag is reached. Forgetting to put in the closing tag can yield unsightly results.

<html> and <body> tags

Two very important tags normally appear at the beginning of any HTML page or e-mail. The first one is absolutely necessary and looks like this:

```
<html>
```

As with all HTML tags, it doesn't matter whether or not you capitalize the <html> tag. Throughout this chapter, I write tags in lowercase.

The <html> tag informs WebTV that what follows is not plain text, but text with HTML tags inserted for formatting. Without the <html> tag, all subsequent tags are displayed in raw form, with the brackets, and have no formatting effect. It's not a pretty sight, so don't forget to start every HTML document with the <html> tag.

The <html> tag must be the very first thing you type when you start creating your HTML document. Don't let any typed characters appear before it. I find it a good idea to put the <html> tag on its own line at the top of the page, so that I can see at a glance that it's there and nothing lies before it.

The second important tag isn't necessary but is common and powerful. This is what it looks like:

```
<body    >
```

Notice that I typed a few spaces before the second bracket. In this example, the spaces represent other specifications that typically follow the word *body*. The <body> tag contains at least one formatting specification and usually several; otherwise, the <body> tag wouldn't be there at all. Here are some common formatting specifications placed in the <body> tag:

- ✔ **Font size.** WebTV recognizes seven different font (type) sizes, where size 1 is the smallest and size 7 is the largest. Here's how the font size tag appears for size 5:

  ```
  <body font size=5   >
  ```

  Again, I left spaces in the <body> tag for more formatting commands. You can stuff quite a few of them in there.

- ✔ **Font color.** WebTV recognizes many font colors. They're identified either by a specific color name or by an individual code comprised of letters and numbers. (See the "Backgrounds" section of the Directory to find sites that display available colors, names, and codes.) Here's how the font color tag appears if you want your letters to appear blue:

  ```
  <body font color="blue">
  ```

  The quotes surrounding the word *blue* are necessary.

- ✔ **Background color.** You can change the background color of your e-mails, your e-mail signature, or your Web page by using the background color tag. Suppose that you want a green background. (Almost 200 background colors are available. See the "Backgrounds" section of the Directory for sites that display them.) The tag would look like this:

  ```
  <body bgcolor="green">
  ```

  The quotes surrounding the word *green* are necessary.

✔ **Background image.** If you prefer, instead of changing the background color, you may replace it with a picture or a tiled background texture. The "Backgrounds" section of the Directory lists several sites that allow you to link directly to the images at that site for creating background pictures on your Web page or e-mail. The tag must include the URL of the linked image; for example:

```
<body background="http://webpage/image.gif">
```

This example assumes that the background image you're linking to is a GIF image, with the .gif file extension — most background images are indeed GIFs. Some, however, are JPEG images and end with the .jpg extension.

As you can see, the <body> tag can be a complex, yet powerful, little beast. It can define to a large extent what your HTML page looks like. Let's assume, as an example, that you're going for a background using the dark olive green color, white letters, and size 3 text throughout the body of your HTML page. This is what the <body> tag would look like:

```
<body bgcolor="darkolivegreen" font color="white" font size=3>
```

Following are a few important notes about the all-important <body> tag:

✔ You should place the <body> tag immediately after the opening <html> tag. You may place it on a new line and even separate it from the <html> tag by a blank line for clarity. (The blank line doesn't affect the formatting.)

✔ The closing tag for <body> is not necessary. Because the <body> tag is a defining tag for the entire body of your page, it's assumed to last until the end. You may, however, use the </body> closing tag whenever you want to bring its formatting attributes to an end.

✔ You may use the elements of the <body> tag independently, whenever you like. For example, you may change the color of a single line of text by placing these opening and closing tags before and after that line:

```
<font color="blue"> </font color>
```

Fun with fonts

You can change the appearance of the typeface on your Web page, e-mail, or e-mail signature by making creative use of the font tags. Following are five basic font attributes you may command:

✔ **Bold.** Bold text is darker and a bit thicker than regular text. You may make text of any color **bold** by placing the following tags around it:

```
<b> </b>
```

✔ **Blackface.** A kind of superbold, blackface darkens and thickens text even more than the bold attribute. Use the following opening and closing tags:

```
<blackface> </blackface>
```

✔ **Italics.** Italic fonts are slanted sideways, *like this*. Use the italics tags, which appear as follows:

```
<i> </i>
```

✔ **Underline.** You may <u>underline</u> text by using the underline tags:

```
<u> </u>
```

✔ **Strikethrough.** Strikethrough text looks `like this`. Use the following tags:

```
<s> </s>
```

Here are a couple notes to keep in mind when using the font tags:

✔ You may mix attributes freely. When mixing font tags, use separate tags, each with its own brackets, and be sure to close each tag when you've finished the formatting. For example, suppose you want to create a sentence with bold and italic text, like this one:

This sentence is bold and italic.

This is how you would create that style with HTML tags:

```
<b><i>This sentence is bold and italic.</i></b>
```

✔ Put your closing tags in the reverse order of the opening tags, as in the preceding example. The first tag opened is the last tag closed.

✔ You may insert font tags around a single word, a whole sentence, a whole paragraph, or the entire text of the page. Just remember to put in the closing tags.

Adding pictures

The Web is a colorful, high-graphics showcase, and it would be a shame if you couldn't add pictures to your own Web designs. Fortunately, it's not hard. In addition to background images, mentioned previously, you can float artwork to the foreground of your Web pages, your e-mail, or even your e-mail signature.

TECHNICAL STUFF

Storing your HTML

So you've decided to jazz up your e-mails by including HTML tags as described in this chapter? It takes some practice, but it's a lot of fun. As you embark on your HTML experience, one trick might come in handy: storing HTML code in your signature.

This trick is on the complex side, but it's worth understanding if you want to use HTML tags in the message body of your e-mails. The more complex your tags, the more you need a way to store them. Otherwise, you must type them manually every time you write an e-mail — an intolerable situation. Manual typing of tags is acceptable only occasionally, such as when you want to emphasize a sentence by putting it in bold type or underlining it.

You can save more complicated HTML tagging in your e-mail signature. Unfortunately, you can't see the HTML tags on the Write a Message screen when composing e-mail. So, for this trick to work, you must copy and paste the HTML from your signature to the Write a Message screen.

Follow these steps carefully:

1. **On the Web Home screen, highlight and select** Setting.

2. **On the Settings screen, select** Mail.

3. **On the Mail Settings screen, select** Signature.

4. **On the Mail Signature screen, type your HTML tags as described in this chapter.**

5. **Highlight and select the** Done **button.**

Remember to use the <html> opening tag and the </html> closing tag. Type whatever tags you'd like to use in the body of your HTML-enhanced letters. You can type both opening and closing tags, or just the opening tags, adding the closing tags when you type the letter. Most signatures have a name in them, of course, and you can add

that, too. The main purpose of this trick is to enhance the body of your e-mail, not the signature, but you can make the code work double-duty. Remember, though, that if you're going to use this code as your signature, you must close all your tags.

Now that you've created some HTML code in your signature, WebTV saves it permanently. You can change it at any time, adding and deleting tags, by repeating the preceding process.

Now you're ready for the second half of this trick. Follow these steps when you want to write an HTML-enhanced e-mail:

1. **Go to the Mail Signature screen as described in the preceding list.**

2. **On the Mail Signature screen, use the Copy and Paste commands described in Chapter 6 to highlight and copy your entire signature.**

3. **Press the Mail key on the keyboard or the Home button on the remote and select** Mail **from the Home screen.**

4. **On the Mail List screen, highlight and select** Write.

5. **On the Write a Message screen, move the cursor down to the message body area and use the Paste command (Cmd+V on the keyboard) to add your signature there.**

6. **Write your e-mail within the HTML tags and then select the** Send **button.**

That last step can get tricky, depending on how many tags you have. After you do this a few times with the same signature, you'll get the hang of it. Basically, you must write your e-mail body between your string of opening tags and your string of closing tags. Make sure the <html> tag is the very first thing in the e-mail body and that your letter ends with the </html> closing tag.

You acquire and use pictures in two basic ways:

✔ **Link to pictures and sounds that you find on the Web.** Every picture on the Web is stored on a *server* (Internet computer) in the form of a *file*. Picture files are a specific type of computer file and can be in one of several *file formats*. In most cases, pictures are stored in GIF format, with the .gif file extension at the end of the filename, such as this:

```
picture.gif
```

GIF-formatted picture files are commonly known as GIFs. The location at which a GIF is stored is identified by a URL, just like Web pages. Here's a hypothetical GIF address:

```
http://www.oursite.com/nicepicture.gif
```

✔ **Transload pictures.** *Transloading* is a process by which you copy a file from one location to another location. Computer users call such a process *downloading and uploading,* and they store the file on the computer's hard drive between the downloading and uploading phases. Because you can't download or upload with WebTV, transloading services do it for you, automatically, at no charge.

What you need to know about transloading

Transloading is a free service provided by a few independent companies (not by WebTV Networks) to help people who are building Web sites without computers. The transloading process copies a file from one server (Internet computer) and places the copy on another server.

What's the point of making such a copy? When your Web page includes a picture, the page must read that picture from a graphics file stored somewhere. You can tell your page to read the file from its original location, or you can transload the file to a new location. Transloading is important because if many Web pages begin reading files from a certain server (a server that stores many beautiful background images, for example), the server is stressed handling all the requests.

Failing to transload the graphics images you use is considered rude at best and unethical at worst. Telling your Web page to read a file from the original server is sometimes referred to as *stealing* or *bandwidth theft*. The proper approach is to transload the file to the server storing your Web page, and then tell your Web page to read the file from there. As a benefit, your page operates more quickly and smoothly because all your files are on the same server.

Some Web sites offer collections of linkable files and invite people to link directly to them, bypassing the transloading process. In some cases, this invitation is made to only WebTV users by WebTV-friendly sites. This is convenient, though you might want to eventually transload the file so your site displays more quickly. Above all, check the site from which you intend to use an image or a sound file, and look for its policy on linking. If no such invitation exists, Netiquette requires that you transload the image to the host server of your Web page.

By far, the most popular transloading service among WebTVers is Star Boulevard, which is at the following URL: `transload.starblvd.net`.

The Directory portion of this book lists several collections of graphics images on the Web, some of which invite direct linking. After you've selected an image to present on your Web page, you need to use the correct HTML tags to display it. Before you can tag the image, you need to know its URL. You may have transloaded the image file to the same server as your Web page, or you may be linking directly to its location in a graphics collection. If you're creating HTML for e-mail, you're most likely linking to the file's original location.

One way or the other, you should make note of the URL at which the picture is stored. With that information in hand, here's the tag with a made-up URL:

```
<img src="http://www.ourworld.com/nicepicture.gif">
```

Remember to use the quotation marks; they're necessary.

Adding music

You can add music to your Web page, e-mail letters, or e-mail signature as easily as adding pictures. All the same principles apply. You must

1. **Find a music file you like.**

   The Directory can help; check the "MIDI Files" section.

2. **Transload the file to your host server if necessary and possible.**

   This is not necessary if you're creating an e-mail signature.

3. **Tag the file in your HTML document.**

Here's the tag to use for linking to sound files, with a made-up URL:

```
<embed src="http://www.oursite.com/nicemusic.mid">
```

 MIDI files are not the only type of music file, but they're the most convenient. MIDI files are much smaller than other music file types and, therefore, load and play sooner than others. If you use any other sound format, you inconvenience your viewers by making them wait for the file to load. Such a delay is especially annoying with e-mail.

Special HTML tags

A number of HTML tags work only through WebTV. They're fun to incorporate into your pages, even if only other WebTV users can see their effects. Here are two such tags.

Transition effects

Transition effect tags create special effects when viewers move from one page to another. Place one of these commands into your <body> formatting tag to make the page display with a flourish. Here's the code for making your page slide onto the screen from right to left:

```
<body transition="slideleft">
```

Other transition commands are self-explanatory, and can be used in place of the `slideleft` command. Here they are:

```
Slideup, slidedown, slideright, slideleft, wipeup, wipedown,
wiperight, wipeleft, blackfade, wiperighttop, wipelefttop,
wiperightbottom, wipeleftbottom
```

Transparency

You can make images on your Web page appear with a varying degree of transparency. This effect is great if you want the background of your page to show through the picture. Selecting a high degree of transparency makes the image's presence subtle, even ghostly.

The `transparency` command works in cooperation with the `img src` command described in a previous section. You determine the degree of transparency on a scale between 0 and 100. (Setting 0 transparency would be pointless.) Here's an example:

```
<img src=http://www.oursite.com transparency="80">
```

A transparency of 80 makes the picture very light and see-through but still distinguishable.

All about Page Builder

Page Builder — WebTV's site-creation feature — is the most important upgrade addition to come along between the second and third editions of this book. Although it was possible to make Web pages through WebTV before Page Builder, and many subscribers did, this tool eases the learning curve for anyone who doesn't care to learn the underlying code of Web design.

The truth is, you can type HTML tags into Page Builder if you want to. But the beauty of the feature's modular, plug-and-view approach is that you don't have to. You can create attractive, basic Web pages without knowing a darn thing except how to navigate with the keyboard and follow instructions.

Page Builder is one of those WebTV features, like e-mail, that really benefits from the optional wireless keyboard. Strictly speaking, you don't need the keyboard to create a page but having one sure quickens the process. The more text on your page (as opposed to pictures), the more the keyboard comes in handy.

Page Builder presents a two-step design-and-publish process. Don't worry about accidentally putting up a Web page that doesn't look good or shows your inexperience. WebTV doesn't make your page public until you explicitly tell it to. It's pretty much impossible to accidentally publish a page. But even if you do, not many people are likely to find it if you don't send them a link. Furthermore, you can change and improve your page as often as you like, whenever you like.

The first step is to visit the Page Builder section. These steps, and all steps in this section, refer to both the Plus and Classic service:

1. **On the Web Home screen, highlight and select** Community.

2. **On the Community screen, select** Page Builder.

Unlike other WebTV features such as Mail and Search, the Page Builder portion has some arcane legal language attached to it. The reason for the Page Builder license agreement is that Page Builder is a publishing application that enables you to put yourself on the Web and, in so doing, represent WebTV Networks as well. Most computer software programs that are downloaded contain licensing agreements that you must click through to indicate your agreement. You don't need to download Page Builder, but you do need to agree to its license terms. These are the salient points:

✔ You get 3 megabytes of Web space. That's sufficient for most purposes, unless you use many, many pictures.

✔ WebTV owns your page address (URL) — so you can't sell it to your dry cleaner.

✔ If your account isn't in good standing, WebTV can pull your page.

✔ WebTV has the right to place banner ads on your page. That right is exercised — at this writing, just one ad appears on most pages.

✔ You must not use your page for any commercial purpose, such as selling merchandise.

✔ You're legally liable for the content of your site, and certain content categories (pornography, libel, hate, promotion of hacking, and others) are prohibited.

✔ You may not use your page to infringe copyright, such as by copying a portion of a book or magazine article to the page.

✔ If any single household account violates any of the license terms, WebTV has the right to yank the Web pages for all that household's accounts.

This summary covers the main points of the Page Builder license agreement, but you shouldn't consider yourself well informed about the document until you read it yourself. Whether you actually read it or not, you must highlight and select the I Accept button to get past it and begin building your page.

Choosing a Page Design

The first step in creating a page is choosing a template that serves as your basic page design. Actually, though I'm putting this step first, the fact is that you can change your basic page design at any time, even after plugging in your page's text and graphic content. Some people prefer writing the text and putting in the links first and plugging everything into a template second. You can do that — my feelings won't be hurt. Well, maybe a little hurt. Anyway, this chapter must present this feature in some order, and this is the way I prefer to do things.

When you first enter the Page Builder area, you land on the Page Builder Index. To choose your page design, follow these steps:

1. **On the Page Builder Index screen, highlight and select** Create.

2. **On the Choose a Page Style screen, highlight and select any thumbnail image of a page template.**

   You have 36 page styles to choose from. Select the plus sign in the upper-right corner of the screen to view the next group of styles.

   You can change to a different style at any time without disrupting your page's content. Some of the styles carry distinct themes (such as baseball) and others are colorfully unspecific.

WebTV automatically saves your page design. You don't actually see it on your screen until you add some content items to your page. You may add six item categories to pages:

- ✔ Headings
- ✔ Text
- ✔ Pictures
- ✔ Links
- ✔ Lists
- ✔ Page breaks

A separate screen exists for adding each of these item types, as described in the next sections.

Adding a heading

Each page can have multiple headings, which serve to divide the page into portions. Whether those portions contain text, links, pictures, or a mix of features is up to you. The first step is to create a heading for your page's first portion.

When planning and designing Web pages, it's helpful to get out some old-fashioned aids — paper and pencil. There's nothing like drawing pictures to clarify how you want your page laid out. You don't need to write all your text by hand, but try outlining the basic portions of your site on paper before diving into Page Builder.

You can add a heading (and other items) at any time. After choosing your page style as described previously, you see the Choose an Item to Change or Remove It screen. Either proceed from there or, if you are starting in a new session, follow these steps:

1. **On the Page Builder Index screen (the first screen you see when entering Page Builder), highlight and select the page you want to add a header to.**

   WebTV stores multiple pages under construction, so you might have several, or just one, page to choose from.

2. **On the Page Settings screen, highlight and select** Change Page.

3. **On the Choose an Item to Change or Remove It screen, highlight and select** Add an Item **(see Figure 13-1).**

4. **On the Add an Item to Your Page screen, select** Heading.

5. **On the Add a Heading to Your Document screen, type a heading.**

   Headings should be short — not more than a few words. If you want a longer heading, consider making the text size small as described in the next step.

6. **Select** Small, Medium, **or** Large **for your heading size.**

7. **Select whether you want a divider line and if so whether you want it before or after the heading.**

   If this heading is not your first heading for the page, use the Move Up and Move Down buttons to shift the order in which the headings are listed.

8. **Highlight and select the** Done **button.**

When you finish this process, Page Builder displays your page as it looks so far. At this point (which recurs often as you continue to add items), you may highlight and select any item (header, text, picture, link — whatever) to change it or remove it.

Figure 13-1:
Choose Add
an Item
to add
text, lists,
pictures,
links,
headings,
and page
breaks to
your page.

Adding text to your page

Text is a major part of most Web pages. If you really don't like writing, you might want to just place pictures in your page. That's perfectly fine for a family album, for example. But even picture-intensive pages have some text to describe the pictures. Follow these steps to add text to your page:

1. **On the Page Builder Index screen (the first screen you see when entering Page Builder), highlight and select the page you want to add a header to.**

2. **On the Page Settings screen, highlight and select** Change Page.

3. **On the Choose an Item to Change or Remove It screen, highlight and select** Add an Item.

4. **On the Add an Item to Your Page screen, select** Text.

5. **On the Change Text screen, type a title for the text you're about to add.**

   This title is like a Heading (see the previous section), but doesn't eliminate or supplant any headings you've already put in. Think of it as a subheading that applies specifically to the block of text you're adding. Or feel free to leave that space blank, especially if you've already placed a heading for this portion of text.

6. **In the Type Your Text Here window, type some text.**

7. **Highlight and select** Small, Medium, **or** Large **for your text font size.**

8. **Highlight and select** Plain, Bold, **or** Italic **for your text font style.**

9. **Highlight and select the** Done **button.**

There is no limit (aside from the endurance of your fingers) to the amount of text you can put in. (There's the 3-megabyte total size limit to your Web page, but it would take an astonishing amount of text to reach that ceiling.)

Adding pictures to your page

This section describes the most complicated part of Page Builder. It doesn't need to be complicated, actually, but it can be if you want. And believe me, lots of people put up with complexity to get the pictures they want on their pages. Adding pictures is complicated because the graphics can come from a variety of sources, and sometimes it takes a few steps to make everything work correctly.

The first thing you need to know is that you can pull your graphics from two primary warehouses of pictures:

- The WebTV Art Gallery
- Your Page Builder Scrapbook

The WebTV Art Gallery holds more than a hundred clip art images in various categories. The pictures are cute, in some cases, and can be used decoratively. Upon trying a couple, it quickly becomes apparent that their actual size is much larger than they appear in the Art Gallery thumbnails. Truthfully, the Art Gallery images are not very popular.

The Scrapbook is another story. This repository is blank at first — use it to store images you might want to use on your page. These selected images can come from two basic sources:

- The Web
- E-mail pictures people send you

Possibilities abound. The next sections describe how to select pictures from the WebTV Art Gallery, load up your scrapbook, and select images from your Scrapbook.

Raiding the WebTV Art Gallery

Art Gallery: It sounds like a museum, doesn't it? No such luck. These drawings, in the style of clip art, serve a decorative function on most Web pages. Follow these steps to use the Art Gallery:

1. **On the Page Builder Index screen (the first screen you see when entering Page Builder), highlight and select the page you want to add a header to.**

2. **On the Page Settings screen, highlight and select** Change Page.

3. **On the Choose an Item to Change or Remove It screen, highlight and select** Add an Item.

4. **On the Add an Item to Your Page screen, select** Picture.

5. **On the Add a Picture to Your Document screen, highlight and select** WebTV Art Gallery.

6. **On the Art Gallery screen, select any image.**

   Use the plus sign in the upper-right corner of the screen to view more selections, and use the minus sign (or the Back button) to backtrack.

7. **On the Change Picture and Caption screen, type a title for the picture.**

   The title appears above the picture on your Web page. Picture titles are usually short.

8. **Type a caption for the picture.**

   The caption ends up beneath the picture and can be as long as you want.

   Note the Replace this Picture and View this Picture links above the caption and title windows. Select Replace this Picture if you have a last-minute change of mind, and remember that you can replace pictures at any time in the future. Select View this Picture to see a full-screen (and somewhat distorted) image of the picture. There's really no point in viewing the picture in full-screen size because you can see it on this screen anyway.

9. **Highlight and select the** Done **button.**

Adding a picture to your Scrapbook from Mail

You can easily add to your Page Builder Scrapbook any pictures sent to you in e-mail, as attachments. This handy feature makes sharing family photos through the Web a breeze. Any family member with e-mail (not necessarily WebTV e-mail) can send you photos as e-mail attachments, which you can then put into your Scrapbook and eventually onto your Web page, which then can be viewed by the entire family.

If you receive a photo through e-mail, follow these steps to add it to your Scrapbook:

1. **On the Web Home screen, highlight and select** Mail.

2. **On the Mail List screen, select the e-mail that has an attached picture.**

3. **On the Message screen, highlight and select** Scrapbook.

   The Scrapbook option appears on the left selection bar only when the e-mail you're viewing has an attached picture.

4. **On the panel that appears, select** Add to Scrapbook.

5. **On the next panel, notifying you that the image was saved, select** Continue **to select another e-mail attachment or** View Scrapbook **to see the contents of your Scrapbook.**

Plus users can add a picture from the television or VCR through e-mail. Follow the instructions in Chapter 6 for clipping an image from the TV or VCR in e-mail, and send that mail to yourself. You then have the attachment ready for adding to your Scrapbook as described in the preceding list.

Adding a picture to your Scrapbook from the Web

You can stock your Scrapbook with images found on the Web by using a process called transloading, discussed earlier in this chapter. Transloading is easier when the destination is the Page Builder Scrapbook than when you're creating a page outside WebTV. That's welcome news, because transloading is perhaps the most complex operation most WebTV users attempt.

Transloading into your Scrapbook is fairly easily accomplished using a service called WebScissors. This site is not an official WebTV service, but it is recommended by WebTV — and by me. The beauty of WebScissors is that it knows where your Scrapbook is and deposits your desired pictures right into it with little fuss on your part.

WebScissors can determine the previous URL you visited, which means that your life is made easier by visiting WebScissors immediately after viewing a picture you want to add to the Scrapbook. Here is the easy-to-remember URL for WebScissors:

```
www.webscissors.com
```

You can always enter that address using the Go To feature on the Options panel. I recommend you save the WebScissors site to Favorites. If you plan to use it a lot while cruising around the Web, snapping up pictures right and left, you'd do best to assign the WebScissors Favorite a dedicated F-key, as described in Chapter 7. That way, you're one keypress away from adding a picture to your Scrapbook at all times.

Now to get down to the nuts and bolts. Here's how to transload a picture from the Web into your Scrapbook using WebScissors:

1. **Anywhere on the Web, highlight and select a picture you'd like to add to your Scrapbook.**

   This step doesn't work with every picture you see because not all pictures are links. And some pictures that *are* links lead to entire pages, not just to the picture display. Assuming you get your Scrapbook images from picture warehouses that invite transloading (see the WebTV Directory section), selecting a picture image displays the picture by itself, with its own URL. That's what you want.

2. **Go immediately to the WebScissors site.**

   Either enter the WebScissors URL or use a preset F-key that you assigned to your WebScissors Favorite. If you must make a stop between viewing the picture and viewing WebScissors (such as to your Favorites), use the Info selection of the Options panel to write down the URL of the picture you want to transload. One way or another, WebScissors needs to know that URL.

3. **On the WebScissors screen (see Figure 13-2), enter the URL of the picture you'd like to add.**

   If you go directly to WebScissors from viewing your desired image, highlight and select the Show Last URL Visited link. If not, type the URL of the picture you want.

4. **Highlight and select the** Show Images **button.**

5. **On the panel that appears, select** Add to Scrapbook.

6. **On the next panel, highlight and select** Continue **to resume surfing the Web or** View Scrapbook **to check out your scrapbook.**

After this process, the image you selected is copied from its original location to your Scrapbook. Remember, as explained earlier in this chapter, it's best to take picture only from sites that give you permission.

Adding a picture from your Scrapbook to your page

After you've acquired some pictures from the Web in your Scrapbook, assigning them to your page is similar to choosing from the Art Gallery:

1. **On the Page Builder Index screen (the first screen you see when entering Page Builder), highlight and select the page to which you want to add a header.**

2. **On the Page Settings screen, highlight and select** Change Page.

3. **On the Choose an Item to Change or Remove It screen, highlight and select** Add an Item.

4. **On the Add an Item to Your Page screen, select** Picture.

5. **On the Add a Picture screen, select** Your Scrapbook.

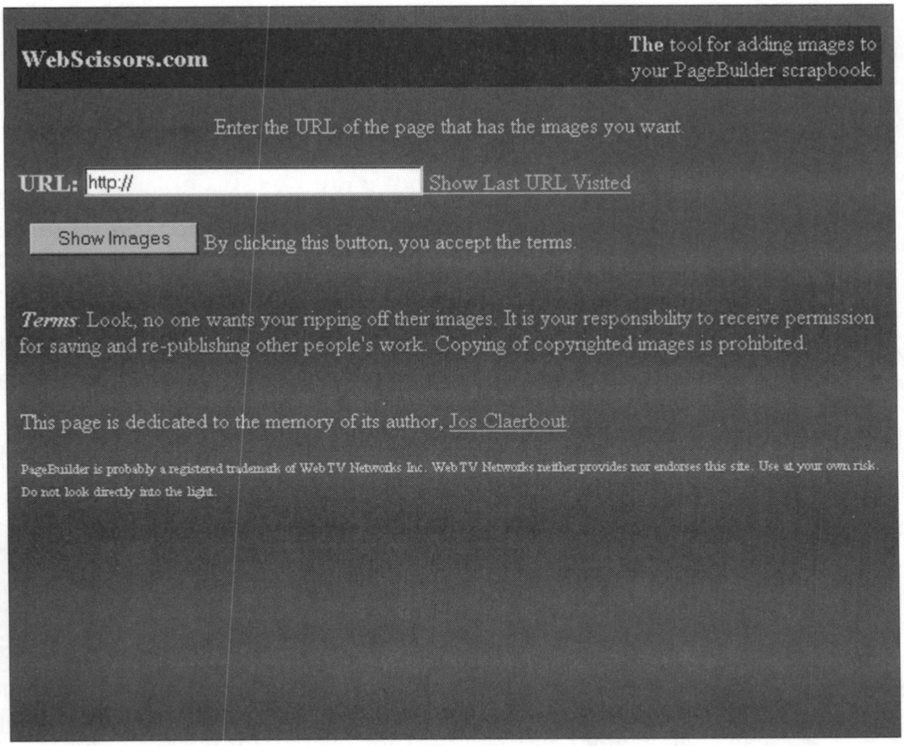

WebScissors.com

The tool for adding images to your PageBuilder scrapbook.

Enter the URL of the page that has the images you want.

URL: http://   Show Last URL Visited

Show Images   By clicking this button, you accept the terms.

Terms: Look, no one wants your ripping off their images. It is your responsibility to receive permission for saving and re-publishing other people's work. Copying of copyrighted images is prohibited.

This page is dedicated to the memory of its author, Jos Claerbout.

PageBuilder is probably a registered trademark of WebTV Networks Inc. WebTV Networks neither provides nor endorses this site. Use at your own risk. Do not look directly into the light.

Figure 13-2:
The
WebScissors
transload
site.

6. **On the Your Scrapbook screen, highlight and select a picture to add.**

7. **On the Change Picture and Caption screen, type a title and caption for the picture.**

8. **Highlight and select the** Done **button.**

Adding links to your page

Lists of Web links have been popular page features for years. Page Builder makes it easy to assemble such lists:

1. **On the Page Builder Index screen (the first screen you see when entering Page Builder), highlight and select the page to which you want to add a header.**

2. **On the Page Settings screen, highlight and select** Change Page.

3. **On the Choose an Item to Change or Remove It screen, highlight and select** Add an Item.

4. **On the Add an Item to Your Page screen, select** Links.

5. **On the Add a List of Links to Your Document screen, type a title for this list.**

   The title may or may not be inserted instead of a heading. You may have both a title and a heading. It's usually easier to make a title here than to use a heading because a heading must be created on a different screen.

6. **Type a short description for each link on your list.**

   The description is what visitors see in the list, not the Web address.

7. **Type the Web address (URL) for each link on your list.**

   You may import URLs from your Favorites collection by selecting the Add from Favorites button. Select sites to appear on your list from the Add from Your Favorites screen and then select the Done button.

8. **Highlight and select the** Done **button.**

Adding a list to your page

You may use bullets to offset lists from the rest of your text content. Your link lists have bullets, and you can designate a list that isn't links, also. These lists can contain anything, really — they're great for recipes or for making a series of brief points. Here's how to build a list of non-links onto your page:

1. **On the Page Builder Index screen (the first screen you see when entering Page Builder), highlight and select the page to which you want to add a header.**

2. **On the Page Settings screen, highlight and select** Change Page.

3. **On the Choose an Item to Change or Remove It screen, highlight and select** Add an Item.

4. **On the Add an Item to Your Page screen, select** List.

5. **On the Add a List to Your Document screen, type a title for the list.**

6. **In the spaces provided, type your list items as you want them to appear on your page.**

   If you need more than the four lines provided, highlight and select the Add a Line button; a new line appears magically. Continue to use that button if you need to.

7. **Highlight and select the** Done **button.**

Adding page breaks

There's no limit to how long a Web page can be, but there is a limit to how long one *should* be. If you've ever visited a page that's a mile long, you know how inconvenient the endless scrolling can be. Don't put your visitors through the same experience. Use page breaks to divide one long page into two or more pages.

Televisions don't have long screens, and Page Builder uses rather large type, even at the small setting. Using pictures and lists adds to the page's length even more than adding text. What I'm getting at here is that it's better to break up the page too often rather than too infrequently. Small pages look good on WebTV.

When you add a page break, Page Builder automatically places a next page link on each page but the last and a previous page link on each page but the first. To add a page break, follow along:

1. **On the Page Builder Index screen (the first screen you see when entering Page Builder), highlight and select the page to which you want to add a page break.**

2. **On the Page Settings screen, highlight and select** Change Page.

3. **On the Choose an Item to Change or Remove It screen, highlight and select** Add an Item.

4. **On the Add n Item to Your Page screen, select** Page Break.

5. **On the Break One Page Into Two screen, use the move up and move down buttons to specify where the page break is located.**

   Page breaks are items just like lists, pictures, and other page items. Imagine the break as a visual item that you place between two other items. That's where the page will break.

6. **Highlight and select the** Done **button.**

Previewing and Publishing Your Page

This is where your Web site moves from the privacy of Page Builder to the public realm of the Internet. Now don't be nervous — you can make it private at any time. It's common to take a page off the Net to work on it and then put a revised version back into public view.

This section describes how to preview your page after making alterations in Page Builder and how to publish it on the Web.

Previewing

Every time you add, delete, or alter an item on your Web page, Page Builder displays the whole page after you select the Done button. That's a sort of preview, but it shows the page within the context of Page Builder, with the left selection bar still showing. A dedicated Preview feature can display your page at any time exactly as it will appear to visitors. Follow these steps:

1. **Make any additions or changes as described in previous sections.**

2. **Highlight and select the** Done **button of whatever screen you're using.**

3. **On the Choose an Item to Change or Remove it Screen, select** Preview **from the left selection bar.**

You can see your page exactly as it will appear to visitors after you publish it, with the exception of a notice at the top of the screen: "You are previewing you page. Press Back to return to editing it." You can even see, at the bottom, the banner ad that appears on all published pages.

At this point, only you can see the page; no one else has access to it. After you've previewed your page, press the Back button to make further changes or to publish the page.

Publishing

Ready to go live? Publishing your page means putting it up on the Web, getting a URL assigned to it, and (if you want) having it listed in your public list of pages. Here's the process:

1. **Make any additions or changes as described in previous sections.**

2. **Highlight and select the** Done **button of whatever screen you are using.**

3. **On the Choose an Item to Change or Remove it Screen, select** Publish **from the left selection bar.**

4. **On the Title and Description for Your Page screen, type a title.**

   The title appears at the top of your page and also in the information bar at the bottom of the screen when your page is viewed.

5. **Type a description.**

   The description appears when your page is listed in your public list of pages, which is optional.

6. **Highlight and select the** Continue **button.**

7. **On the Ready to Publish screen, select the** Include in Public List **box if you'd like to your page to appear in your public directory of Web pages.**

    You can have more than one Web page. When you have two or more published pages that are selected to appear in your public list, WebTV automatically generates a directory of your pages. That directory is always located at this URL:

    http://community.webtv.net/*yourname*

8. **On the Congratulations! Screen, make note of the URL of your published page.**

9. **If you'd like to send an e-mail announcement of your page, select** Send Mail Announcing Your Page.

    The Write a Message screen is displayed, with a link to your page included at the bottom of the e-mail. Just fill in the recipient's address, write a note (if you want), and send it off.

10. **If you'd like to add a link to your page to your e-mail signature, highlight and select** Add Its Address to Your Mail Signature. **Select** OK.

    The addition is made automatically, and a panel appears confirming the change to your signature. You can, of course, remove the link from your signature at any time.

11. **If you'd like to change the title or description of the page at this time, select** Change the Title or Description.

    You can alter the title and description, and anything else on the page, at any time.

12. **Highlight and select the** Done **button.**

You can make a private page public or a public page private at any time. Whether a page appears on your public list is completely up to you. The switch that adds and removes your page from your public list is on the Page Settings screen. You need to republish a page to make the switch. Here's how to make a private page public:

1. **On the Page Builder Index screen (the first screen you see when entering Page Builder), highlight and select the page you'd like to make private.**

2. **On the Page Settings screen, select** Change Public Listing.

3. **On the Title and Description for Your Page screen, highlight and select the** Include this Page in Your Public List of Pages **box.**

    Selecting this check box toggles between public and private. You can go either way.

4. **Highlight and select the** Done **button.**

Un-publishing and discarding

The time may come when you no longer want your page to be public. This is a different decision than wanting to remove a page from your public list. Removing a page from the public list does not remove the page from the Web.

Two more drastic removals are available:

- **Un-publishing.** Takes down your page, making it unavailable to visitors but keeping it in your Page Builder section for further work.

- **Discarding.** Deletes the page entirely, sending it into the great virtual void where all pages go eventually.

Both these actions are accomplished on the Page Settings screen. Here's what to do:

1. **On the Page Builder Index screen (the first screen you see when entering Page Builder), highlight and select the page you'd like to un-publish or discard.**

2. **On the Page Settings screen, select** Un-publish Page **to remove your page from the Web and continue storing it in Page Builder or select** Discard Page **to remove all traces of the page from Page Builder.**

   Discarding a published page un-publishes it, naturally.

3. **If you chose** Discard Page, **select** Discard **or, if you have a sudden change of heart,** Don't Discard **on the panel that appears,**

When you've discarded a page, you're returned to the Page Builder Index screen, where the discarded page is now missing from your collection of pages.

If you have many pages, published and un-published, Page Builder can seem like a cluttered mess. Cleaning it up one page at a time, following the preceding procedure, is a chore I wouldn't wish on anyone. Fortunately, you can discard multiple pages quickly, using the Clean Up feature:

1. **On the Page Builder Index screen, highlight and select** Clean Up **from the left selection bar.**

2. **On the Clean Up Web Documents, highlight and select the check boxes next to any pages you want to discard.**

Remember a few things here. First, this feature discards the pages, whether they're published or not. They will be Gone (with a capital *G*) if you do this. Irretrievable. Vanished. Get the picture? This isn't un-publishing; this is bulk discarding. Both published and un-published pages appear on this screen. By the way, you can check the memory allotment at the top of this screen — it shows, as a percentage, how much of your 3-megabyte storage allowance is currently occupied.

3. **Highlight and select** Discard **from the left selection bar.**

4. **On the panel that appears, highlight and select** Discard. **Or select** Don't Discard **if you change your mind.**

5. **Still on the Clean Up Web Documents screen, highlight and select** Scrapbook **to clean up your Scrapbook collection in the same fashion.**

Moving Items around Your Page

Page Builder relates to everything you put on the page — such as a picture, a heading, a list of links, or a block of text — as an *item*. Note that a list, for example, is not several items — the entire list is a single item. Each thing is added to the Add a . . . screen and incorporated onto your page as an item.

You can move items around on your page by shuffling them up or down the master list of items. This maneuver is accomplished on the Add a . . . screen related to that item. Suppose you want to move a picture, which is currently the fourth item down on your page, up to the third position. Here's what you do:

1. **On the Page Builder Index screen (the first screen you see when entering Page Builder), highlight and select the page you want to change.**

2. **On the Page Settings screen, select** Change Page.

3. **On the Choose an Item to Change or Remove It screen, scroll down to highlight and select the picture (or other item) you want to move.**

   The highlight box makes it easy to distinguish items. It jumps from item to item as you press the Down -arrow on the remote or the keyboard.

4. **On the Change Picture and Caption screen (if you chose a picture), highlight and select the** Move Up **button at the bottom of the screen.**

   The Move Up button is next to the Move Down button, and naturally you can select either one. Just above the buttons, a line of text tells you where the selected item (the picture) is on your total list — for example, "item 4 (of 9)." After selecting the Move Up button, that line of text quickly changes to "item 3 (of 9)."

5. **Highlight and select the** Done **button.**

About Your Page URL

All pages created with Page Builder are addressed with similar URLs. Your public list (which exists if you have two or more pages marked for your public list) is always at this URL:

```
http://community.webtv.net/YourName
```

Actual page addresses use that entire URL with an added element at the end that identifies your page title, like this:

```
http://community.webtv.net/YourName/PageTitle
```

Chapter 14

The Internet's Potential

My friends sometimes ask me how I can take the online world so seriously and whether it's as real to me as . . . well, real life. Little do they know I don't have a real life. That drawback notwithstanding, I do believe in the Internet's capacity to make substantial improvements in the quality and convenience of life. Furthermore, in my many years as a citizen of the Net, including my subscribing to online services such as CompuServe and America Online, I have known people for whom online access is much more than just a fun diversion.

A few hundred people from all over the world suffering from rare and debilitating forms of brain cancer still manage to talk each day by means of an e-mail support group. A woman with unusual religious convictions, living in a rural area and isolated from kindred souls, finds a second home in a message-based spirituality forum. Two people, wandering among online chat rooms, meet and establish a friendship that continues over weeks and months. Their connection deepens, they meet in person, and amazingly, a year after meeting in cyberspace, they get married.

For all the great success stories that hype the Internet's value (and I can rattle them off all day, believe me), there are just as many — and probably more — stories of people who pursue their passions in personal, private ways.

The pleasure of online personal interaction, heightened on WebTV with the addition of MSN Instant Messenger (see Chapter 8), isn't the whole story. Meeting people is perhaps the highest fulfillment of new technology, but the Internet has two other broad functions. Taken as a whole, these three aspects of the online experience constitute the Internet's potential:

✔ **Information.** The Internet still is and probably always will be an awesome source of information. The sheer amount of knowledge available on nearly every subject imaginable is a remarkable aspect of 21st-century life.

✔ **Community.** More than in its early years, and increasingly, the Internet is a meeting place for people. The Net is like an enormous hub into which we connect like spokes.

✔ **Service.** As the Internet has grown more commercial, it has begun to adopt a service-oriented tone. Whether you're looking for information delivery through e-mail or clothes shopping in a virtual store, the Net offers a growing variety of services to the cyber community.

This chapter discusses the potentials of the Internet in broad terms. For recommended sites, see the *WebTV For Dummies* Internet Directory — the yellow pages of this book. Several sections of the Directory starting with *WWW* highlight news, finance, portal, shopping, entertainment, and other sites.

Depth versus variety on the Internet

When approaching the Internet, one big choice you have is whether to go for variety or depth.

The *variety approach* is when you gobble up as many Web sites as possible; keep track of new developments and explore them at the first opportunity; keep a Favorites collection two miles long; and prowl around constantly looking for new treats. Your hunger for variety rarely lets you settle in one place for long or get deeply acquainted with the people who frequent it. A person who seeks variety derives satisfaction from a wide grasp of the Net, perhaps checking into a few dozen Web sites every day or reading dozens of Usenet newsgroups without posting anything.

The *depth approach* is just the opposite. You look for the gems and then treasure them. The emphasis of the in-depth experience is finding a few good homes on the Net and then living in them consistently. Maybe you give your personal e-mail box most of the attention. Maybe you visit a few Web sites for news, a couple of Usenet bulletin boards where you participate actively, and a particular online game.

Obviously, neither approach is better than the other. Your choice depends on your taste. If you feel scattered when you log on, as if you can't quite hold it all together, try deepening your approach. If you feel bored or in a rut, you probably need more variety and should go browsing.

News at 11:00 (or 12:00, or 1:00, or . . .)

Television, newspapers, radio, and now the Internet make us the best-informed society in history. The digital age has ensured that news and information will never be in short supply. With news not only easily available but seemingly thrown in your face at every turn, why would you want to use the Web as yet another news source?

Well, the Web is not just another news source; its unique features can actually help with the problem of information overload. The Web puts the flow of information under your control to a greater degree — no news anchor is yapping at you about who-knows-what while you wait for him or her to get to the news you want to hear.

Although WebTV uses your television set, the idea is to enhance TV programs, not replace them. I find it valuable to understand the strengths of both TV and the Web in delivering news. Television has a few things going for it:

- ✓ **Ease.** TV news is about as easy as it gets. Turn it on and watch it. You don't have to decide what's important or do any research. Nothing on the Web is ever quite as effortless because you must at least select links to get from one screen to another. Granted, highlighting and selecting links on the screen isn't hard labor, but it does require more than the television stare.

- ✓ **Multimedia.** Television brings the world into the home with video presentations of news events, no matter where in the world they originate. The Internet is more static, and generally, you read news rather than absorb streams of video and sound.

- ✓ **Personality.** The smiling anchorperson packages the day's unsavory events with a personable, if somewhat prefabricated, style. The Web has no talking heads, and the style with which information is delivered amounts to nice page design.

Complementing these TV strengths, news on the Web shines in these areas:

- ✓ **Depth.** When you reach a subject on the Web and decide to learn more, you find virtually no limit to how deep you can go. With television news, your level of understanding is decided for you by news producers who are trying to squeeze the world into 60 minutes (many of which are taken up by commercials).

    Using TV and WebTV together, however, you can see a brief report about a political candidate on TV and then switch to the Web to find, for example, the candidate's voting record and biography; learn about how the branches of government work; read a bit about the history of the electoral process; and discover how leaders are chosen in other countries.

✔ **Variety.** You can learn about many more world events on the Web than through television. In particular, international news gets more play on the Internet, which is, after all, an international network.

✔ **Selectivity.** You get to choose what kind of news you see on the Web. This is more interactive than TV and should come as a relief to anyone who has sat through a seemingly endless sports report (non-sports fans especially) just to get to the weather. Similarly, the selectivity of the Web lets you avoid local TV news broadcast coverage of gutter and tabloid-type "news" stories in favor of stories on national and international issues, if you like. WebTV emphasizes the selectivity of the Web as it applies to news coverage by offering the Find option. (See Chapter 3 for a frolic through all the choices you have with the Options button on the remote.) Using Find, you can search any Web page for a particular word or word *string* (group of letters).

✔ **Availability.** WebTV is never off the air, and its "programs" are always running. You never need to wait until 11:00 to get the news — unless, of course, your teenager is tying up the phone all evening.

WebTV Plus users get another dimension to online news, thanks to interactive TV programming from such shows as NBC Nightly News, Dateline, Newshour with Jim Lehrer, and MSNBC programs. See Chapter 11 for a discussion of WebTV interactive television.

Internet News: What to Expect

News on the Web comes in a large variety of sources, publications, and services:

✔ **Internet news sources** are agencies that organize and write news for wide distribution, both online and offline. Wire services are the prime example, and you can find wire service reports all over the Web, almost without looking for them. Wire service reports are news stories in raw form, often sold for use in newspapers under the byline of AP (Associated Press), UPI (United Press International), Reuters, and others. They are likewise used in Web sites that provide news to visitors.

✔ **News publications on the Web** include many of the same newspapers and magazines you find on a newsstand. The Web editions sometimes replicate the printed versions; in addition, they sometimes include interactive features that work especially well on the Web.

✔ **Web-based news services** bring it all together by packaging and delivering news. The services they offer take different forms. Some are topically oriented, such as business news services; others are more general. Some sites include a special feature such as e-mail delivery of news reports or the option of setting up a news clipping folder right on the site, which automatically collects stories with keywords of your choice.

The cost of Web news

The best news is that most Web news is free news. Information about current events is so plentiful on the Internet that it doesn't make sense for any site to charge for it. Some service sites, however, do charge subscription fees for the use of the whole site, a portion of it, or specific features.

Sites that charge for news services come in two basic flavors:

- **Those that offer a particularly useful and convenient service, such as e-mail delivery.** E-mail delivery is just one example, and not all e-mail delivery services cost money. Other services include database access to archives of special interest and access to specialized wire services that are expensive for the Web site to carry. One well-known and popular news service on the Web, NewsPage (`www.newspage.com`), offers levels of subscription (including free) according to the level of access you desire. For no money, you can read basic wire services; at the uppermost subscription level, you can get the most exclusive and pricey articles.

- **Those that provide specialized news with valuable authority.** An example is *The Wall Street Journal* (`interactive.wsj.com`), which charges a subscription to access its Web publication. *The Journal* gets away with these charges because of the prestige and added value of its brand name and the quality of its business news.

News on the Web is mostly free, with certain services or features of added value, which may or may not be worth your subscription dollars. Web subscriptions, where they do exist, are sometimes more expensive than the respective print subscriptions.

Unlike the usual yearly subscription to a magazine, Web subscriptions are usually by the month — similar to subscribing to home newspaper delivery but without the broken windows. Typical Web subscription rates range from $3 to $10. In some cases, you might find the high cost justified by the interactivity of the Web, which lets you tailor an online news service to your needs. In addition, online services are updated constantly, making them inherently more valuable as news sources (the news is newer) than printed publications.

Many news Web sites require you to register before getting to the news services. Don't confuse registration with subscription! All subscriptions require registration, but not all registrations require paid subscriptions. The overwhelming majority of site registrations are free and exist only so that the company that owns the site can keep a database of its members. Don't be put off by a registration request — you don't lose any money unless you enter your credit card information. Rest assured that site registration does not add cost to your WebTV account. If you're considering a paid monthly subscription to a news service, remember that you can often get a free trial subscription to help you evaluate whether the service is worth the cost.

The three levels of Web news

Using WebTV to get news from the Internet can be as brief or as lengthy and as shallow or as deep as you like. You can graze, munch, or gorge on news on the Web:

- ✔ **Scan headlines.** Scanning takes only a minute or two and can give you an overview of what's happening. You should go to the news sources, some of which I list as examples later in this chapter, to graze the headlines. You can easily go into more depth from there if you like or keep it quick and superficial.

- ✔ **Read stories.** Reading the stories, akin to reading a newspaper, is the next step, but you don't have to fumble through flimsy paper sections to get the whole thing. Stories are often displayed after selecting headline links in Web news publications.

- ✔ **Going deeper on the Web.** The news services often provide databases for going deep into a story. Furthermore, and even easier, the best Web news publications often offer links to background and research sites that can give you an understanding of the larger picture.

  For example, a movie review might contain links to the studio's Web site, the lead actors' pages, and a site specializing in the history of motion pictures. Or a story on a local election could link you to background sites on state history, legislative issues, candidate comparisons, and other related topics. Bouncing back and forth between these external links and the main story is an interactive, easy way to broaden your understanding of the story, and it's one of the best advantages to getting your news from the Web.

The preceding list might make the Web seem better organized than it is. In fact, the list reflects my personal mania for organization. Dividing news on the Web into sources, publications, and services is a peek into my compulsive brain. The distinctions are useful, but I don't want you thinking that you find headlines only in source sites, stories only in publications, and deeper coverage only in news services. All kinds of Web-based news sites contain news of varying depth. The divisions I outline can help you get a grip on the enormity of the Web's information potential.

Online Finances

If you're interested in money management, investing, and personal finances, you might watch TV news programs that deliver updates and daily summaries of the financial world. Some cable channels deliver continual play-by-play of the stock market. On TV, financial news programs tend to run 30 or 60 minutes and include roundups, summaries, forecasts, and opinions. The strong points of financial television programming are as follows:

✔ **Experts.** Financial news shows are always corralling university theorists and experts from brokerage houses and grilling them for their predictions of market activity and general economic performance. The Web offers plenty of opinion, too, but much of it is expressed by knowledgeable amateurs, and you can't always verify the credentials of the people whose opinions you read.

✔ **Synthesis.** Financial TV shows are great at boiling down complex situations into digestible news bites. You come away from financial programs feeling like you generally understand what's going on in the money world, even if the particulars are too complicated to grasp without a degree in economics.

By contrast, the Web shines as a financial information resource in these areas:

✔ **Interactivity.** You can do more than just watch and listen on the Web — in fact, in most cases you *have* to do more. If you really get into the interactive spirit and if you search the Web assiduously for financial service sites, you can manage your money entirely using online services through WebTV.

✔ **Personal research.** The Web doesn't always boil things down for you like TV does, but it opens up worlds of information for the motivated researcher. On the Web, you can find your own news, make your own conclusions, and get your hands on much of the same raw data that the experts use.

✔ **Services.** Learning about finances is one thing; conducting your finances is another. On the Web you can open online accounts, invest through the Internet, do your banking on-screen, and shop for insurance and loans on the Net.

✔ **More information.** One big advantage to the Internet is that it simply offers more financial information than the tube. Finance is a huge subject of interest to many Netizens, and many Web sites deal with issues of money and investing.

✔ **Personal networking.** The Web is a two-way street. In addition to participating in interactive Web sites, you can meet people from around the world who share your interests and communicate with them on message boards and through e-mail.

As in other areas of interest to the WebTV user, the financial news strengths of TV and the Web complement each other perfectly. The television is great for following economic news, trends, and opinions; the Web is useful for taking action on your personal finances or getting more information.

What Can You Do with Money on the Web?

The Internet can be a useful tool for personal finances in four ways:

✔ **Learn about it.** Financial information is plentiful, for beginners and veterans alike. You can use WebTV to get primers about investing, economics, marketplaces, and other aspects of the financial world. More experienced people can learn about tracking companies and managing personal portfolios. By poking around a bit (starting with the sites I describe in the "WWW Financial Sites" section of the Directory), anyone can increase his or her understanding of how money works and how to manage it.

✔ **Invest it.** Believe it or not, you can use the Internet in place of a living, breathing money broker. You can buy securities, trade in options, and do everything else that you used to need a real broker for. Investing online takes more expertise than letting a broker advise you, so beginners should beware.

✔ **Bank it.** Online banks provide bang-up services in many regards, with one thing lacking — the personal service of walk-in branch offices. But even physical banks increasingly offer online services, so you can balance your checkbook and pay bills online.

✔ **Follow it.** Tracking markets and economic trends is a task perfectly suited to the information-intensive realm of the Internet. From charting individual stock performances over the past five years to managing a complex personal portfolio, the option of following the market can make WebTV pay for itself.

✔ **Discuss it.** On Internet message boards and through e-mail, online investors love talking about money.

Family Surfing

Until the invention of WebTV, using the Internet had been largely a solitary activity. Computers are usually located in the study or a bedroom and are most often used by one person at a time. WebTV brings the Internet into living rooms, dens, and TV rooms, where groups of people and families can use it together.

Web entertainment of the future

The online phenomenon has sprung upon us quickly, unexpectedly, and sometimes it seems, overwhelmingly. The Internet is evolving at a lightning pace and speculating about the future is irresistible. Netizens have a lot to look forward to. All signs indicate that the Web will continue to get better in terms of content, speed, and technological frills over the next several years.

If you become a total Net addict like me, and if you browse the Web with WebTV for substantial periods of time almost every day, you can easily see the Web improve. The content of Web sites gets better all the time. Remember, the Web today is in a state of development similar to television in the 1950s. But you find much more variety on the Web these days than you saw on TV in its early years, thanks largely to the Web's egalitarian nature.

All it takes to be a Web programmer is a few skills, a bit of motivation, and some time. (See Chapter 13 for pointers on how to create a Web site through WebTV.) This means that as a Web surfer, you sometimes have to wade through bad sites to get to good ones, but it also means that everyone is on an equal ground and many unique voices are heard. No one can tell creative individuals to "get off the air," no matter how opinions about their Web sites might differ. No rating systems exist that would cause a Web site developer to cancel a site because of insufficient revenues. Instead, the content on the Web is largely driven by the identities of the people and corporations who publish there. In addition, as the corporations and individuals responsible for Web content continue to learn viewer preferences, the quality of those sites improves, becoming more attractive, more useful, and more entertaining. It makes sense to assume that the trends of improvement along with individuality will continue.

Technologically, today's entertainment on the Web is hampered by limitations in the underlying communications system. The Web's infrastructure, as it is sometimes called, primarily refers to the phone lines most people use to connect to the Internet. WebTV and most computers use a standard home phone line. The phone line is excellent for voice communications and for transmitting small information nuggets, such as e-mail.

Pictures, though, are slightly larger computer nuggets that take a bit longer to transmit — as you no doubt notice when you land on an especially picture-laden Web site. Video clips are even larger than static pictures and take even longer to transmit. And when it comes to streaming moving pictures in real time through the phone lines — well, forget it. The phone lines we currently use don't have enough *bandwidth* (technospeak for the capacity of a given data line) to deliver the kind of smooth picture and sound you see on television.

Larger bandwidth is the number-one improvement to look forward to for Web entertainment of the future. For now, Web programmers work with text, pictures, and sound in the form of RealAudio or MIDI. When the bandwidth expands and most people get on the Web through *broadband* (high-capacity data line) access, Web programmers will be able to stream moving pictures right through to our living rooms, just like television. (See Chapter 12 if you want to know more about MIDI and RealAudio WebTV features, as well as streaming media.)

(continued)

(continued)

The main difference between the Web of the future and TV? Anyone with a computer can put programming on the Web. Consider, too, that about one billion pages are now on the Web. And you thought you received a lot of channels through your cable system!

I leave it for you to decide whether the future scenario is a hideous prospect or the promised land of consumer choice. The real question is, when is it likely to become reality? Bandwidth expansion through better cables essentially amounts to rewiring the entire residential population of the country (or the world, depending on how global your outlook is) with better lines for transmitting computer data. If the job were mine, it would take me an entire weekend, at least. That's why some people predict the bandwidth revolution will be in wireless form, using satellites. Whatever the means, and however long it takes, the impact on our recreational habits and possibilities will be immense. In the meantime, we have the satisfaction of being in the forefront of a new technology, just like consumers of the 1950s who plugged in their first television sets.

Family Web surfing? I know — you have enough trouble sharing the TV remote. But group Web surfing is easier. Remember, deciding what television show to watch together requires a group commitment of at least 30 minutes. With the Web, you can check out one site for a few minutes, dart to another, hand the remote off to a spouse or a child and follow his or her lead for a few minutes, and then all decide to check out movie reviews, sports scores, or the family e-mail. In some ways, the Internet lends itself to family viewing even more than television does.

Shop Till You Drop (the Remote)

The Net is a glorious place for consumers. And it didn't just start yesterday or with the advent of the Web. The world was wired long before that, especially in the United States, where the credit card network makes remote access to funds as easy as slicing a piece of pie. The Internet is, among many other things, a potential extension of the financial and banking networks that already handle just about everyone's dollars.

The Web offers uncountable opportunities to whip out your wallet, whether for essential services or indulgent products. Far more useful than the shop-at-home cable channels, the Web lets you search for what you want, and it often provides a means of getting it quickly without ever leaving the house (or your couch, with WebTV). And if you're not looking to buy, electronic window-shopping can be singularly satisfying.

Technology makes the temptation to buy stuff more intense. The convergence of digital technology and rampant consumerism is leading to a greater choice when it comes to methods of payment (except for the choice to not pay, of course). But just as bank checks were an innovation when first introduced and then credit cards provided a new level of convenience, consumers are again on the threshold of new ways to empty their bank accounts — buying goods over the Net.

Buying the old-fashioned way

Even for people who are open to the information superhighway but resistant to new (and somewhat remote) forms of ordering and paying for goods, the Web is nonetheless a great shopping tool. Many manufacturers, stores, and product catalogs display their wares on Web sites, as alternate showrooms. (In most cases, you may purchase those goods and services over the phone, by mail, or in a store.)

Watch the next car commercial you see on TV closely to see whether a Web site's URL (with the `http://` or `www` prefix) is displayed near the end of the commercial. The URL is an invitation to visit a virtual showroom without leaving your house — quite a convenience if you think about it. Here's how shopping for a new car usually goes: You travel around to all the local dealers getting basic price and model information, straggle home trailing those slick brochures that don't tell you much (but have exciting pictures), exhausted even before you get down to the serious business of test driving, haggling, and basking in the attention of fawning salespeople eager to send their kids to college on the commission they'll get from your new car purchase. On the Web, you can accomplish the same thing at home, provided the cars you want to check out have decent Web sites. You can do all kinds of product research on the Web, including asking other Netizens what they think of the products or services you're considering.

When it comes time to buy, you might feel that the Web isn't the best way. Even with items smaller than a car, you can use the Web to contact a company and then resort to the tried-and-true methods of sending a check or ordering over the telephone with a credit card. And, of course, you can still go to a store — I think. (I haven't been outside for a while.)

Credit cards on the Net

Credit cards are overwhelmingly the most prevalent way to make a purchase on the Internet — for now, at least. The future may tell a different story. (Your WebTV set-top box has a smart-card slot and, at some point, that thing will actually become useful.) Paying for something on the Net with a credit card is similar to paying with credit in a store or over the phone. On the Web, you typically type your card information plus your mailing address (to both verify your credit card and to have the item delivered to your home). Many online stores allow you to set up an account so that your credit card information can be kept on file.

Is it safe to use a credit card on the Internet?

You often hear and see warnings about credit card fraud on the Internet. The fear that a so-called third party can observe your credit card number as it zips along the phone lines is a real one, though such an event is relatively unlikely. Keep the following points in mind:

✔ More care is exerted to keep credit card transactions private on the Internet than in most other situations where we use those little plastic devils. Consider the risk associated with your trash can full of credit card bills and receipts, your phone lines when you make a purchase over the phone, or even your mailbox when a new card arrives — the Internet is certainly no less safe.

✔ You may be hesitant to enter your credit card information into a computer, where it will be stored and presumably available for hackers or system administrators to see. But remember that your credit information is already stored in multiple locations in all kinds of networks, including the one operated by the bank that issued your card, all of which would make better targets for the credit card defrauder. The very act of opening a credit account puts you in a somewhat exposed position.

✔ Computer hacking is a reality, and crimes involving the digital theft of credit information have been committed. Hacking, however, is not an easy skill that just anyone can learn. Hackers pursue a highly technical, difficult, and arcane enterprise that usually takes years of practice and a great deal of knowledge. With the kind of investment necessary to defeat a typical network's security, high-level hackers are more interested in a bigger score than your personal credit line. Nevertheless, the information superhighway is not without its version of highway robbery.

✔ The most important thing in any transaction is peace of mind. You must be comfortable with any use of your credit card, whether you're online or offline. Credit card theft and fraud are realities of our modern world both within cyberspace and outside it. If a Web site (just as with an individual) seems sketchy, don't make the purchase. Trustworthy sites have other ways to conduct your transaction.

Smart cards

Smart cards are part of the payment technology of the future. Actually, they are very much part of the present technology in some European countries, and many people expect that they will swim over to U.S. shores before too long. WebTV is ready for them with the smart-card slot in the front of your set-top box. All you need to complete the equation is for banks and merchants to adopt the smart-card standard. Okay, that's a big step, granted. But most people in the computer and financial industries think that the smart-card era is going to be upon us soon.

Smart cards look somewhat like credit cards — both are small rectangles of plastic — but they operate differently. In most cases, when you use a credit card, you are borrowing money. Smart cards are paid in advance by "loading" them with cash. You go to a convenience store or to a local bank to load your smart card. After it's loaded, much like a prepaid telephone calling card, the card can be used to buy any product or service that accepts smart-card payments.

The advantage of smart cards is that no confidential information is transferred at any point during a purchase. The card itself, which contains a computer chip, does all the bookkeeping. The smart card is a self-contained accounting system that stores your balance of payments and available cash. When the cards are finally used over the Internet, you should have no worries about digital eavesdroppers or hackers. With WebTV, the smart card will be read through the smart-card slot, and online transactions will be risk-free.

E-cash

Electronic cash, or *e-cash,* is still mostly a theoretical method of payment. Experimental systems are popping up here and there on the Web, but so far, no online merchants have embraced any one method. E-cash is basically a money substitute that exists only in cyberspace but is accounted for and used like credit money in the offline world.

Some of the largest financial institutions are developing electronic cash systems, and it might become a more widespread reality in the near future. The success of e-cash is a bit harder to predict than the use of smart cards — both in terms of the technological feasibility and whether the system is going to catch on in the Internet community.

Fitting the Internet into Your Life and Schedule

The Internet is so beguiling to some people that it practically takes over their lives (not good). For others, its potential is never realized, and it is underused (harmless, but still not good). Some people have kept Internet use in balance while letting it partly take the place of previous interests, such as TV or magazines. Others use the Internet cleverly to make their lives easier or to access information that they can't get in other ways, but they keep its presence in their lives to a minimum.

Not too long ago, a psychologist coined the concept of *Internet addiction,* and then later denied that such a thing existed clinically. I'm in no position to evaluate psychological categories. But as someone who recognized his own deep infatuation with online services early on and managed to turn the compulsion into a profession, I recognize several layers of Internet dependence:

- ✔ **Occasional.** The light user treats the Internet like a can opener. It has a clearly defined role in life and is used only when needed for a specific task. That role could be e-mail, visiting a few sites for information, collecting news electronically, doing job-related research (or homework), or occasional mild curiosity. The light user checks e-mail every few days or even just once a week.

- ✔ **Moderately recreational or task oriented.** The moderate user sees substantial value in the Internet and enjoys it recreationally as a regular but unobtrusive activity. E-mail is relied upon for social and maybe professional communication and is always checked within a few days. This person might use e-mail to stay in touch with family members. The moderate user enjoys surfing the Web for its own sake when idle time is available to do so, but doesn't go out of his or her way to make that time and doesn't sacrifice other social possibilities. This user probably participates informally in message boards.

- ✔ **Frequent.** The frequent user has crossed a line by prioritizing the Internet above many other social opportunities at least some of the time. E-mail is always checked daily, sometimes both morning and evening. A dedicated phone line is a possibility, so that access to the Net is never denied. Such a person is pursuing online friendships on message boards and enjoys real-time Internet chatting. E-mail correspondences are important, and the frequent user tends to refer to them in conversation as often as he or she refers to phone calls or face-to-face conversations. Web surfing is a high recreational priority, and the frequent user has a great interest in and enthusiasm for Web site design.

- ✔ **Dependent.** The dependent user, even if not clinically addicted, has forgotten some aspects of life for the thrill of online connectedness. Like someone who has moved to another planet, he or she loses touch with the outside world to a large extent. E-mail and message boards are checked compulsively for personal messages. In some cases, real-time chatting is the lure, soaking up hours at a time. Web surfing can likewise be a black hole. The dependent user is accurately portrayed as staring at the screen deep into the night.

Everyone involved with the Internet has experienced, from time to time, that moment of revelation: "Oh brother, am I wasting time!" The moment is often accompanied by a quick shake of the head and swift disconnection from the Net. If you think, over the long run, that you're placing a bit too much importance on your connection to the Internet, consider these simple safety measures:

- Don't take food intravenously. Eat real meals.

- Don't let those meals consist of only pretzels, cookies, and soda. Cook something.

- Pick up the phone — it's that other device connected to the wall — and talk to someone.

- Ban the words *Internet, Web, e-mail, chat room,* and *cyber*-anything from your vocabulary for an entire day. All right, an entire hour.

- Don't check your e-mail one night. Left unread for a few hours, it won't explode. At least, I don't think so. (I've never tried it.)

- Invite someone to join you in a WebTV session — preferably, someone saner than you.

Part IV
The Part of Tens

The 5th Wave   By Rich Tennant

"It's amazing how they always fell asleep during 'Matlock', but this is their third hour surfing forensic Web sites."

In this part . . .

Here, I continue the grand ...*For Dummies* tradition of chapters describing ten of this and ten of that. In this edition, it's tips galore! I've compiled a truckload of hints, bits of advice, unofficial (but useful) tricks, and key reminders of important points sprinkled through the book. You'll laugh. You'll cry. Or neither. My hope is that you'll come back to these chapters repeatedly and discover something new each time.

Chapter 15

Ten Tips for Better WebTVing

*W*ebTV is a unique product. As such, WebTV users should be equipped with unique skills for getting the most out of it. This chapter gives you several tricks for enhancing your Internet experience. Some of the following tips hold true for computer access to the Web, whereas others are strictly for folks using WebTV Internet terminals.

Try the Wireless Keyboard as Your Remote

Most of the time, you don't need to type a lot on the Web. You get around by selecting hyperlinks, and the WebTV remote is perfect for that. It fits nicely into the hand, and the Arrow buttons are positioned conveniently under your thumb. Navigating the Internet with a single finger takes full advantage of the easy hyperlink environment of the Web.

For some people, however, typing can be a big part of the Web. Of course, e-mail and even minimal typing such as entering keywords into Search is much easier with the wireless keyboard than with the on-screen keyboard. But what some people don't realize is that the wireless keyboard can replace the remote entirely, and that sometimes it's more convenient. For example, you already use the keyboard when you write your e-mail — try to use the keyboard also to move around the various pages of the e-mail section. Normally, you would use the remote to select different screens and letters, but you can do the same things on the keyboard with the Arrow buttons (to move the highlight box) and the Return key (to select links) and avoid fumbling back and forth between the keyboard and remote.

Another reason to use the wireless keyboard for basic Web navigation is that some WebTV features that require a few button-pushes on the remote are immediately accessible with dedicated keys on the keyboard. Using the remote is not hard labor, but the keyboard makes it easier by offering each option (except for Reload) as a separate key. For example, if you want to send a Web page to someone's e-mail box using the Send option, just follow this abbreviated procedure on the keyboard:

1. **Press the Send key.**

2. **Type the e-mail address of the mailbox to which you're sending the page.**

3. **Press Return.**

Using the remote, you'd need to press the Options button, select Send, switch to the keyboard to type the e-mail address, and then go back to the remote to fire away the e-mail.

The downside to using the keyboard all the time is that it's not as convenient to hold — especially when you want to lounge — because if you're lying down, you can't easily put the keyboard on your lap. But try it some time when you're sitting up, and you might find that you like the extra control and features it gives you.

Don't Beat Your Head against a Wall — Just Head to Another Site

I was surfing the Web on the prowl for a good online shopping venue for music CDs. I found one well-known outlet and began exploring its many Web pages. It was a tangle and confusingly laid out, and many of the links didn't work. Pages loaded very slowly, sometimes stalling halfway through. I struggled with this site (which shall remain nameless) for 20 or 30 minutes, determined to get the hang of it, before I finally realized that I wasn't the problem — the site was the problem. Some Web sites are just too slow or too confusing.

Immediately after giving up on that horrendous Internet music store, I found another one — the Tower Records site, a terrific place to buy music online. Remember that the Web is huge, and if you have trouble with one site, you can quite likely find another similar, better site right around the virtual corner. Don't bang your head against a Web wall — just move on to something better. Oh, by the way, here's the URL for Tower Records:

```
www.towerrecords.com
```

Give Your Feedback!

If you scroll to the bottom of the home page of many Web sites, you find an invitation. The invitation is to send an e-mail message with suggestions or feedback to the individual or organization that created and runs the Web site. The invitation is in the form of a link — highlight and select it to display the Write a Message screen, where you can compose your e-mail.

Be assured that responses with feedback don't go unnoticed. The Web is a highly interactive place, and when a *Webmaster* (that's what Web site administrators are called) asks for feedback, he or she takes it seriously. You will probably get a response acknowledging your letter and even discussing your suggestions. In addition to the personal satisfaction of participating, even in a small way, in the development of a Web site, you're helping to improve the Web overall.

One suggestion: If something about the Web site bothers you, make your e-mail feedback constructive. Suggest changes or politely point out problems or bugs at the site. Tempting though it may be to write angry letters, especially if the site is chronically slow or some of its links don't work, you get better results if you don't flame the Webmaster's e-mail box. You feel better in the long run, too.

Save It Now!

Let me tell you about a failing that most Netizens are prone to. It's a certain kind of complacency. Here's how it goes: You're surfing the Web one evening. You might be searching for something in particular or just idly nosing around. You come across a great-looking extreme sports site — the home page has loads of interesting links covering remote mountain snowboarding, rocket skateboarding, cordless bungee jumping, and many other thrilling methods of recreational suicide. You think to yourself, "Wow, I'm going to save this site! But first, I'll just check out this link. . . ."

There's your downfall — that "first . . ." leads to a second and a third, and before you know it, you push deep into the site, lose track of the home page, and end your session having forgotten to save the site. Can you find it again? Can you find the same needle a second time in the proverbial haystack that's the Web? The rule is: Save now, explore later. Make it a habit to press that Options button and select Save (or just press the Save key on the keyboard) as soon as you see a site that you might want to visit again. You'll have a much easier time deleting a site from Favorites than finding an unsaved site.

Send Sites to Yourself

The preceding section recommends that you save promising sites to your Favorites collection without a second thought, keeping in mind that you can delete items from Favorites if the area gets too cluttered. I stand by that suggestion — I learned as a result of years of hard, regret-filled, bitter experience in which I lost many a site because I forgot to save it. Do I hear a violin in the background?

But I also have another suggestion that can help you avoid Favorites clutter in the first place. Use the Send option to mail Web site addresses to yourself. Sending a site to yourself is a convenient way to remember favorite sites or mark a site for a future visit without adding it to Favorites. Just follow these steps:

1. **When you encounter a Web site that you might want to visit again, press the Options button on the remote.**

2. **When the Options panel appears on the screen, highlight and select** Send.

   You may combine Steps 1 and 2 by using the Send button on the keyboard.

3. **When the Send panel appears on-screen, enter your own WebTV e-mail address, using either the on-screen or wireless keyboard.**

   Your address is your screen name plus the WebTV domain name in this format: screenname@webtv.net. (Chapter 6 has all the details about e-mail addresses.)

4. **Highlight and select the** Send **button.**

Within seconds, the e-mail arrives in your box, with a link to the page you are on. Conveniently, the subject of the e-mail message is automatically listed as the title of the Web page, so you can see at a glance where your favorite Web links are stored in your e-mail collection.

If you send yourself enough Web pages, one thing becomes apparent: The page title, which appears as the subject of the e-mail in your mailbox, occasionally has nothing to do with the subject of the page. The discrepancy is due to sloppy page coding on the part of the individual who created it. You can make a note of the page title (in the lower-left corner of the screen) when you're parked there, before or just after you send the page to yourself, if you notice that the title isn't memory-jogging enough for the page's content. Another trick is to forward the e-mail to yourself after you receive it the first time, and change the Subject line to a title that refers more closely to the page content. This second method involves a bit more effort but works better in the long run if you want to keep the e-mail link in your mailbox for a while.

To retrieve the message and use the link, follow these steps:

1. **Go to the Mail area from the Home screen.**

2. **When the Mail List screen appears, notice that the titles of some e-mail messages correspond to Web sites you've saved in this fashion.**

3. **Select the Web site (e-mail subject) you would like to visit.**

4. **When the Message for *YourName* screen appears, look for the link in the body of the message.**

   The link is the only thing in the body of the message.

5. **Highlight and select the link to visit the site.**

The big advantage to storing favorite Web sites this way is that you can see many at once by scanning your list of stored e-mail messages. The disadvantage is that you don't have thumbnail pictures of the home page as you do in Favorites.

Keep Your Waiting Time to a Minimum

For something called an information superhighway, the Web can be dreadfully slow. Sometime it resembles the information parking lot. The Contacting Publisher box that appears when WebTV is connecting to a Web site can seem to hang on forever. Although you can't do anything to speed up a slow-loading page, you do have a way to minimize your overall delay: Simply don't wait! (Revolutionary, huh?) Remember that the Back button can get you out of any jam. If a page is taking too long to load, just back your way out of it.

Many people don't realize that Web delays are quirky and that delays are sometimes the result of trying to access the site at just the wrong moment. In other words, if you experience a delay, you might have had better luck by simply arriving at the site a little earlier or later.

Experienced Web surfers never wait more than ten seconds for an indication that a page is loading smoothly. If you see the on-screen panel with the spinning globe in the upper-left portion of the screen and a jagged, moving line in the lower-right corner, the page is loading. Without both those indicators, don't sit waiting for long — just press that Back button and try the link again. Pages often load immediately on the second try.

One final speed hint: Remember that when you use the Back button to retrace your steps through several previous pages, you don't have to wait for each page to reload before pressing the Back button again. Just wait long enough for the new (previous) page to begin appearing on the screen and then whisk it away with the Back button.

Take the High Road (Speed Choices)

With some sites, you have another way to increase your speed on the Web. You often run into sites that give you a choice of pathways through the site, such as text only, high bandwidth, or low bandwidth. If a text-only link is offered, that's your fastest route. Because pictures take longer to load than text, text-only paths are usually free of delays.

Another choice is sometimes offered between high bandwidth and low bandwidth. High-bandwidth paths are designed for cable modems, DSL lines, and other very-high-speed Internet connections. WebTV Plus uses the fastest possible dial-up modem, but it's still much slower than a cable modem or DSL. Generally, choosing the low-bandwidth option is the best bet for both Classic and Plus users. But if you're in no hurry and want to try some dazzling pages, choose high bandwidth.

Stay Logged on with Audio

The automatic ten-minute timeout can be a headache. If you don't select a link or check your mail for at least ten minutes while using the Web, the WebTV service decides you've fallen asleep and terminates your connection. It's not as rude as it might sound, because most online services have the same policy with varying timeout durations. But it can be inconvenient to leave the TV for ten or fifteen minutes and then log back on to continue your session.

You can fool WebTV into thinking you're alertly watching the screen by activating some audio content that streams continually through your connection. A RealAudio radio station is a good bet. (See Chapter 12 for a rousing discussion of multimedia and RealAudio.) After you get an Internet radio station going, WebTV won't log you off.

The difficulty with this tricky solution is that it's a hassle to find and activate an Internet radio station every time you want to take a fifteen-minute break. Make it easier by saving a RealAudio page to your Favorites collection. That way, you're always just a few selections away from streaming some audio.

Here's the URL for a radio directory page from which you can select any number of audio streams:

```
http://realguide.real.com/?f=stations
```

I know that's not the easiest URL in the world to copy. But if you type it once into the Go To panel of Options (see Chapter 3), you can then save the page to Favorites and never type the URL again.

The Ever-Present Home Button Shortcut

Two things are worth remembering: First, the Home screen puts you two clicks of the remote away from just about every major feature of the WebTV Network. Second, the remote has a Home button. This means you're never more than three remote-clicks away from any important feature of E-mail, Explore, Search, Favorites, Community, and Around Town. In a cyberspace as vast as the Internet, that's quite a shortcut. It's easy to get addicted to the Back button of the remote to backstep your way through a session. Don't forget to use that Home button to get where you're going.

Be Part of the Family

Many WebTVers enjoy meeting each other and talking by means of the WebTV bulletin board in the Community area. (See Chapter 8 to find out about Community.) Here's how to join in:

1. **On the Home Screen, highlight and select** Community.

2. **On the Community screen, highlight and select** Discuss.

3. **On the Welcome to Discuss screen, highlight and select** Begin Using Discuss.

4. **On the Featured discussions screen, highlight and select** WebTV.

5. **On the Group: Webtv.users screen, highlight and select** messages to read, **and use the Reply function as described in Chapter 4.**

The WebTV discussion group is always full of lively message board conversation, including praises and complaints about the WebTV system. It's a good place to pick up hints and meet your cyber-brethren.

Chapter 16

Ten More Tips for Better WebTVing

*B*ecause I'm a caring and connected individual, a new-millennium man of sensitivity and charm, I've assembled ten more tips to supplement the preceding chapter. Actually, I'm no more sensitive than the average block of wood, and most people who meet me don't hit the charm-alert button. But never mind all that. It's the tips that count. Shortcuts, new ideas, helpful reminders. Here they are.

See the Next Address

You can always see what Web address you're currently viewing by using the Info selection of the Options panel. Sometimes it can be useful to see the address of a Web page you're about to link to, before visiting it. You can do so by using a certain keyboard combination.

Seeing an address in advance is handy in determining whether or not to try the link. For example, if you see that the link takes you outside the site you're currently exploring, you might not care to select it. Whatever the reason might be, seeing the address of any link currently in the highlight box is as easy as pressing the Ctrl and Cmd keys of the keyboard simultaneously. The address of the highlighted link appears in the status bar at the bottom of your screen.

I check about half my links before selecting them — mostly out of sheer curiosity and because it's so quick and easy to do.

Create an Audioscope

This tip is for anyone creating a Web page or e-mail signature who enjoys on-screen gadgets. An *audioscope* responds to streaming sound with wavy lines. You can see a small audioscope in action at the bottom-right corner of your screen when playing a RealAudio or MP3 file. The audioscope HTML tag is special to WebTV and doesn't work through non-WebTV systems — but it doesn't hurt them, either. WebTV audioscopes simply don't appear on computer screens.

Chapter 13 provides a tutorial on HTML code, the underlying system of tags for all Web pages. Use the following code to place an audioscope on your page or e-mail signature:

```
<audioscope bgcolor=black width=200 height=50 gain=3
    leftoffset=-5 rightoffset=5 leftcolor=white
    rightcolor=red></audioscope>
```

In the preceding example, I assigned eight attributes to the audioscope:

- **bgcolor** is the background color.
- **width** is the width in pixels; for best results, keep this number below 400.
- **height** is the height of the audioscope; this should be smaller than the width.
- **gain** specifies the jumpiness of the lines of the audioscope.
- **leftoffset** is the distance from the left border of your page.
- **rightoffset** is the distance from the right border of your page.
- **leftcolor** is the color of the left-channel audio band (on top).
- **rightcolor** is the color of the right-channel audio band (on bottom).

The audioscope comes to life only when music is playing. There's no point putting it on your page or e-mail signature if you don't also embed a MIDI file or some other audio element.

Jump through Scroll Lists

Some Web page designers have an annoying habit of presenting long drop-down lists of choices on pages with fill-in forms. The prevalent example is when you must type in your state. You'd think the American population didn't know their state abbreviations and weren't capable of typing them. Instead, we must scroll tediously through the long alphabetical lists of states until we come to the correct one and then select it. The process is especially torturous for those poor souls living in Virginia, West Virginia, and Washington. Not to forget Wyoming.

Anyway, here's a tip that gets you through those lists in snappier fashion. When you encounter such a drop-down list, highlight and select it. Then type the first letter of the item you need — such as *W* for Wyoming. The list zooms down to where the Ws are, and you avoid a lot of scrolling.

Save Your Communities

Sounds like I'm recommending a bit of social service in your spare time. Although that would be politically correct, it would take precious time away from the TV and the Internet and is therefore an unacceptable use of energy. No, I'm referring to saving your online community screens.

I praise the convenience of WebTV Favorites throughout this book. And I continually preach the value of saving pages to Favorites early and often. Like my Great-aunt Violet always said, "It's easier to delete a Favorite than to find a lost page." (I don't have a Great-aunt Violet, but if I did, and if she ever said such a thing, she would be correct.)

Most people think of saving Web pages, but don't bother saving chat rooms or bulletin boards. Why not? Because they haven't read this gold-plated tip telling them to do just that — put favorite chat rooms and message boards into Favorites folders.

The Community portions of WebTV are a little hard to get to. The easiest chat room requires four link selections from anywhere on the Web. Message boards can take many more selections if they're buried deep in the directory. (See Chapter 8 for heart-pounding instructions on all of this.)

The solution, if you enjoy frequent chatting and message-board discussion, is to simply save your favorite, oft-visited communities.

When saving a message board, remember to save the first screen of message headers. It's the first screen that displays the most recent message, so that's the screen you want to link to.

Rename Your Favorites

Neither you nor WebTV has any control over what captions appear under the thumbnails of Web sites saved to Favorites. The captions say whatever the page title happens to be, as determined by the person who created the page. Sad to say, most people don't create pages with an eye to how they might appear in your Favorites folder. The result is that the puzzling captions often give little clue to what the heck the page is or why you saved it.

The answer is to rename your Favorites. The process is part of the Organize in Favorites, described with stunning imagery in Chapter 7. The point of this tip is to recommend, in particular, renaming any WebTV service screens stashed in your Favorites section. These in-house pages have the worst captions of all.

When renaming, remember that there's a 25-character limit to Favorites captions. If you attempt the caption, "Great page in the MoneyCentral site where I can search for undervalued stocks and become as rich as Uncle Geoffrey who always gives me shoelaces for Christmas, the jerk" it'll be reduced to "Great page in the MoneyCe..." Which might be just as well.

Use Simple Web Addresses

WebTV makes an important assumption about Web addressees, and that is that they always contain *www* at the beginning and *com* at the end. Both these items follow the *http://* prefix, which is always present when you use the Go To selection of the Options panel.

The importance of this assumption is that it saves you typing. If the address you want to visit does indeed contain *www* and *com,* you need to type only what goes between. An example is the AltaVista site. The full address of the Alta Vista home page is

```
http://www.altavista.com
```

You don't need to type the *http://* because it's already in the Go To window. You don't need to type *www* or *com* because they're both assumed. So you type only

```
altavista
```

Keep in mind that if your Web address doesn't have *www* or *com,* you need to type the whole address after the *http://* prefix. Here are two examples:

```
cbs.marketwatch.com
www.webtv.net
```

Use Simple E-Mail Addresses

Just as WebTV makes an important assumption about Web addresses (see the preceding section), so too does it make an assumption about e-mail addresses. WebTV assumes everyone in the world has a WebTV address. Now don't get me wrong — you can easily send messages to anyone on the Internet, no matter who that person's mail provider is. WebTV is completely fluent with standard WebTV e-mail addresses.

But when you're mailing another WebTV subscriber, you can leave off the WebTV signifier — that's the *@webtv.net* portion — from the e-mail address. You can abbreviate the address in this fashion no matter where you enter it, whether you're in the Mail section or sending a Web page. Just type the recipient's WebTV screen name and select the Send button.

Skip from Link to Link

Maybe it doesn't bug you, but it bugs me. On a Web page with lots of links, using the arrow keys to navigate from link to link can be aggravating. I always end up hitting the wrong arrow key and moving sideways when I meant to move down or jumping the highlight box upward when I wanted to move it to the left.

The Tab key of the keyboard (which doesn't exist on the remote) causes the highlight box to jump to the next link, no matter where that link is located. If you're good with the arrow keys, this tip might cause you more annoyance than it saves.

Use the Keyboard to Move the TV Window

This tip is for Plus users only. (Sorry, Classicians. Classicons? Whatever.) When using the built-in picture-in-picture feature, with the small TV screen displayed as you surf the Web, you can slide the TV image from side to side using the Enter button on the remote. (Chapter 3 explains this whole picture-in-picture business.) If you're a keyboard surfer, reaching for the remote every time you want to shift the TV picture over is a nuisance. As we all know, nuisance leads to aggravation and aggravation leads to gnashing of teeth and rending of garments. It must be avoided.

Dental health and sartorial integrity are maintained by a simple keyboard command. When you want to move the TV window to the other side of the screen, press the Cmd and M keys at the same time. Use Cmd+M to toggle the TV screen back and forth to your heart's content. I'll use any excuse to write the word *toggle*.

Go Easy on the HTML

I spend an entire chapter illustrating HTML code and the ways it can be used. (That would be Chapter 13.) What I say here might seem to contradict my enthusiasm for HTML and my admiration for the remarkable resourcefulness of the WebTV community in stretching the boundaries of the WebTV system. But WebTV is more than a service provider; it's a community within a larger community. As such, it benefits all WebTVers to be aware of their relationship to the online universe and especially to Internet computer users whose online lives intersect WebTV at certain points.

I'm specifically referring to the use of HTML in e-mail signatures and message-board posts. This issue is a touchy one for WebTVers who are aware of it, but many more are simply not aware of how non-WebTV folks regard HTML in these environments.

Almost universally, HTML is unwelcome in newsgroups. (Newsgroups are the original bulletin boards of the Internet, completely accessible through WebTV. See Chapter 8 for more on newsgroups.) Unwelcome is putting it graciously — HTML is roundly despised in the newsgroup environment, which is traditionally a text-only domain for sharing discussions. Even modest HTML is likely to draw angry flames, and the widespread practice among WebTVers of linking HTML code to pictures and sound files brings tempers quickly to a boiling point. An angry schism has developed between computer users and WebTVers on this point.

I omitted all discussion of this issue from the second edition of this book, not wanting to appear critical, or worse, hypocritical. During the period between book editions, the resentment that simmers between computer newsgroup users and WebTV users has intensified, and I want to at least bring some awareness to the portions of the WebTV community that aren't aware of the effect their HTML creations have.

There's an easy solution for anyone who cares about newsgroup protocol. (And it's worth caring about. Remember, newsgroups have existed for decades. You're contributing to an online culture with long traditions.) Simply turn your signature off when posting to a newsgroup — especially a newsgroup that isn't primarily for WebTV. It's easy to think you're cozily enclosed within the WebTV family at all times, but when writing to most newsgroups, you're out there on the Net, surrounded by computer users.

Some discretion might be called for when using e-mail, too. In e-mail, though, you're mostly writing to friends and not inflicting long download times and unexpected multimedia outbursts on strangers. One situation in which you might consider turning off your e-mail signature is when sending group mailings (circulating jokes, for example) whose recipients include computer users. In e-mail, just as in the newsgroups, the graphics and music that are so much fun in WebTV are unwelcome surprises to many computer users.

Chapter 17

Ten Tips about Mail, Chat, and Messaging

*T*he suggestions in this chapter deal mainly with communication — chatting, e-mail, your Web site (if you have one), and message boards. There's a bit of common sense and a dollop of weirdness in the following sections, as well as nuggets of advice and a shortcut or two. Mix together, bake for twenty minutes, and out comes a tray of delicious brownies. I wish.

Fun with Weird Characters

I'm not talking about the characters you meet in chat rooms, though they can be fun too. I'm talking about typed characters that diverge from the standard alphabet. That's right — you're not limited to the letters you see on the keyboard. However, you *must* use the optional wireless keyboard to attain the utter coolness of alternate characters.

Why would anyone want to make seemingly nonsense characters appear in an e-mail, a message-board post, or a chat room? Sheer silliness is one good reason. Some people string together weird characters that resemble regular letters, making up words that are oddly recognizable.

All of the following special characters are created with the Alt key of the keyboard (which doesn't exist on the remote). Some of them require another key to be pressed with the Alt key. In all cases, press the two (or three) keys simultaneously (except where instructed otherwise) and watch the alternate character appear on your screen. It sounds confusing but is very easy to accomplish. Try a few to get the swing of it.

The best way to try these symbols is in Mail, on the Write a Message screen. The message body of an outgoing letter provides a blank palette for experimenting. You probably don't want to actually send your keyboard experiments (unless you're feeling hostile toward somebody who's easily confused), so don't fill in the To: field.

First, start with Alt+*letter* combinations. These characters range from the copyright symbol to the trademark symbol to bits of indescribable oddity. The Alt+*letter* combinations in Figure 17-1 are printed with uppercase letters for clarity but work the same way with lowercase letters.

Figure 17-1:
Making
alternate
characters
with
Alt+*letter*
combina-
tions.

Alt+A=å	Alt+O=ø
Alt+B=™	Alt+P=¶
Alt+C=ç	Alt+Q=æ
Alt+D=ð	Alt+R=®
Alt+F=*f*	Alt+S=ß
Alt+G=©	Alt+T=þ
Alt+H=ª	Alt+V=‚
Alt+J=°	Alt+W=œ
Alt+K=†	Alt+X=×
Alt+L=¬	Alt+Y=¥
Alt+M=µ	Alt+Z=§

Different characters result when you use Alt+Shift+*letter*, as shown in Figure 17-2. Press all three keys at the same time, but don't hold the letter key down, or you'll get multiple repetitions of the symbol.

Figure 17-2:
Making
alternate
characters
with
Alt+Shift+
letter com-
binations.

Alt+Shift+A=Å
Alt+Shift+C=Ç
Alt+Shift+D=Đ
Alt+Shift+H=,
Alt+Shift+J=,,
Alt+Shift+K=‡
Alt+Shift+L=¯
Alt+Shift+O=Ø
Alt+Shift+Q=Æ
Alt+Shift+T=Þ
Alt+Shift+W=Œ

Now try some numbers. The characters in Figure 17-3 result from the Alt+*number* method. Don't use the Shift key.

Figure 17-3:
Making
alternate
characters
with
Alt+*number*
combina-
tions.

Alt+1=^{1}
Alt+2=^{2}
Alt+3=^{3}
Alt+4=¢
Alt+5=¼
Alt+6=½
Alt+7=¾
Alt+8=·
Alt+0=°

Figure 17-4 shows you the list of symbols you get by pressing Alt+Shift+*number*.

Figure 17-4:
Making
alternate
characters
with
Alt+Shift+
number
combina-
tions.

Alt+Shift+1=¡
Alt+Shift+3=£
Alt+Shift+4=¤
Alt+Shift+5=‰
Alt+Shift+9=€

Multilingual, are you? Congratulations. It probably drives you crazy to type in European languages without placing the proper accents above vowels. The characters in Figure 17-5 can help. Many of these require more complicated keyboard tricks. For all these characters, you press Alt and the letter, then release those two keys and press the single letter. For example, Alt+E, A means you press Alt+E together, then release those two keys, and then press A. With all the methods in Figure 17-5, you can get the same accents over uppercase versions of all the letters by using Shift+*letter* in the second step instead of the letter by itself.

Figure 17-5:
Making
accents
over letters.

Alt+N,N=ñ	Alt+I,A=â	Alt+U,A=ä
Alt+E,A=á	Alt+I,E=ê	Alt+U,E=ë
Alt+E,E=é	Alt+I,I=î	Alt+U,I=ï
Alt+E,I=í	Alt+I,O=ô	Alt+U,O=ö
Alt+E,O=ó	Alt+I,U=û	Alt+U,U=ü
Alt+E,U=ú		Alt+U,Y=ÿ
Alt+E,Y=ý		

Finally, just two more alternate characters to impress your friends, or at least convince them that you've gone over the edge:

✔ Alt + < = «

✔ Alt + > = »

Send an E-Mail from Anywhere

You can send e-mail from anywhere — anywhere on the Web, that is. You know about sending a Web page's link to an e-mail recipient. (That is, you know about it if you read Chapter 3. If you haven't read it yet, just imagine the good times that lie ahead.)

But what about sending a full-fledged e-mail letter while surfing the Web, without going into the Mail section? You'll be glad (or perhaps utterly indifferent) to know that you can do so in two ways.

First, you can use the aforementioned Send feature, as follows:

1. **On any Web page, press the Options key on the keyboard or the remote.**

2. **Highlight and select** Send.

   An alternative to these two steps is to simply press the Send key on the keyboard.

3. **Type the address of your recipient.**

4. **Highlight and select the** `Edit Message` **button of the on-screen panel.**

   WebTV displays the Write a Message screen, with the link to the Web page you're sending included at the bottom of the message.

5. **Write your message and select the** `Send` **button.**

This process works fine if you want to send the link to the Web page. But what about when you have a sudden urge to dash off a letter completely unrelated to your Web surfing? You don't want to send a page; you just want to write. Here's a shortcut:

1. **On any screen whatsoever, press the Options key.**

2. **Highlight and select** `Go To`.

3. **On the panel that appears, type your recipient's address preceded by the** `mailto:` **qualifier.**

   Whoa. Now we're getting a little technical. Here's the deal. That `mailto:` thing is a standard link element that directs programs to e-mail. In this case, it directs WebTV to route your Go To request to the Mail section. Here is what you should type:

   `mailto:recipient@address.com`

   Note that there's no space between `mailto:` and the e-mail address.

   You need to use the Delete key of the keyboard to erase the `http://` in the `Address` field of the `Go To` panel. The `mailto:` command replaces the `http://` prefix.

4. **Highlight and select the** `Go to Page` **button or press the Return key of the keyboard.**

5. **On the Write a Message screen, compose your e-mail in the normal fashion and select the** `Send` **button.**

Using this procedure doesn't bypass the Mail section or the Write a Message screen — there's no way to do that when sending a letter. But it gives you a quick way of getting there. Then, after you've sent your note, just press the Back button to return to the Web page you were viewing when overcome by the whole letter-writing inspiration.

Be Careful when Using WebTV's Name

This tip is directed toward folks setting up Web sites about WebTV — not necessarily *on* WebTV through Page Builder but *about* the service in some way. Many WebTV users enjoy sharing their experiences and knowledge about WebTV through Web pages. In so doing, some people have learned the hard way not to borrow the WebTV name or logos too liberally.

In particular, don't use WebTV in a domain name that you register. A URL such as www.webtvhints.com resides in a legal grey area, and WebTV Networks takes these legalities seriously. The company is nice about such trademark infringements at first, requesting that the domain name be discontinued and granting a little time to create a new home for your pages before taking legal action (Domain names are not free, so don't waste the money.)

Likewise, don't use the WebTV logo on your pages. Well-intentioned as it might seem to promote the company's logo, it's legally risky.

Use Chat Commands

When in a chat room (see Chapter 8), you might notice that the lines of text scrolling up the screen are in different colors and imply more than just public chatting. Some of those lines describe actions, for example. How do people make these differently hued lines? It's not hard.

The first chat command you might want to try is one that lets you send a private message to another person in the chat room. The message isn't e-mail; it appears right on the recipient's chat screen and nobody else's. It's called *whispering*, and the whisper command link is located to the left of the main chat window. Here's how to whisper:

1. **In any chat room, highlight and select** Whisper **in the left selection bar.**

   A two-window panel appears. The left window contains the screen names of people in the room. The right window is blank, awaiting your whisper.

2. **In the left window of the two-window panel, highlight and select the name to whom you want to whisper.**

3. **In the right panel, type your message.**

4. **Highlight and select the** Whisper Message **button.**

   Your whispered message appears on the recipient's screen. That person knows it's a private, whispered greeting because it appears in orange letters with a parenthetical to you like this:

   YourName (to you): Hi, it's me!

You can shorten the preceding multistep procedure by using a manual command for whispering. Like other chatting commands described in this section, the whisper (or message) command is preceded by a forward slash — the forward slash key is located below the question mark of the keyboard.

To whisper using a keyboard command, you need to type the command followed by the recipient's screen name and then your message:

```
/msg YourRecipient hi, how are you?
```

Three other commands frequently come in handy:

- **Ignore.** You can block text lines from any individual in the chat room. Use the /ignore command, followed by the screen name of the person you don't want to see. Ignoring isn't two-way; that person can still see your chat lines as long as you aren't ignored by that person. The only way to readmit someone to your chat screen is to leave the room and come back in. There is no de-ignore command.

- **Who.** Find out who is in the room with the /who command. Just type /who and press the Return key. Alternatively, you can highlight and select People on the left selection bar.

- **Action.** You can send a line into the chat room that reports any action you type. The /me command is popular, and you see the results of it in any chat room within seconds, as people use it. Type /me followed by an action, and your screen name will replace the /me command when the line appears in the chat room. So, the line

```
/me waves to the room
```

appears in the room as

```
YourName waves to the room.
```

The action appears in grey type.

Deal with Flames and Trolls

The Internet isn't always as polite as a gracious and elegant dinner party. And it's on the message boards that tempers run highest. Two manifestations of irascible human nature are common in the discussion forums:

- **Flaming.** Arguments that get personal are flames. Personal attacks, conducted in the safety of the verbal realm, can be vicious and vulgar.

- **Trolling.** Trolls are individuals intent on disrupting a discussion board with insulting or wildly off-topic messages.

Both flames and trolls bring out the sporting spirit in some people and disgust in others. If you don't care for hard-edged banter, your best bet is to ignore trolls and inflamed discussions. Fortunately, it's often the trolls who get flamed most intensely.

Use the Send Key in Mail

Here's a handy shortcut that should become second nature if you forward a lot of mail. Families, especially, tend to forward mail from member to member. You can always use the Forward option as described in Chapter 6. But in general, it's easier to use a keyboard command than to move the highlight box around the screen.

The Send key on the keyboard provides a shortcut to forwarding any e-mail message you're reading. This is how to do it:

1. **On the Message screen, showing a letter you've received, press the Send button on the keyboard.**

2. **On the displayed panel, select the** Forward **button.**

3. **On the Forward a Message screen, fill in the recipient's address and select the** Send **button.**

The Send key functions elsewhere in Mail to display the Write a Message screen. Here's how that works:

1. **On the Mail List screen, where you view received letter titles, press the Send key.**

2. **On the displayed panel, select the** Write **button.**

3. **On the Write a Message screen, address and write your letter and then select the** Send **button.**

Include Messages when Sending Pages

Sending a Web page (actually the link, as described in Chapter 3) is a nifty feature but limited. The result is a somewhat enigmatic e-mail with a link in the message body. You can always use the Edit Message option of the Send Page panel, but there's also a sly trick for squeezing a quick message into the header of an e-mail. Follow these steps:

1. **On any Web page (not a WebTV service screen), press the Options key and select** Send.

   Alternatively, simply press the Send key on the keyboard.

2. **On the displayed panel, type the recipient's address and press the spacebar once, so that there's a single space after the address.**

3. **Type a short message in parentheses.**

   The parentheses are necessary so WebTV doesn't mistake your message for part of the e-mail address. The message won't get sent without those parentheses.

4. **Highlight and select the** Send Page **button.**

   Your e-mail is delivered to the recipient with the short message, parentheses and all, in the To: field of the e-mail header. Recipients don't see the message in the e-mail's subject line.

Insert Spaces in Chat

Must every tip have earth-shaking significance and immortal usefulness? I think not. I hope not . . . because this one is on the trivial side but irresistible.

When chatting through WebTV, any spaces you place before your line of text are ignored and eliminated by the system. Your line appears in the chat window immediately after your screen name. No big deal, but on some occasions, for emphasis or dramatic effect, you might want to separate your line of text from your name.

You can accomplish this tectonic effect by using the Alt key with the spacebar. Just hold down the Alt key as you make your spaces, and those spaces appear in the chat window, separating your text line from your name.

Make Groups of Addresses

Your WebTV address book is a convenient way to store e-mail addresses without having to write them down. It also makes it easy to add recipients to an outgoing letter, as explained with charm and refinement in Chapter 6.

If you have a family, or a group of online friends, or for any other reason like to send letters to multiple recipients simultaneously, organizing certain addresses into groups is more convenient than shoes when walking on hot coals.

You can create address-book groups with these steps:

1. **On the Mail List screen, highlight and select** Addresses **from the left selection bar.**

2. **On the Addresses for** *YourName* **screen, highlight and select** Add **from the left selection bar.**

3. **In the** Name **window of the Add an Entry screen, type the group name.**

4. **In the** E-mail **window, type the e-mail address of each group member.**

   Separate the addresses with semicolons.

5. **Highlight and select the** Add **button.**

A group in your address book can be placed in the To: line of an outgoing e-mail, and everyone in the group receives the mail.

Try the Tips Index

Want more tips? Of course you do. Who doesn't? Remember that there's a Tips Index in WebTV Today, in the right selection bar. Go to WebTV Today from the Home screen, and select Tips Index.

The list of tip subjects covers almost every aspect of the WebTV service. Many suggestions are rudimentary, but it's good to be reminded of features you might not have used in a while.

Chapter 18

Ten Sites from My Favorites Folder

*N*arrowing down my favorite sites to a list of ten is a terrible challenge. That's why I copped out and spread twenty selections over two chapters — this one and the next. Even twenty sites is too few, and I regretfully leave out many excellent and worthy Favorites candidates. This list should give you some ideas, and maybe a few Favorites of your own.

Yahoo!

www.yahoo.com

Yahoo! is more than a Web site; it's a complete online service. I've referred to it many times in this book, and here I describe the parts of it I use the most. I also describe why it remains my number one Web site, as it has been from the first day that I discovered it. Yahoo! started long ago, near the beginning of the Web, just when people were starting to need help finding things. At first, it was merely a Web directory, and that was useful enough. Over time, however, Yahoo! evolved into far more than a simple map of the Web. Now you can dive into Yahoo! for news, sports, finances, personals, yellow pages, clubs, and much more.

My day on the Web usually begins with Yahoo!, specifically with Today's News link. You can find other sites that deliver deeper news, but for speed, nothing beats Yahoo!'s headlines.

Investors use the Yahoo! Finance section constantly. (Select the `StockQuotes` link on the home page.) I have the Finance page saved to my Favorites for easy access. On the Finance page, you can enter any stock market trading symbol and receive a quick price quote (usually about 20 minutes behind the actual market), in simple or detailed form. The detailed version (see Figure 18-1) gives a table of information that's relevant to investors. Yahoo! even offers price charts showing the stock's movement over time, and all this is seamlessly linked to wire service news releases about the stock you're investigating. Many online investors stay plugged into Yahoo! for breaking news about publicly traded companies.

The Yahoo! Sports section is also the quickest way on the Web to check sports scores. You can explore its fast-moving screens by selecting the `Sports` link on the home page.

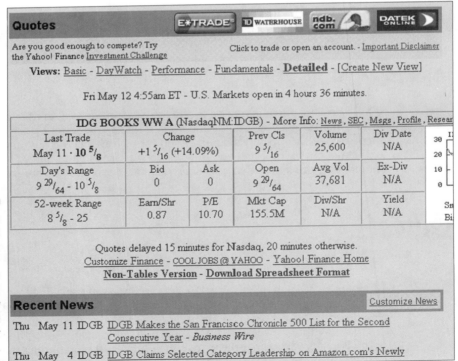

Figure 18-1:
Stock quotes in Yahoo! Finance are quick and clear. Every online investor uses them.

The `Live Net Events` link is the best way to find out what's happening on a given day on the Web. The link is like a town bulletin board for the Internet, where people can put up notices of live events. Live chats and conferences with special guests are listed, and best of all, it's a great way to find out what RealAudio events have just been released. You can find listings of radio interviews released to the Web as RealAudio presentations, news shows broadcast regularly, and much more. I like to check in once a day to see what's going on. You can also look ahead, on a day-by-day basis, to see what's scheduled a week in advance.

It's impossible to adequately describe the depth and value of Yahoo!. Visit. Explore.

Wired News

    www.wired.com

Providing news of the emerging networked world, *Wired News* borrows the sensibility of *Wired*, the neon-paged monthly manifesto of the technology-enhanced lifestyle. *Wired News* is a completely original publication, with little overlap of *Wired*'s content. The articles and features in *Wired News* represent cutting-edge thought and the sensibility of the digital generation, and it's a good read for anyone interested in what's really going on in the global Internet scene. It's not a particularly technical publication, although it does assume a certain experience with the features of the online world. *Wired News* is a site for Netizens; if you're a newcomer, it's a fine way to get up to speed (high speed) with Net culture.

Wired News is on the cutting edge in every way, including the design features it uses. The site is still a good experience for WebTV users, though, because most of the content is in plain (if brightly colored) text. Some cosmetic features might not appear through WebTV, but you still get all the content. One aspect that comes through loud and clear is the stunning color design, which is similar to the retina-scalding pages of *Wired*.

Yodlee and OnMoney

    www.yodlee.com
    www.onmoney.com

These two sites are *personalization portals* that specialize in garbling the conversation of anyone who tries to pronounce that phrase. What does it mean? Both these sites began as services that consolidated online finance accounts — their users could access their online account balances, online brokerage positions, credit card bills, and other accounts all from a single page. Not bad, but a little arcane for many people. Both sites, especially Yodlee, have broadened their appeal recently.

If you open online accounts, OnMoney and Yodlee are still great places to manage those accounts free of charge. Furthermore, users can access their online shopping accounts, travel accounts, Web-based e-mail accounts, and more. In short, these sites are like secretaries for busy and involved Internet citizens.

In my opinion, Yodlee (see Figure 18-2) is a little easier to navigate, displays its screens more clearly, and operates somewhat faster. Start there, but remember OnMoney, which offers unique features of its own.

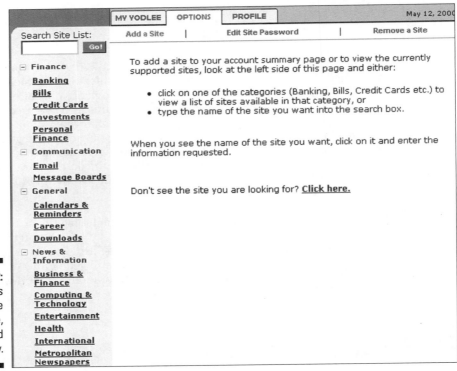

Figure 18-2:
Yodlee helps organize the online life, clearly and simply.

The BigHub

`www.thebighub.com`

One of the most remarkable research sites on the Internet, The BigHub is a collection of about 1,500 distinct search engines, each one prowling through a unique database of information.

Start your visit by scrolling down to the Specialty Search Categories section, and start browsing through the directory. Notice that each category provides a number of search-engine forms inviting you to enter search keywords. Don't neglect the left sidebars, where the directory subcategories lurk. This thing is deep, and although it might seem dry or academic, The BigHub is actually fun to play with. The sense of power is palpable when you have access to so many databases at your fingertips.

To experience the lighter side of this massive research tool, go into the Entertainment portion of the directory (see Figure 18-3). You can search through back issues of *Entertainment Weekly,* data files of certain TV shows, the thousands of Web pages at Viacom, the All-Music Guide, a gigantic database of song lyrics, Rolling Stone Network, Roger Ebert's movie reviews from 1985, and tons more.

You simply must try The BigHub to believe it.

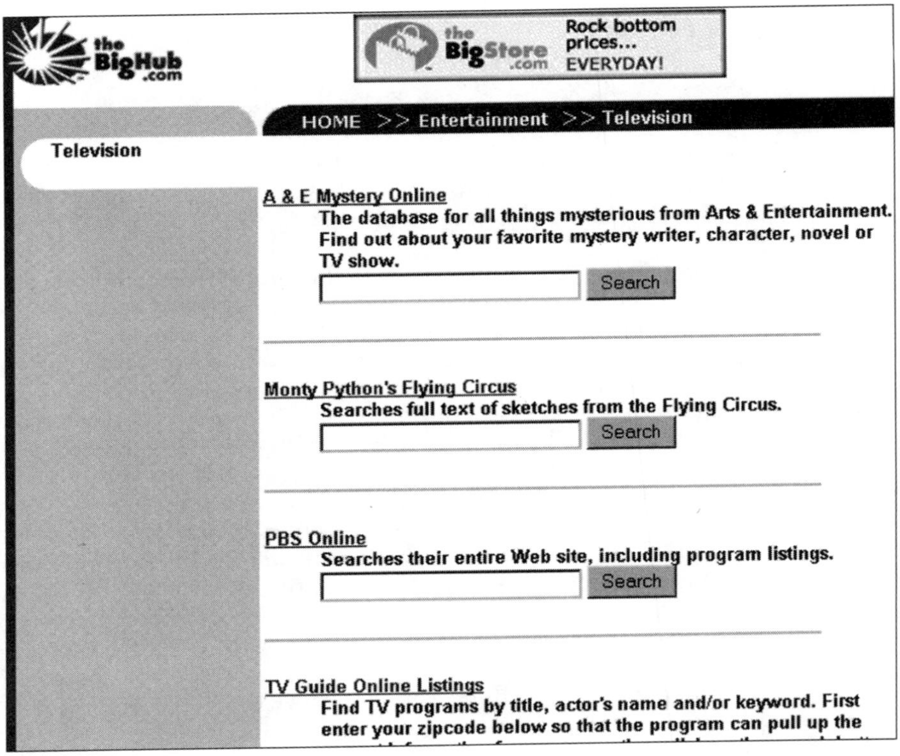

Figure 18-3:
The
BigHub's
collection of
search
engines
makes
prowling for
information
fun.

MP3.com

www.mp3.com

Now we're talking dynamic. Now we're talking controversial. And now, with WebTV's upgraded audio capability, we're talking about something WebTVers can participate in more easily. It's digital music — the online revolution shaking up record companies and delighting music lovers.

You might be familiar with MP3 as a buzzword representing the electronic distribution of songs over the Internet. MP3.com is one of the seminal sites in this revolution, helping thousands of "indie" artists and bands gain wider audiences by presenting their music online. Unlike some other MP3 and digital-music sites, MP3.com presents its downloadable MP3 files legally, sanctioned by the artists who put their music on the site.

Now, you might wonder why I'm recommending a site famous for its down-loads to a community of users who can't download anything to their WebTV units. Never mind the downloads. Almost every song at this site (and it has hundreds of thousands of them) is represented by a *streaming* version that you can listen to instead of downloading. In many cases, the streaming songs are presented in both Lo Fi and Hi Fi versions — always select the Lo Fi choice (see Figure 18-4), unless you fancy watching your nails grow as you wait for the stream to begin.

The upshot? MP3.com is a terrific place to join the digital music scene and find new artists who aren't in the mainstream, pop-centric, star-oriented music biz. You can buy CDs of MP3.com artists here, too.

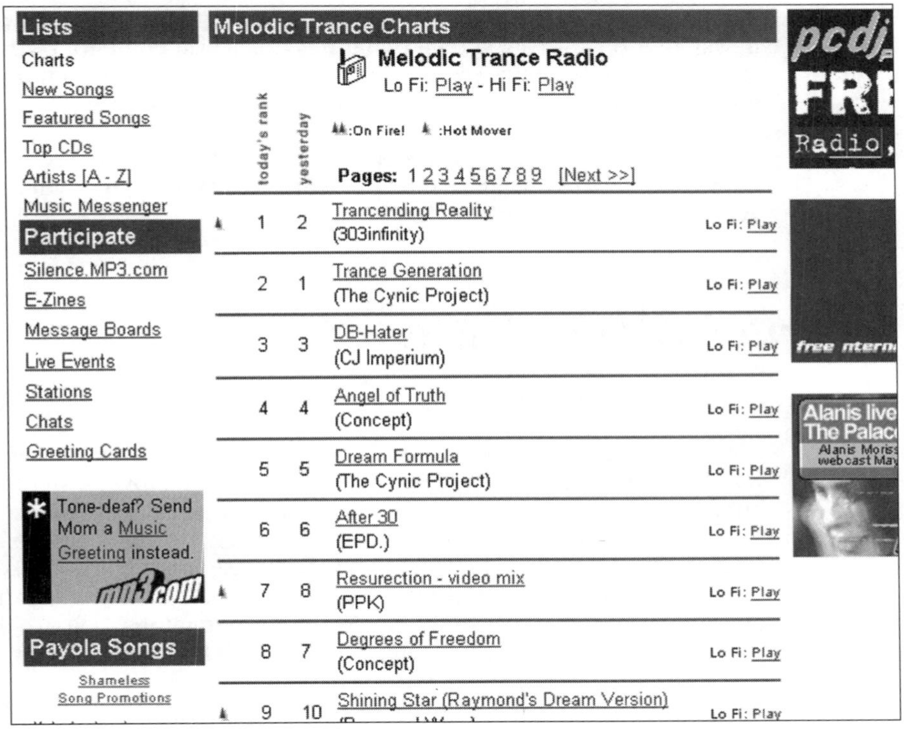

Figure 18-4: WebTV can usually play the Lo Fi songs pre-sented by MP3.com. It's a great way to find new music.

The New York Times

www.nytimes.com

A few years ago *The New York Times* held a contest to determine a new slogan for its online edition. The newspaper slogan, "All the News That's Fit to Print," seemed unseemly for a publication that isn't actually printed. Many thousands of submissions were considered, but in the end none were deemed adequate. So no slogan at all appears on the electronic edition. But if the printed paper contains all worthwhile news, the Web edition somehow manages to be even more valuable.

In addition to posting almost all the printed stories, the Web site adds continual updates throughout the day. Even if you don't like the idea of reading a newspaper on your TV screen (what has this world come to?), you have to respect the global news resources of *The New York Times* organization and its generosity in creating a comprehensive, no-charge site.

Read fast, though. The *Times* keeps its stories "live" for only twenty-four hours. After that you can search a five-day free archive, but older stories are available only on a pay-per-view basis.

Internet Movie Database

www.imdb.com

I can't tell you what a comfort this site is to me. Before the Web, when I watched a movie, I often suffered the frustration of knowing an actor's face but failing to place *how* I knew it. The gnawing tip-of-the-tongue feeling distracted me throughout the whole movie. Now I know that I can go home and look up the actor in the Internet Movie Database (see Figure 18-5). Sanity is preserved (though you might not agree after reading portions of this book). Countless times I've reassured movie-going companions, "Oh, we'll look it up later." It's always the IMDb (as it's affectionately known) that I have in mind.

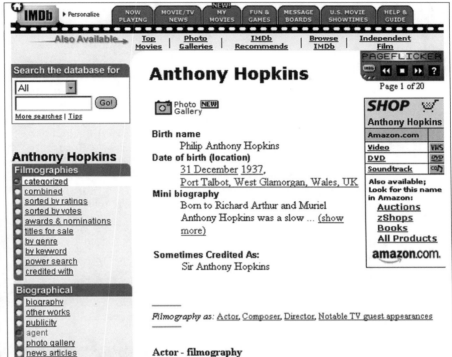

Figure 18-5:
The Internet
Movie
Database is
an essential
resource of
actors and
their work.

The IMDb is incredible. You can search for any actor, any film, any director, any film character, and even TV shows. The cross-referencing provides easy connections and catalysts to faltering memory. Each actor's roles are listed, and you can link directly to every movie on the list to see who else is in it. Television appearances are usually included in the actors' filmographies.

The Internet Movie Database isn't the place to go for pictures or fan gossip. It's well-organized, hard-core information all the way.

TV Guide Online

www.tvguide.com

What could be more natural? Browsing through an interactive edition of *TV Guide* using your interactive-TV, Internet-enhanced information appliance. (That would be WebTV.) This generous site puts up feature articles and frequently updated gossip and other articles, with only gentle efforts to get you subscribed to the magazine. Read transcripts of the many live chats held every week at the site. Browse through the cover gallery.

Oh — and the listings (see Figure 18-6). Punch in your ZIP code and see what's on. On-screen listings might not appeal to Plus users, who have their own sophisticated program lineups, but Classic owners can really benefit.

Figure 18-6:
TV Guide
Online
provides
listings for
any location
in the U.S.,
complete
with cable-
company
channels.

39B E!	<< Paid Programming			
39B BET	Off Air	Off Air	Marilyn Hickey	Kenneth Copeland
40B NICK	Dick Van Dyke	Wonder Years	Bars & Tone	Phred on Your Head
41B A&E	<< McMillan and Wife		Simon & Simon	
42B TWC	First Outlook			
43B USA	Bloomberg Information Television >>			
44B CNBC	Today's Business			
45B MTV	<< Videos		Videos	
46B ESPN	SportsCenter		SportsCenter	
47B MSG	<< Golf		Last Word	Sports Geniuses
48B FSNY	<< New Product Showcase		Sports News	
49B FX	<< Paid Programming			
50B CNN	Ahead of the Curve			
51B TNT	< Kung Fu	Gilligan's Island (TV-G)	Wild Wild West	
52B ESPN2	Legends of Hockey		Backroads with Ron and Raven	Sportsman's Quest
53B DISNEY	Ink and Paint Club		Mouse Tracks (TV-Y)	DuckTales (TV-Y)
54B AMC	<< Reds (PG)			Riders of the Range (NR) >
55B HN	<< Headline News >>			
56B FOOD	Paid Programming >>			
57B TVLAND	Hogan's Heroes	Hogan's Heroes	I Dream of Jeannie	I Dream of Jeannie
58B MSNBC	Special Edition		Imus >>	
59B HIST	Year by Year (TV-G)		Classroom (TV-G)	
60B TLC	<< Paid Programming		Mother Nature (TV-Y)	Salty's Lighthouse
61B CBMART	<< Cable-Mart: Photo Advertising for Local Businesses-Real Estate, Auto, Retail, Professional Services & more. Call Bill Sturman at 908-431-0848. >>			

CBS MarketWatch

cbs.marketwatch.com

One of the preeminent, top-flight finance sites, CBS MarketWatch is an astonishing online resource for investors (see Figure 18-7). Stock-market play-by-play is covered with high journalistic standards, but that's just the front page of this profoundly informative site. Keep scrolling down the page, paying attention to the left sidebar and all the links at the bottom. Dozens upon dozens of links spin off into bunches of content that, by themselves, would do most sites proud.

All-star columnists and a large writing staff give this site the resources to cover emerging news while ruminating on less transitory topics. You can pick your speed with CBS MarketWatch. Of course you can get stock quotes here, but frankly I'd stick to Yahoo! Finance (finance.yahoo.com) for those. Besides that one area of information, CBS MarketWatch is unparalleled for delivering a potent combination of hard-hitting journalism and in-depth reporting.

Figure 18-7: CBS MarketWatch is the gold standard of online stock-market reporting.

The Onion

`www.theonion.com`

Don't talk to me when I'm reading *The Onion*. I'm usually too incapacitated with laughter to reply. Undoubtedly the sharpest and most literate satirical newspaper in America, the Web edition of *The Onion* duplicates the printed paper. If you saw the millennial book called *Our Dumb Century,* you've gotten a taste of the no-boundaries send-ups that characterize *The Onion's* fake news articles. Written in a flawless faux-journalistic style, these examinations of the absurd raise the mundane to ridiculous heights.

Beware. *The Onion* never shies away from vulgarity. This site isn't for kids or for adults who don't favor the off-color rambunctiousness of a comedy club. The spicy language, juxtaposed against the formal wire-service style heightens the hilarity, but only if you have invulnerable sensibilities.

I hope you like *The Onion*. If so, make your visit a mid-week habit. New editions are usually posted on Wednesday.

Chapter 19

Ten More Sites from My Favorites Folder

*T*he hits keep coming. The sites featured in this chapter are every bit as important and excellent as those of Chapter 18. Visit often. Go early and stay late. Learn stuff, buy things, and get enlightened. Remember that you can save more than just home pages in Favorites. As you prowl through these destinations, most of which are sizable, throw valuable inner pages into your Favorites folders before you lose track of where they are. You can always weed them out later.

C|Net

www.cnet.com

C|Net is an awesome domain of information related to technology in general and computers specifically. Some of its spin-off sites are of little use to WebTV-only users — especially the renowned Download.com. But there's much more to C|Net than acquiring programs for a computer. For one thing, if you're considering buying a computer or you use one at work, C|Net puts truckloads of comparative information about hardware and software at your disposal.

I want to direct your attention to the news portion of C|Net (see Figure 19-1), which enjoys the following enviable URL:

```
www.news.com
```

News.com is perhaps the best destination for gleaning current events in the technology universe. More accessible than Wired.com (featured in the previous chapter) and more technical than a general news publication, News.com gives the play-by-play for e-commerce, online services, Web content, and the online business sector. When there's news about WebTV Networks, News.com is among the first publications to report it. I check News.com every day, without fail.

Figure 19-1: News.com, a division of C|Net, provides superb coverage of technology news.

Slate

www.slate.com

A product of Microsoft, *Slate* can be considered *The New Yorker* of the Internet, with an edge of informality befitting the online milieu. Edited by Michael Kinsley, who, in fact, interviewed for the top editorial position at *The New Yorker* when Tina Brown stepped down, this e-zine is literate, funny, scathing, cultured, and — it wasn't always this way — absolutely free. Slate dumped its subscription plan a while back and now dishes up its entertaining pages to any visitor who walks in the virtual door.

One of the most long-running and consistently popular features of *Slate* is Today's Papers (see Figure 19-2), a rundown of features and editorial attitudes of several major U.S. papers. There's no better way (short of reading all those papers yourself) to get a quick grip on current events and current editorial opinion. Scroll down the main Slate page to find Today's Papers; each day's column is posted at about 4:00 A.M. Eastern U.S. time.

Figure 19-2: Today's Papers, an enduringly popular feature of literary e-zine *Slate*.

Real.com

www.real.com

Real.com (see Figure 19-3) became much more fun after WebTV was upgraded to RealAudio G2, a relatively modern version of the prevalent Internet audio format. This portal is a good destination for finding online radio stations and other audio locations.

Much of this crowded home page is dedicated to promoting downloadable software products and must be ignored by WebTVers. Scroll down the page, keeping your eyes on the left sidebar. Several links — Music, Radio/TV Stations, Entertainment, and Live — take you to directories of listenable content.

RealAudio through WebTV is much improved since pre-May 2000 days. Still, at this writing, a recent version of RealAudio (version 7) doesn't work through WebTV, and even newer iterations are sure to follow. The upshot is that there might always be some virtual radio stations and other music streams that WebTV chokes on. Currently, and I hope for a good long time, WebTV handles most RealAudio quite well, and Real.com is a starting point for finding programming.

Figure 19-3: Scroll down Real.com's busy home page to see the Find It Here First section.

Silicon Investor and Raging Bull

www.siliconinvestor.com
www.ragingbull.com

If you're an investor or even if you're just interested in investing — or, for that matter, you just enjoy controversial online discussions — check out one or both of these watering holes.

Silicon Investor is one of the oldest online investing communities, and it remains the gold standard. A subscription service, you must pay a fairly hefty annual fee for the privilege of posting messages. Anyone, however, can waltz in and read the boards without posting. A message board exists for almost every major American stock in existence plus other investing topics. The membership is savvy, and most people take their stock trading with dead seriousness. The subscription fee scares off the disruptive types, by and large, leaving intense, knowledgeable discussions of stocks and their trends.

Raging Bull (see Figure 19-4) is a late arrival on the scene compared to Silicon Investor and has gained great popularity. Part of the site's attraction is the lack of any fee for participating; another appeal is the editorial content (daily articles and columns). In addition, the messaging software is powerful and fun to use.

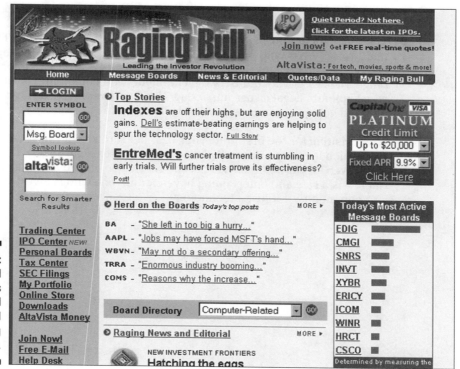

Figure 19-4: Raging Bull offers editorial content and a raging community.

SmartPlanet

www.smartplanet.com

What started as ZDU (Ziff-Davis University), a small education site where average people could learn computer skills, has evolved into a massive catalog of online learning about all kinds of topics.

SmartPlanet is a WebTV-friendly destination that offers subscription access to its complete curriculum. The inexpensive subscription fee can be paid monthly or annually (for a discount) and entitles you to an unlimited number of classes. The "classrooms" are actually message boards, and you might be surprised what a good learning environment that can be. The boards afford each student a chance to ask questions and get individual attention from the instructor. Some people prefer to audit classes silently.

Continuing Education credits are offered for many of the courses taught at SmartPlanet.

Net4TV

www.net4tv.com

The preeminent information site for WebTV and other interactive-TV systems, Net4TV has cultivated its editorial voice and emerged as a sophisticated advocate of convergence technology and its users. With impressive range, Net4TV covers industry developments and community issues with equal aplomb. Legal issues impacting WebTV are reported, as are the comings and goings of prominent individual members.

When visiting for the first time, your best bet is to select the Net4TV Voice link, which leads to a menu of current articles (see Figure 19-5). Editorials about WebTV bar no holds against the service on controversial issues. Net4TV is a safe and entertaining haven for anyone who is invested in WebTV as a community, not just a technology.

Figure 19-5:
Net4TV
presents
information
about all
kinds of
interactive
TV,
including
WebTV.

eBay

www.ebay.com

Of all the headline-grabbing, Internet-related developments over the years, the emergence of eBay (see Figure 19-6) has to be one of the most startling, dramatic, intriguing, and culture-altering. Started as a gigantic online auction, eBay now resembles a global garage sale. Populated primarily by individuals selling possessions from their attics, eBay is also the virtual home to small retail businesses auctioning their inventory.

Even if you have no interest in the various forms of e-commerce or buying anything over the Internet, eBay is a must-see destination. I treat it like a museum. If you haven't given the site the exploration it deserves, visit and be utterly astounded at the range of stuff to be found here.

But beware: eBay addiction is a real affliction.

Figure 19-6:
The auction house-cum-museum, eBay.

Amazon.com

www.amazon.com

The first big Internet retailing brand name, Amazon, like eBay (see the pre-ceding item), can be regarded as a shopping experience or a community experience. Amazon (see Figure 19-7) began as a bookseller, quickly expanded to music CDs, and later evolved into a multifaceted department store selling nearly everything from electronics to patio furniture. Amazon has an auction department, too.

The core attraction is still books. I use Amazon to browse even when I have no intention of buying. (Although I hasten to point out that purchasing through Amazon is a good experience — this company knows how to do e-commerce right.) The readers' reviews were a good idea years ago and have built this domain into what resembles a gigantic book club.

Obviously, the best thing a visitor can do at Amazon.com is buy one of my books. That goes without saying. But after that, enjoy a top-flight browsing experience.

Figure 19-7:
Amazon.com, once merely an online bookstore, now is a full-fledged virtual department store.

U.S. News Online

www.usnews.com

U.S. News Online is the cyberspace nest of *U.S. News and World Report.* Others prefer Time.com, which I also admire. But this site got its virtual act together early in the game, and I got in the habit of visiting for my regular dose of newsweekly-style current events.

The News You Can Use feature lends itself especially well to online publication and is divided on the site into five categories: Money, Health, Tech, Travel, and Work. Each area contains tutorials, tips, and a search engine for finding more.

The site features various interactive perks, but you might want to visit just for the articles — U.S. News shares most of the current newsstand publication with online visitors free of charge.

About.com

www.about.com

A unique resource, About.com is almost an online service in its own right. The idea behind this site is to gather experts in various fields and give each one a site to manage. The result is hundreds of sites (Figure 19-8 shows one), each constructed from the same design template, giving the entire domain a consistent look and feel.

The experts, called Guides, are encouraged to develop their sites into deep, informative destinations. The topics range from broad portal topics such as investing to tiny niche specialties like soap making. Each site is a community, an information resource, and a carefully cultivated experience led by a single committed person. Many About.com destinations are outstanding and there's a bottom-line level of professional to all sites, even those of lesser quality.

Figure 19-8: Investing for Women, one of over 700 special-interest sites at About.com.

WebTV For Dummies
Online Directory

The 5th Wave
By Rich Tennant

SINCE THEN WE DISCONNECT THE ONLINE SHOPPING FUNCTION DURING THE HOURS "LIFESTYLES OF THE RICH AND FAMOUS" IS ON.

In this directory . . .

The WebTV community amazes me. As a long-time computer user, I'm accustomed to other computer users getting to the bottom of new technologies and using them in personal ways. WebTV users don't have nearly the task-oriented tools that computer users do, yet they are one of the most innovative and resourceful groups of online citizens I've ever encountered. The degree to which WebTVers have joined the Internet community with Web pages is astounding.

The first several sections of this directory consist of sites about WebTV, produced by WebTV users, or helpful to the experience of WebTV. I dedicate these sections to WebTV members, the early adopters of a new technology who have improved the system through their intelligence, creativity, curiosity, and resourcefulness.

The last few sections, beginning with *WWW*, contain Web sites of general interest in certain categories. I've included Web portals, search engines, finance sites, and shopping destinations.

To visit any of these sites, you must type the URL in the Go To feature of the Options panel. Some URLs are on the complex side, requiring careful typing. It's important, then, to quickly save to Favorites any site you might want to return to. Don't force yourself to type that URL more than once. It's better to save too many sites and then weed them down later.

About This Directory

You should know a few crucial points about certain sites as quickly as possible. To help get the gist of some sites, I include in this directory a few micons — small graphics that tell you something important at a glance. Here they are:

★★ Particularly attractive or well-designed sites are flagged with this micon.

Some sites in this directory ask for your name, e-mail address, and perhaps some other information before you can view all the site's screens.

The Directory is loaded with free graphics, backgrounds, and MIDI files for use in home pages and WebTV e-mail. Some of these collections invite WebTVers to link directly to the file's location, bypassing the transloading process (see Chapter 13).

Some sites are so useful, have such a great selection of files, or are so unique in their design that they beg to be added to your Favorites collection. This micon is a top honor.

Backgrounds

The Web has a brisk, exciting, and basically free market for background images. Background images can be a simple wash of one color or an elaborate piece of artwork that lies underneath a Web page's text. WebTVers sometimes place a graphic background underneath their e-mails or e-mail signatures (see Chapter 13).

The simplest form of background is to define an HTML color as part of an HTML tag. (Again, see Chapter 14.) The next step up is to acquire a background tile. *Background tiles* are designed to appear as a seamless design when placed against each other. (The tiling is automatic.) Finally, a large background image can be acquired, such as an outer space field of stars or an image of clouds drifting through a blue sky.

This section is an adjunct to Chapter 14, which instructs you in linking and transloading background images. This section mostly lists graphic collections, but also features some link sites that themselves are directories to image archives.

1001 Background Graphics

marketwizz.com/backgrounds/index0002. html

★★
★★

I didn't actually count them, but I'll take the site's word for it. Organized onto 63 pages, each screen displays the actual background tile, not just a link to it. This, thankfully, cuts down on the number of selections you must make to see the backgrounds. To get to the next page in the cycle, scroll down and select the Next icon near the bottom of the page. The quality of the backgrounds? A dazzling collection of textures grouped by color and theme.

Backgrounds Index

www.camalott.com/~tspaar/bgindex.html

Fantasy art meets background textures at this index. The result is one of the wildest, yet most strangely beautiful, collections of backgrounds you'll ever see. These art creations are not tiles, but full-screen backgrounds. The problem with using these images is that their vibrant colors make it difficult to place legible text on top of them. But it's worth experimenting with and, if nothing else, definitely worth gazing at these index pages.

Big Daddy's Free Backgrounds

www.geocities.com/SoHo/Gallery/7752

Simplicity and a wide range of hues characterize Big Daddy's background collection. From black to light grey, this archive provides basic and stylish background tiles, none of which are garish or too attention grabbing. Well, almost none. The entire collection used to be listed on the home page, but has grown to the point of needing additional pages. Still, the site is simply laid out and easy to navigate.

Celine's Original GIFs

www.specialweb.com/original/bgrounds. html

A striking collection of carefully crafted background tiles. Some are subtle and others, if you use them, will grab your visitors by the eyeballs and refuse to let go. Names such as Deep Blue Wind, Stone Smudges, Red Flower Power, and Grey Groovy Flow indicate that Celine is a free spirit with a talent for digital design. Celine has continued her excellent design experiments since the last edition. My only wish is that she'd display the backgrounds tiled over a full page.

The Elated Web Toolbox

★ ★
★ ★

www.elated.com/toolbox

A high-end graphics site, The Elated Web Toolbox features kits for adding certain graphic elements to a Web page. The texture kits, for example, provide background textures; the button kits offer stylized buttons of various sizes that give a common design theme to a Web page. You should avoid one type of kit, though — called the page kits — because they furnish entire Web page templates that are useful only on a computer. The other kits are fine for WebTV.

Holiday Backgrounds

www.cpsweb.com/hdayback.htm

This site suggests a great idea. Around the holidays, why not change the background imagery of your Web page to match the jubilant spirit? In truth, the only holiday addressed at this site seems to be Christmas, and only 16 background tiles are available. But the site uses mostly soft pastel colors, making them suitable for lying under text, especially text with the bold tag, <b>. (See Chapter 13.) Come December, give this page a look.

HTML Color Names

pages.prodigy.com/reck/colnmes.htm

Putting a background color behind your WebTV e-mail signature or your Web page is one of the most attractive — and easy — design choices you can make. Easy, that is, if you know the official name of the color you want to use. Each color recognized by the WebTV system (and most computer systems) is identified by a name and an HTML code, which is a combination of letters, numbers, or both. It doesn't matter whether you use the name or the code, but you must use one or the other. HTML Color Names is a big chart of colors that gives each hue's name and code. Very useful.

Over the Rainbow

www.geocities.com/SiliconValley/Heights/ 1272/index.html

Don't go into this site if you're enjoying a bad mood — the optimism and good cheer is overwhelming. Advertising text-friendly backgrounds, Over the Rainbow delivers with gorgeous color screens and fading hues that accommodate text perfectly. Try the Conservative Backgrounds collection for the most text-friendly of all. Batik Backgrounds are absolutely lovely, though some of them don't hold text easily. It's obvious that great care has gone into the creation of these background images, and the site is a treasure.

Scream Design

http://www.screamdesign.com/freebies.
html

From brick walls to wood paneling to less describable psychedelic statements, Scream Design provides an uninhibited collection of art. More than just backgrounds, you also find GIFs, buttons, numbers, letters, and miscellaneous graphics. The interface isn't optimized for WebTV, so the tile images appear to be scattered randomly across a black surface.

Other Stuff to Check Out

members.tripod.com/~SeaCup/ohhno.html
www3.islandnet.com/~luree/custom.html
www.geocities.com/SoHo/9695/
background1.html
www.geocities.com/SouthBeach/Surf/1057/
index.html

Free Web Pages

The Page Builder service lets you put a site right on WebTV computers. If that's your choice, you don't need any of the sites in this section. Some folks, however, prefer to go outside WebTV for site hosting. The Page Builder tools, though convenient for beginners, are limiting for those with more experience. Many companies have entered the marketplace as Web site hosting services. The best news is that the service is often free.

The sites listed here all offer ready-made communities of Web page owners. The "city" and "neighborhood" models are often cleverly implemented, in the hope that members feel a real sense of belonging. Each offers a certain amount of host computer memory for storing Web pages, measured in *megs* (megabytes). Unless you are creating a library of graphics and music files on your Web pages, the amounts of memory provided by these sites should be ample.

Another service offered to some degree by each of these listed sites is online Web-page-building help. This means you don't need access to a word processor or HTML editor. Chapter 13 can help you with many of the HTML tags you may need to know to complete the process at any one of these hosting services.

AngelFire

www.angelfire.com

AngelFire is popular with WebTV subscribers. One selling point: AngelFire provides a library of images and sounds for your pages. Because they're already on the same server as your site, they don't need to be transloaded. AngelFire gives up to 30 megabytes of site storage, up from a previous 5 megs.

FortuneCity

www2.fortunecity.com

A popular and classy Web site community, FortuneCity has much to offer. 100 megabytes of Web page memory is exceptionally generous, and the community is spiced with dozens of neighborhood communities with names such as Benny Hills, Campus, Rainbow Park, Underworld, Wembley, and The Jail. You can also find free e-mail, chatting, and lots of site promotion opportunities.

Freetown

www.freetown.com

Freetown is a virtual community that takes the town model to the max. Freetown incorporates many elements of an actual town in its directory, including a post office (e-mail), newspaper (news headlines), a police station (lists the whereabouts of everyone currently chatting), a mall (online shopping), and neighborhoods (where free Web pages are stored). The free Web page builder includes a Construction Company and Home Improvements center. The analogy might get overbearingly cute, but it works.

The Globe

www.theglobe.com

25 megs of Web page memory lags behind some of the other communities (though it's more than you get at Yahoo! Geocities), but The Globe makes up for it in other ways. (Besides, unless you're stuffing massive graphics onto your site at a record pace, 25 megs is likely all you need.) The Globe is positioned as one of the leading Internet communities. Members receive e-mail updates of Globe events, some of which involve celebrity meets. The site-design and publishing tools are a strong point here.

TalkCity

www.talkcity.com

A leading and well-rounded online community service, TalkCity enhances its status as a foremost chat center by now offering free home pages with an industry-lagging 12 megabytes of storage. The community structure and neighborhood system is relatively undeveloped compared to GeoCities, Tripod, and FortuneCity. Live chat events and clubs are the main community venues here; free Web pages are icing on the cake.

Tripod

www.tripod.com/

Tripod is part of the Lycos online portal, and has improved greatly since the last edition of this book. Gone is the chaotic home page. However, don't expect that much

storage space — in this regard Tripod is still mired in the past, providing 11 megabytes. But don't disregard Tripod's benefits. Millions of members populate about a hundred community neighborhoods — this is a bustling virtual society. Great home-page-building support has made Tripod popular with WebTVers and others. This is a community to sink your teeth into.

Xoom

xoom.com/home/

Xoom's home page doesn't come across well on the WebTV screen, but don't let that unimportant fact blind you from the benefits of this service as a Web host. Attacking the stinginess of its competitors, Xoom boldly offers 500 megabytes of free storage — an industry-leading gesture. The Sharehouse feature isn't of use to WebTVers without access to a computer, so don't be swayed by all the hype about that service.

Yahoo! GeoCities

geocities.yahoo.com

The granddaddy of Web communities, GeoCities is the most populated free Web page society and one of the most controversial as well. The virtual community is all the more in the cyberspace mainstream after being acquired by Yahoo!. The Yahoo! purchase has toned down GeoCities's rampant advertising policy on member pages, a source of past infuriation among its residents. GeoCities has one of the clearest home pages in the business and gives you 15 megs of storage. GeoCities has been doing this for a long time, and it knows the business. The partnership with Yahoo! lends clarity and efficiency to the sign-up process.

Other Stuff to Check Out

www.freeyellow.com
www.freeservers.com

WebTV Game Sites

Games can present a problem for the WebTV interface if they require a smooth mouse interface, which computers have. Also, clicking and dragging (a maneuver performed with a computer mouse to move on-screen game pieces around) is not supported by WebTV, so games such as chess, which normally require dragging as a way of moving pieces, can't be played on WebTV.

This section lists game sites that work perfectly through WebTV, including one chess site.

Astrology Online

www.astrology-online.com/zodiac.htm

If you take astrology seriously, forgive me for placing this site in the "WebTV Game Sites" section. The folks who maintain this site are obviously dedicated to planetary alignments and their indications, and they furnish daily and weekly horoscopes for all sun signs. That's the recreational aspect of the site. Beyond the forecasts is a wealth of background about the ancient art.

Bill's Games

www.billsgames.com

What a wealth of great WebTV-playable games Bill Kendrick has assembled on one site: hangman, Plaid Libs (a variation on Mad Libs, in which you make up hilariously word-displaced stories), a word scramble, brain teasers, Tic-Tac-Web, a Concentration-style memory game, Websweeper, mazes, and much more. This is the WebTVers ideal central gaming site and a great family

favorite. Congratulations to Bill for setting up his own domain; all game-loving WebTVers hope for his continued success.

Crossword Puzzles

ed.webtv.net/~tpark/new/crosswordpub/ general/

The home page isn't much to look at — it's just a list of puzzles by filename. It looks kind of geekish, but don't let that dissuade you from choosing one. The puzzles themselves are beautiful and surprisingly smooth to operate. It's helpful to have an optional keyboard for these puzzles. Use the arrow keys to move around the puzzle squares. The puzzles I've tried are of an intermediate level, which suits me just fine. Various subjects are offered. The design of the puzzles isn't necessarily symmetrical, which is a surprise but a trivial complaint. Try them!

Earth: 2025

www.eesite.com

An extremely ambitious game screen, Earth: 2025 is a country-building game that you can play, tournament-style, with thousands of other players. Or, less competitively, you may play the Standard game. Or both. (One account for each game is allowed. Registration is required but free.)

Funplanet

www.funplanet.com/us/index.html

Funplanet is a game and trivia center that's partially accessible to WebTV. Stay away from the Comet game because it requires Java, an Internet feature not implemented on WebTV. But there's plenty to select from without that game, including blackjack, Superpoker, a word hunt, and quizzes about movies, sports, and music.

Gamesville

www.bingozone.com/html_gv/gv_login.
htm

Gamesville is a jewel of the Lycos network crown, long renowned as a premiere gaming site for low-tech play. Many of the games carry prizes, some of them substantial. I recommend Bingo as a good place to start through WebTV. Most games work in the WebTV interface, but you never know when a Java interface will trip you up. If that happens, just Back-button your way out and try another game.

Guess the TV Theme Songs

users.southeast.net/~oct24/tvgame.htm

You must try this. I insist. The quiz consists of three sets of about ten TV themes each. You listen to one after the other, using drop-down menus to select which song goes with which show. The game is timed, so quick identification is part of the fun. Scroll down to the bottom of the page and select the Check Answers button to find your score. The songs are played through MIDI arrangements and are really quite excellent. It's a hum-worthy trip down memory lane.

IQ Test

www2.iqtest.com

For some, an IQ test might not seem like a game. But this site claims to have the most entertaining IQ test on the Internet, so it qualifies for the "WebTV Game Sites" section of the Directory. The tests are shorter than a real IQ test, so you don't need to devote much time to this exercise. The site goes out of its way to reassure us that IQ isn't necessarily related to success in life. In fact, the site goes too far out of its way, before letting you get to the test, to make sure you understand that this is *all in fun*. Yadda, yadda, yadda — bring on the test, already. Finally, after a quick registration process, you can match wits with the test questions.

duJour

www.dujour.com

The duJour site offers several games played with points. You can only gain points, never lose them. At the end of each day, the person with the highest point total wins a prize. Because of the distribution of prizes, registration is necessary but free.

Rags to Riches

www.headbone.com/wtvrags/

★★ ★★

Rags to Riches is a sophisticated fantasy-career-building game whose complexities probably make it unsuitable for kids under 12. The goal here is to manage a rock group to stardom, making management choices for them and booking the band on a world tour.

Rewind

www.80s.com/Entertainment/Music/
Rewind/

From a site dedicated to cultural artifacts of the 1980s, Rewind is a name-that-tune game featuring — you guessed it — songs of the 1980s. Manic Medley is a similar game, and the Rewind page also links to a movie quote quiz. Scroll down to see both those links.

Robbie's WebTV Games Galore

www.angelfire.com/ca/kidstown/
page1.html

As the name implies, Robbie has put together a link site to WebTV-playable games around the Net. From quizzes to adventure games, bingo to casino games, Robbie seems to have an unslakable thirst for games, which is fortunate for the rest of us.

Other Stuff to Check Out

www.blueberry.co.uk/gid-bin/berries
www.brain.com
www.facade.com/attraction/tarot
www.puzzledepot.com

GIFs for Web Pages

GIF stands for Graphic Interchange Format, and now that I told you that, I suggest you forget it. Basically, a GIF file is a picture file, and pictures suitable for use on a Web page are commonly known as GIFs. GIF files have a .gif file extension at the end of the filename. Another common graphic file type is JPEG, with the .jpg file extension, and some of these sites contain JPEG archives in addition to GIFs.

GIFs are sometimes used as background images for Web pages, and some GIF artwork is featured in the foreground. This section doesn't discriminate between background and foreground but provides several picture collections for browsing, linking, and transloading. (See Chapter 13 for information on transloading and linking pictures.)

The Cottage

members.tripod.com/~JC1035

A pleasing, down-home atmosphere pervades this site, with a relaxed attitude that includes an invitation to link directly to its images without transloading them. Imaginative library names include The Basement (background images), The Kitchen (food images), The Library (signs and graphic alphabets), The Garden (flower images), and The Attic (lines, bars, and other design elements).

Danny's Collection of Animated GIFs

www.geocities.com/SoHo/3505

★ ★
★ ★

Danny has been hard at work, apparently. Formerly Danny's "Little" Collection, the site has grown. Just browsing through this site's treasure-trove of animated images can be addictive. The available categories are in the middle of the screen; just select one to see a list of images. The categories promise an unusual selection, including animated GIFs, and you won't be disappointed. Even the home page has been cleaned up and whipped into a more professional format since the last edition of this book — much improved.

Dr. Fun's Animated GIFs

www.drfun.com/ani.htm

His name is Dr. Cosmo Fun (no doubt his real name), and he specializes in animated graphics files for home pages. This is a somewhat odd site that clearly caters to WebTV users, yet displays messily on the WebTV screen. There is a Help message board for WebTV users. The images here are meant for transloading, not for direct linking.

Draac's Free GIFs 123

members.tripod.com/~gifs123/index.html

  ★ ★
★ ★

Draac is almost legendary among WebTV users. A special section of helpful resources for designing WebTV e-mail is probably unique on the Web. It's rare that a Web site is optimized according to WebTV display parameters, and this one does a beautiful job. It's modeled after the WebTV Web Home screen (a bit satirically, in fact), and is almost as attractive. Draac offers a cogent explanation of how to link to his images, along with permission to do so without transloading. The tutorial is usable, and the images are mostly static pictures. The site operates fairly quickly on the Tripod server (see the URL) and is a good bet for linking. Have fun!

Fancymay's Links

members.tripod.com/~Fancymay

Fancymay, for all the capriciousness of her name, is a serious collector of graphic resources for home-page building. Her site is a directory of links to other sites for acquiring textured backgrounds, GIF pictures, and MIDI sound files. The design is simple and clear, and the range of links is impressive. She has a tremendous list of background-only sites. A great Favorites selection.

Free GIFs for WebTV

www.angelfire.com/pa/freegifs/index.
  html

This collection isn't the largest in the world, but it has some unusual and clever pictures and animations. Check out the dancing raisin, for example. Felix the Cat, worriedly pacing, is also fun. The Monster Mailbox animation gobbles mail voraciously. Background images are offered here in addition to the animations. The Free GIFs for WebTV collection can be used by any computer user but has been built by a WebTV subscriber and is obviously meant to cater to other WebTVers.

GIFPILE

www.geocities.com/SoHo/Gallery/2681/
  home.html

A pile of GIFs? It's certainly not an understatement — what we have here is a *big* pile of graphic elements for enlivening any Web page. From backgrounds to banners, animations to static pictures, this site collects nifty graphics from all over the Web. The site is copied at three distinct Web locations — it doesn't matter which one you

choose from the home page. In addition to its own incredible graphic collection, GIF-PILE is a good hub site for finding all kinds of graphics stuff on the Web.

Graphics and Stuff

www.geocities.com/SiliconValley/Horizon/
  7489/gifs.html

An excellent jumping-off point in your search for Web images, Graphics and Stuff links to other hub sites as well as original image collections and transloading services. Created by Alan Y., a WebTV member, Graphics and Stuff is part of his extensive Web-based WebTV Guide.

Patrick's Free Graphics for Webbers

www.geocities.com/Heartland/
  Pointe/8961

Having optimized his site for WebTV users, Patrick goes a step further and invites anyone to link freely to any graphics he presents, without transloading it off the server. You still may prefer to transload it into your Web site directory, but you have no moral obligation to do so in this case. The collection is a diverse mix of backgrounds, static images, arrows, buttons, and e-mail symbols. Angels, state flags, music pictures, and Halloween images are some of the more unusual categories. The site may be on the inelegant side, but it's easy to use and has some wonderful material for the taking.

Rozie's Alpha-Bytes

www.geocities.com/HotSprings/3055/
  alphabet.html

Alphabet graphics are not the same as fonts. A *font* is meant to be used throughout an entire portion of text; *alphabet graphics* are highly designed, colorful letters best used one at a time. You can drop in a letter graphic as the first word of a paragraph, for example, to good effect. Rozie's letters are whimsical and even garish, but definitely fun.

WebTV Friends Linkable GIFs

www.geocities.com/ResearchTriangle/Lab/
6510/gif.html

 ★★
★★

Despite a notice saying the site is moving (which might be gone by the time you read this), the GIFs are still available and easily linked. Scroll down the home page to see the links. This site is constructed especially for WebTV viewing, so it operates smoothly and quickly. Furthermore, its invitation to link directly to the images, without transloading them to another server, is WebTV-friendly. The collection itself is pretty large and includes some backgrounds in addition to the standalone GIF pictures and animated GIFs.

Other Stuff to Check Out

members.theglobe.com/seide/default.
html
www.erinet.com/jelane/families

WebTV Help Pages

The WebTV service provides some on-screen technical assistance, but nothing compared to the support provided by WebTV members for each other. An extensive grass-roots movement exists on the Web to expand the consciousness of the average WebTV subscriber. This section lists some of the unofficial sites that help explain how to make the most out of WebTV.

AAA WebTV Forum Site

www.geocities.com/WestHollywood/
Heights/6504/index.html

AAA is a community resource for WebTV users. It's interested only in interactivity community in some form, such as chatting or message boards. The site is optimized for the WebTV screen and is clear and easy to use.

Alan's WebTV Guide

www.geocities.com/SiliconValley/Horizon/
7489/

Alan provides a detailed and wide-ranging service at this site, which is more than just a WebTV guide. In fact, it's a fairly broad Internet guide, linking to Net reference sources, travel and money services online, music, sports, entertainment, and much more. In addition, he groups WebTV-specific pages.

Dave's WebTV Tips and Tricks

www.geocities.com/Area51/Chamber/
4328/index.html

Dave is one sharp techie. He has figured out some nifty backdoor tips and tricks for WebTV users and is careful to say which ones apply only to WebTV Classic. He teaches you how to create backgrounds and offers links to a few help sites. Select the `index page` link (you must scroll down to see it) for a more coherently organized view of all he has to offer. Dave is one of the most knowledgeable and skilled users of WebTV currently publishing Web pages.

Introduction to WebTV

www.geocities.com/ResearchTriangle/
8795/intro.html

Paul Erickson has written a general and basic FAQ (Frequently Asked Questions) page about WebTV. It might be too elementary if you're already a WebTV user, but it's a good page to send a non-user (if that person can receive it on a computer) or to print and give to a family member you're trying to drag online through WebTV.

Net4TV

www.net4tv.com

As spotlighted in Chapter 19, Net4TV is a fantastic site that goes beyond the typical array of help links and recycled information. Net4TV is an editorial powerhouse that speaks on behalf of the WebTV community while covering the entire interactive TV field.

Richie Rich's WebTV Links

members.tripod.com/~richierich_1/

A fantastic launching pad for WebTV-friendly exploration. Richie packages links and specialized search engines on this single page.

Ultimate WebTV Search

www.webtvsearch.com

Libby has created a fine and deep linking resource. Many of her categories apply specifically to WebTV, such as official company pages, WebTV-friendly games, and WebTV message boards. Other categories help with general Internet exploration.

Usenet Advice for WebTV Users

www.watchingyou.com/webtv.html

This informative page is a blast of get-with-it protocol for participating in Usenet newsgroups, the discussion forums of the Internet. The page also spells out WebTV's Terms of Service rules as related to discussion groups.

WebTV Development Help

www.geocities.com/Athens/Acropolis/
2289/webtv.html

Written from the perspective of a GeoCities page owner, WebTV Development Help nonetheless offers constructive tutorials about building a home page with HTML commands no matter where you have your site. One small problem is that the lessons assume that you have access to a computer. Not to worry, though. The basic instruction about HTML commands is useful for non-computer WebTVers — just ignore such instructions as "Now save the file."

WebTV Experts

www.geocities.com/WestHollywood/
Heights/6504/expertlist.html

Power to the people! Gleefully bypassing the official WebTV customer service routes, WebTV Experts is a clearinghouse of WebTV users who specialize in certain aspects of the WebTV experience and are willing to answer questions through e-mail. A few dozen such informal experts are listed by expertise, such as HTML coding, WebTV technical, Internet searching, WebTV Plus setup, and e-mail signature files. Click any name, and a Write a message screen appears, ready to carry your question directly to a self-professed expert's mailbox.

WebTV FAQ

hammer.prohosting.com/~aosw/faq.html

This FAQ (Frequently Asked Questions) page belongs to the Usenet newsgroup alt.online-service.webtv. Unlike most newsgroup FAQs, this one goes way beyond spelling out rules of protocol in the newsgroup and answers many basic questions about the WebTV experience, from hooking up a system to transloading graphics to a Web site.

WebTV Friends

members.tripod.com/~DJACE/ace4.html

WebTV Friends is an all-purpose WebTV user site; I placed it in the "WebTV Help Pages" section of the Directory on the strength of two of its links. The Printing Resource Page features some fun printable screens but far more useful is the WebTV

`Word Processor` — a clever attraction that lets you practice HTML commands. (A brief HTML lesson helps.) The `HTML Resource Page` link is a deeper instruction manual on HTML tags.

WebTV Planet

demo-net.hypermart.net/tricks.html

 ★★
★★

WebTV Planet is a collection of nicely designed pages stuffed to the gills with tips and tricks. The writing is riddled with typos, but don't pay any attention to that. Here you can find hidden codes, keyboard commands, and alternate ways of doing stuff through WebTV. Fair warning: Some of the tips are dated and no longer work. You have to try them to find out. Although a little more upkeep would benefit this site, the sheer volume of tips makes it all worth while.

WebTV SIG

www.webtvsig.com

★★
★★

SIG is an online term from the 1980s meaning Special Interest Group. This page hasn't been around quite that long. The Andresen family constructed it to provide helpful links for WebTV users. When you get to the preceding URL, select the `My Browser is WebTV` link for the best path through the site.

WebTV Tools and Resources

www.geocities.com/Yosemite/Trails/4666/ tools.html

 ★★
★★

A fantastic link page to helpful WebTV-centric sites, WebTV Tools and Resources covers transloading services, online word processors, and many kinds of resource pages. This one should be saved as a Favorite.

Other Stuff to Check Out

www.ruel.net/settop.html

HTML Help

HTML, or Hypertext Markup Language, is the underlying language that creates hyperlinks and screen formatting on the Web. Chapter 13 explains the basics of HTML coding and how to create WebTV e-mail formatting and Web pages with HTML tags. HTML is a subject deserving of an entire book (dozens of such books are out there), and many Web sites tackle portions of the topic. Some of the following sites are designed specially for the WebTV member who wants to begin using HTML or use it more effectively. Other sites are generally helpful to anyone wanting a better understanding of HTML.

Basic Word Processor

www.geocities.com/SiliconValley/Lab/ 1025/word.html

This site is doing itself a disservice by calling its word-processing tool *basic*. Far more than a mere text-input editor, the Basic Word Processor is enhanced with buttons that activate certain HTML tags. When you want to type a line in bold or italics, for example, just select the `Bold` or `Italic` button — no need to know the HTML codes. The buttons cover headings, lists, fonts, and general formatting. An outstanding tool. Be sure to familiarize yourself with the cut-and-paste commands described in Chapter 6.

HTML Text and Word Processor

www.angelfire.com/ny/CodePad/ wordprocess.html

A very nice tool indeed and invaluable for WebTVers designing their own Web page. If you're writing your HTML code manually, this site is especially welcome. A basic word-processing screen allows you to type text, and then the `Preview` button displays the Web page in progress. (Use the `Back` button to return to the word processor after previewing.) This system provides a great way to practice your HTML and cut-and-paste skills (see Chapter 6).

WebTV Word Processor

www.geocities.com/Yosemite/Trails/4666/ word.html

Perhaps the easiest on-screen word processor for WebTVers, this site allows regular text typing and HTML tags and provides dictionary support. As with the other word-processing sites in this section, you need to copy and paste your work as described in Chapter 6.

Other Stuff to Check Out

www.angelfire.com/vt/VirtualXone/ ?site=Enter
www.geocities.com/SoHo/Cafe/9710/ a.WordProcessor.html

MIDI Files

MIDI, the Musical Instrument Digital Interface, is the most convenient music format for use on Web pages. The reason for this is that MIDI files are much smaller than other music files, and they load more quickly. Many WebTVers use MIDI songs as soundtracks for their e-mail or Web pages.

This section lists MIDI song collections that provide music files for linking or transloading. See Chapter 13 for information on transloading files.

Grav's Linkables

www.geocities.com/SouthBeach/Cove/ 8501/index.html

Whoever Grav is, he or she is a generous soul. Link away directly to these MIDI files, and forget about transloading them. (That

invitation is offered to WebTV users only.) Quick tutorials on how to code MIDI playback features into your page or signature file are a welcome feature of this site. The tunes themselves lean toward vintage pop and rock, including the music of Eric Clapton, the Rolling Stones, Kansas, and Steely Dan.

Looney Tunes Sound Source

www.nonstick.com/sounds

Oh, how could I resist this one. This is not a MIDI site, I admit it. But if you're a cartoon fan, you must surf over to this thing immediately. It's stuffed full of audio files — actual recordings — of Bugs Bunny, Daffy Duck, Elmer Fudd, Road Runner, Tweety, Wile E. Coyote, and many other beloveds exclaiming, snorting, gasping, screaming, and otherwise holding forth in superlative sound bites. Sound effects and music links round out the extensive collection. This site is a gem.

MIDI Tunes

www.geocities.com/SunsetStrip/5621/ MidiTunes.html

This highly selective page features only rock, pop, country, and easy listening MIDI files. That may seem like a broad spectrum of music, and indeed it has about 100 pieces, but they're obviously handpicked according to a particular taste. WebTV users are welcome to link directly to any file on this page, without transloading it.

Pipeline: Music Selected for WebTV

tv.iacta.com/wpages/wpipe_midi.htm

A link resource to collections of MIDI music files all over the Web, this site does a good job of covering the most important MIDI archives in cyberspace. Each link is accompanied by a one-paragraph description, much appreciated by those of us who want to know where we're going before we get there.

Sound & Music Galore

www.angelfire.com/ma/MaCBeeR/
mac2.html

An atypical link page to MIDI music sites, Sound & Music Galore features the unusual. Did you know there's a Scottish MIDI music site? You would from the index presented here. From movie themes to classical to karaoke, Sound & Music Galore ferrets it out and links you to it.

Standard MIDI Files on the Net

www.aitech.ac.jp/~ckelly/SMF.html

A somewhat technical presentation of links to MIDI files indexes, Standard MIDI Files on the Net requires some exploration and a bit of an adventurous spirit. (By the way, *standard* MIDI files are the type that play automatically through WebTV. You don't need to be concerned with nonstandard MIDI files.) This site is distinguished by a search engine that allows you to search by a style of music, an artist, or a composer.

Official WebTV Sites

This section lists sites created by WebTV Networks and other companies involved in the WebTV venture.

Club WebTV

webtv.net/corp/clubwebtv/newsletter/
Club WebTV is a monthly newsletter of news, columns, technical information, letters from subscribers, and archived past issues. The site always has an open letter from one of the company's three founders. The Town Square feature highlights items from the webtv.users newsgroup. It's a decent effort to create a club-like feeling

among WebTV subscribers, but the grass-roots clubbiness through home pages and newsgroup postings is much more compelling.

Help Center FAQ

wecare.webtv.net

This list is an outline of the entire Internet side of the WebTV service (the features shared by Classic and Plus), framed as an enormous question-and-answer session. There's a keyword search engine for asking your own questions.

WebTV Home Page

www.webtv.net

★ ★
★ ★

WebTV Networks has toned down the graphics pizzazz of its official site since the last edition of this book, and now offers a quick, attractive roundup of information concerning Classic and Plus services and hardware. You can view charts that compare features of the two systems as well as lists of accepted printers. All the specs are here.

Sites by WebTVers

Here's a collection of sites created by WebTV members. The sites are not necessarily *about* WebTV — plenty of such sites are sprinkled through the rest of the Directory. These sites are primarily recreational and struck my fancy.

Gary & Mary's Cyberpad

www.angelfire.com/tn/gofer/frames.html
Gary and Mary have created an environment that manages to be both homey and celestial. Enlivened by a playful sense of humor (check out the Black Hole link), this site has something for everyone — or at least tries hard. The All-Night Jukebox is

perhaps the most winning feature. As the site says, "Today is the tomorrow we worried about yesterday." I'm not sure what that means, but it sounds wise.

Karen's WebTV Web Ring

www.geocities.com/SouthBeach/Palms/
   3153/karensring.html

Karen started her Web ring with only a single requirement for membership: All ring sites must be created using WebTV. Given that, the sites can be about any topic in the world (any G-rated topic, that is). Exploring her ring is fun; keep her in mind if you've created a page and would like to join. She provides complete instructions.

Pictures and Art on the Web

members.tripod.com/~cholicow

Mostly fantasy art here: Dolphin Child, Space Child, Nite Quest, and others. The artistic values are very clear and appealing. The spacey background adds to the atmosphere.

Semi-Wicked Good Maine Page

members.tripod.com/ayuh

A bright MIDI theme from *Green Acres* should wake you up with a jolt if you drowse into this site. Take the facts about Maine with a grain of salt. There's no mention of fiddleheads, one of that noble state's best spring features. If you have a hankering to read an online Maine newspaper, this is the place to go.

Tom's Attic

members.tripod.com/~tchatterton/webtv.
   html

Tom Chatterton is apparently the world's most dark-addicted night owl. His site, begun as a college project and having grown way out of the test tube, is an eclectic collection of information and humor. The background music is nice, and the pages are unpredictable in design and content. A fun site.

WWW Finance Sites

Money and the Internet — a perfect marriage, but without the music and flower petals. Financial publishing online has grown to vast proportions. This section just scratches the surface, pointing you in directions in which you can continue exploring.

CBS MarketWatch

cbs.marketwatch.com

See the full review in Chapter 18. This is a gold-standard site for comprehensive coverage of the stock and bond markets.

Free Real Time

www.freerealtime.com

Serious investors pay monthly subscription fees for sophisticated stock quotes that instantly reflect exchange pricings. Most consumer stock quotes on the Internet are delayed by fifteen or twenty minutes. Free Real Time is a quote service that delivers exactly what its name promises. After a free registration, you can type any ticker symbol and get an up-to-the-second quote. The limitation of one quote per screen is a handicap, but hey, you get what you pay for.

Gomez.com

www.gomez.com

So many financial service sites now exist that evaluating and choosing services for personal use is a real challenge. Which online broker to use? Which online bank has the best features? Gomez.com takes on the challenge of defining and identifying the best features of online brokers, banks, insurance companies, and mortgage lenders. This site is a must-visit for anyone getting interested in online money management.

InvestorWords

www.investorwords.com

Quick, what is a demand curve? I'm sorry, that's not correct. If you'd like to do better on next week's quiz, make InvestorWords a habit. A legendary glossary of financial terms, the site is almost unbelievably comprehensive. Best of all, the layout makes it easy to find the word you're looking for. Intensive cross-referencing leads to the sort of dictionary browsing that either enthralls you or puts you to sleep. At any rate, InvestorWords is the address to know when you need a word defined.

MSN MoneyCentral

moneycentral.msn.com

Deep, resourceful, and informative, MoneyCentral is one of the great financial portals on the Web. Its boundaries go way beyond investing to cover financial planning, electronic bill-paying, interactive portfolios, mortgage assistance, and much more. Editorial content is not as comprehensive as at some other destinations, but there's no site with broader reach or more well-chosen tools. Some sections require free registration.

SmartMoney

www.smartmoney.com

This online edition of the popular magazine is stuffed with useful editorial and interactive content. A solid emphasis on mutual funds and the personalities behind the stock market distinguishes this site from others, not to mention its efficient and eye-pleasing design. Check out the stock screens for good investing ideas.

TheStreet.com

www.thestreet.com

One of the most respected online investment publications, TheStreet.com is the creation of James Cramer, volatile, cranky, and entertaining Wall Street opinionist. Cramer's take-no-prisoners attitude is all over this site, whose columnists and reporters cover every aspect of the quickly evolving investment scene. Some portions of the site are reserved for paying subscribers.

Yahoo! Finance

finance.yahoo.com

A juggernaut among financial Web sites, Yahoo! Finance provides a quick, easily navigable convergence of quotes, news, fundamental research, stock charts, and investment message boards. Every online investor uses Yahoo! Finance for at least one of its many features. Go to the home page, type a ticker symbol into the quote field, and take it from there. You might not emerge for days.

WWW Portals

Everyone has a nesting impulse — that need for a sense of home. The allure of a home base is as real in cyberspace as it is in the physical world, and it's satisfied by destinations called *portals*. Portals are major online sites that serve as anchors for the entire Internet experience. Providing a variety of news, specialized coverage of lifestyle topics, and various personalization features, these media sites are like virtual home bases.

For WebTV users, WebTV itself is the major portal. The Home screen and its spin-off services — Mail, Search, Community, and MSN Instant Messenger — are a launching pad for further explorations. The sites spotlighted in this Directory section are meant not to replace the WebTV Home-screen experience but to augment it.

AltaVista

www.altavista.com

Once a preeminent portal, AltaVista slipped in prestige for a couple of years and now is on the rebound. The acquisition of Raging Bull (see Chapter 19) as its money-news source gives the site some élan. A full range of news and community features round out the AltaVista experience.

Excite

www.excite.com

Excite is an exceptionally well-designed portal with a wide range of news and lifestyle features. The Start Page system lets you assign certain information elements that you want to appear when you sign in.

Lycos

www.lycos.com

One of the Web's most helpful directories anchors the Lycos portal. Whereas some directories strive for sheer size, Lycos attempts to add usefulness through organization of good sites. In other words, you can find quality Internet destinations with a minimum of hassle here. A range of news personalization features are provided.

Yahoo!

www.yahoo.com

The ultimate Web portal. See the full review in Chapter 18. The My Yahoo! feature offers customized pages of news and infotainment features. Although certain portions of the Yahoo! experience (including My Yahoo!) require registration, everything at Yahoo! is free. Remember that WebTV can't use the downloaded features, such as Companion and Messenger.

Other Stuff to Check Out

www.zdnet.com
www.msn.com
www.go.com
www.netscape.com
www.snap.com
www.infospace.com

WWW Search Engines

WebTV has its own keyword-searching service, described in Chapter 9, with which you can find new Web sites. This feature has a good search engine and is formatted to look nice on the WebTV screen. So why would anyone ever choose to try another search engine, one not specifically formatted for WebTV? Simply because every search engine is different and therefore yields unique results to a keyword query.

Many Internet veterans have favorite search engines and wouldn't think of limiting themselves to a single one. At the very least, it's good to be aware of alternatives and to know where other engines are located. This section highlights some of the popular and effective search destinations.

Excite

www.excite.com

My personal favorite for quick, essential searching, Excite is a time-tested engine that delivers a combination of sorted and unsorted results. Accordingly, you get the best of both worlds — serendipitous findings and organized division of results into categories.

HotBot

www.hotbot.com

A pit bull of a search engine, HotBot relentlessly tracks down the type of site you're looking for and brings back its link in its jaws. Select the Advanced Search button in the left navigation bar to see the extraordinary range of options available to you. HotBot provides a powerful and flexible range of customized search parameters. There's a learning curve here, and the neon colors aren't as pleasant through WebTV as on a computer monitor, but these drawbacks are worth overcoming.

Google

www.google.com

What kind of name is Google for a search engine? A silly one, for sure, but this site has risen to claim a top spot among search engines. The awesome speed of this thing is one great feature — Google delivers your search results faster than you can blink. Granted, that advantage is more noticeable on a computer than through WebTV. But if the speed doesn't impress, try Google for the quality of its results.

Northern Light

www.northernlight.com

Some folks use Northern Light exclusively for searching, thanks to a powerful engine and the useful way the site sorts results. Although most search engines deliver a plain list of Web site links that match your keyword query, Northern Light sorts the results into folders. A search on the keyword *paris*, for example, returns folders labeled Current News, France, Hotels, Museums, Literature, Vacations, Tour de France, and others. In other words, the search engine creates a directory of results for every search. It's a beautiful thing.

Raging.com

www.raging.com

Raging.com is a new search engine from AltaVista, which for a long time was the most sophisticated and most favored search engine on the Web. Raging.com gets right down to business on a home page that features a logo, a keyword entry form, and nothing else. You can customize the search in a number of ways, including searching in twenty-five languages. This engine may not have a pretty face but underneath lurks powerful technology for finding Web sites.

Scour

www.scour.com

Scour is an engine devoted to multimedia files — graphics, video, and sound. Forget about the video files because virtually all of them do not play through WebTV. Sound, however, is another story, especially after the May 2000 upgrade that added Windows Media playback and RealAudio G2. Scour is a great place to find Internet radio stations. Highlight and select the Radio link at the top of the page.

Other Stuff to Check Out

www.yahoo.com
www.lycos.com
search.netscape.com
www.zensearch.com
www.thebighub.com

WWW Shopping Sites

This is what you've been waiting for, isn't it? You can't fool me. That credit card is out; your hand is quivering. No problem. Following are a few sites where you can exercise your proficiency with plastic.

Amazon.com

www.amazon.com

Started as the first big bookstore on the Web, Amazon has grown into the first big department store on the Web. Amazing dedication to customer satisfaction (not to mention great prices) has earned this site ferocious loyalty from its frequent visitors. Register at the site for a more personalized shopping experience. See the full review in Chapter 19.

FTD.com

www.ftd.com

I have used FTD.com numerous times for sending gifts on short notice, and the site always gets a visit from me the week before Mother's Day. Flowers are the focus here, of course, but the virtual store also features coffee mugs, gourmet platters, and various gifts for any season.

J.C. Penney

www.jcpenney.com

★ ★
★ ★

One of the best *click-and-mortar* shops — that is, an offline store with an online branch. J.C. Penney operates the virtual store with élan, sporting an exciting online catalogue, plenty of inventory sales, and reliable delivery. Kmart should visit this site to see e-commerce done right.

uBid

www.ubid.com

An online auction space like eBay (see Chapter 19), uBid differs by auctioning in-house inventory of products from various manufacturers. This isn't person-to-person auctioning of stuff from the attic. At uBid you can buy clothes, jewelry, sports equipment, appliances, and computers. Most of the products are overflow inventory and refurbished equipment. The electronic stuff comes with limited warranties, for the most part.

Other Stuff to Check Out

www.cdnow.com
www.bn.com
www.alibris.com
www.excitestores.com

Index

Notes

Notes

Notes

Notes

Discover Dummies Online!

The Dummies Web Site is your fun and friendly online resource for the latest information about *For Dummies* books and your favorite topics. The Web site is the place to communicate with us, exchange ideas with other *For Dummies* readers, chat with authors, and have fun!

Ten Fun and Useful Things You Can Do at www.dummies.com

1. Win free *For Dummies* books and more!
2. Register your book and be entered in a prize drawing.
3. Meet your favorite authors through the IDG Books Worldwide Author Chat Series.
4. Exchange helpful information with other *For Dummies* readers.
5. Discover other great *For Dummies* books you must have!
6. Purchase Dummieswear® exclusively from our Web site.
7. Buy *For Dummies* books online.
8. Talk to us. Make comments, ask questions, get answers!
9. Download free software.
10. Find additional useful resources from authors.

Link directly to these ten fun and useful things at
http://www.dummies.com/10useful

For other technology titles from IDG Books Worldwide, go to
www.idgbooks.com

Not on the Web yet? It's easy to get started with *Dummies 101*®: *The Internet For Windows*® *98* or *The Internet For Dummies*® at local retailers everywhere.

Find other *For Dummies* books on these topics:

Business • Career • Databases • Food & Beverage • Games • Gardening • Graphics • Hardware
Health & Fitness • Internet and the World Wide Web • Networking • Office Suites
Operating Systems • Personal Finance • Pets • Programming • Recreation • Sports
Spreadsheets • Teacher Resources • Test Prep • Word Processing

The IDG Books Worldwide logo is a registered trademark under exclusive license to IDG Books Worldwide, Inc., from International Data Group, Inc. Dummies.com and the ...For Dummies logo are trademarks, and Dummies Man, For Dummies, Dummieswear, and Dummies 101 are registered trademarks of IDG Books Worldwide, Inc. All other trademarks are the property of their respective owners.

IDG BOOKS WORLDWIDE
BOOK REGISTRATION

We want to hear from you!

Visit **http://my2cents.dummies.com** to register this book and tell us how you liked it!

- ✔ Get entered in our monthly prize giveaway.

- ✔ Give us feedback about this book — tell us what you like best, what you like least, or maybe what you'd like to ask the author and us to change!

- ✔ Let us know any other *For Dummies*® topics that interest you.

Your feedback helps us determine what books to publish, tells us what coverage to add as we revise our books, and lets us know whether we're meeting your needs as a *For Dummies* reader. You're our most valuable resource, and what you have to say is important to us!

Not on the Web yet? It's easy to get started with *Dummies 101*®: *The Internet For Windows*® *98* or *The Internet For Dummies*® at local retailers everywhere.

Or let us know what you think by sending us a letter at the following address:

For Dummies Book Registration
Dummies Press
10475 Crosspoint Blvd.
Indianapolis, IN 46256

BESTSELLING
BOOK SERIES